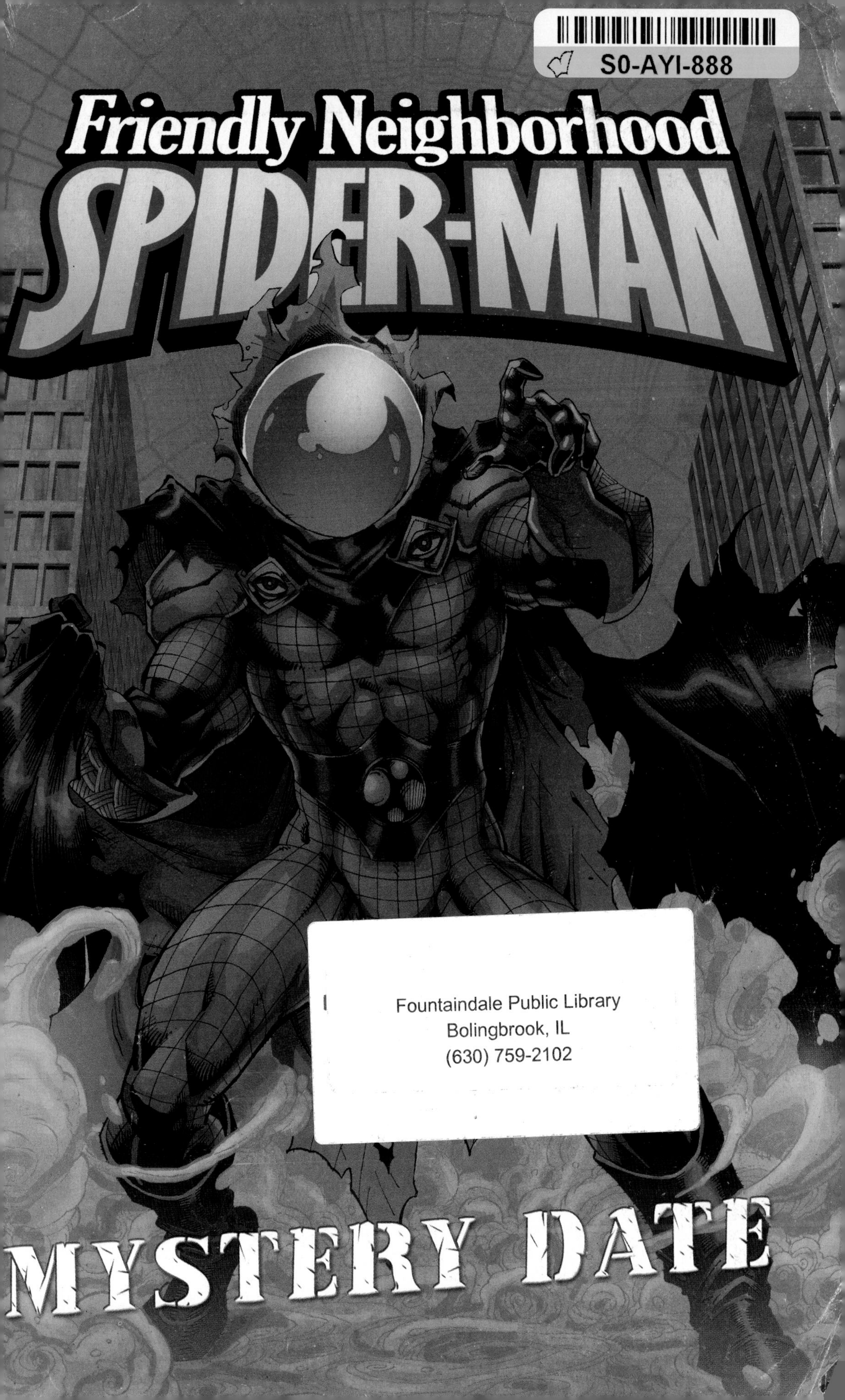
Friendly Neighborhood
SPIDER-MAN
MYSTERY DATE

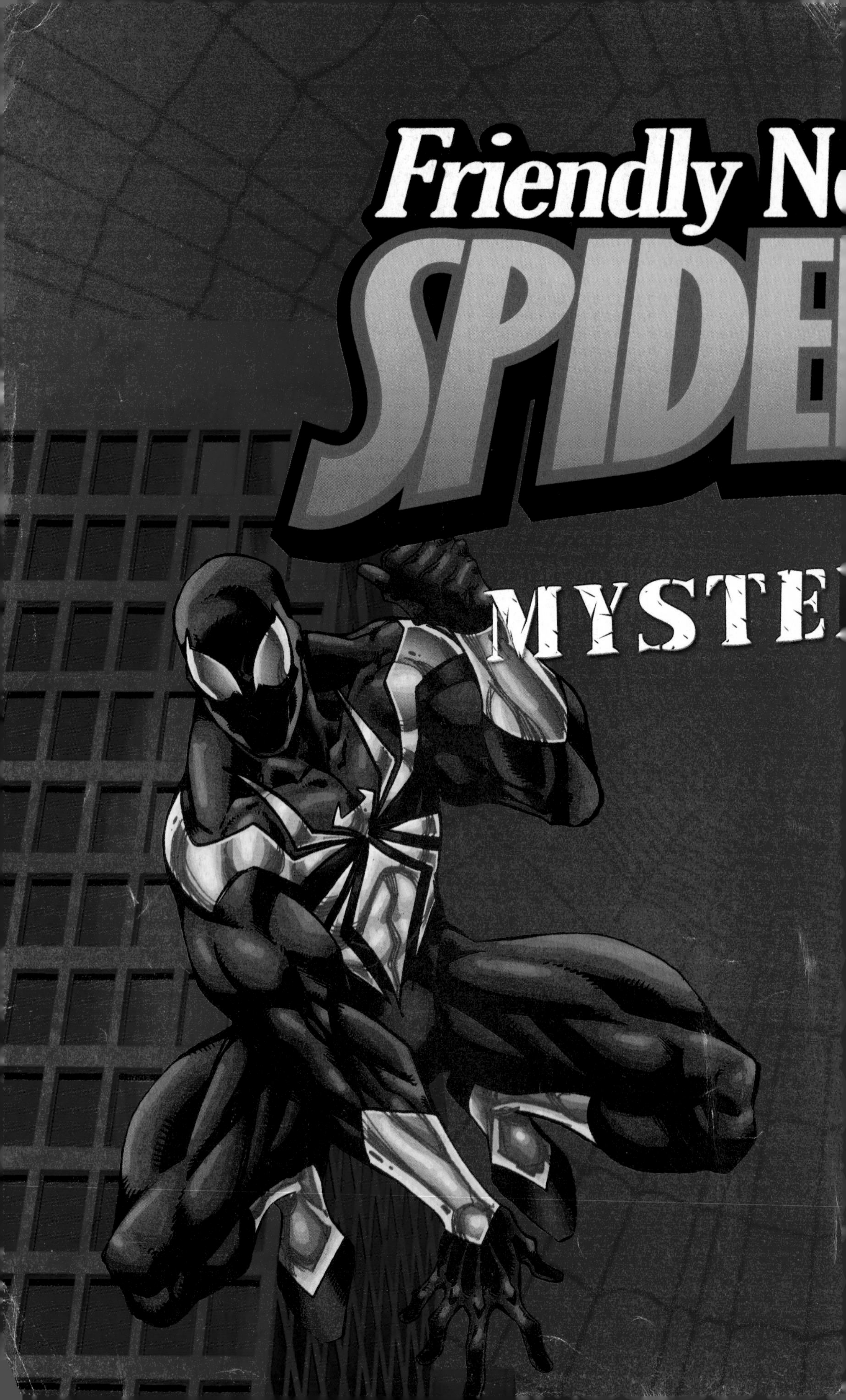
Friendly N
SPIDE
MYSTE

ghborhood
R-MAN

Y DATE

Writer: Peter David

ncils: Todd Nauck & Scot Eaton

ks: Robert Campanella
with Rodney Ramos & John Dell

lors: Lee Loughridge & Matt Milla

tters: Virtual Calligraphy's Cory Petit

ver Art: Mike Wieringo with Mike Manley and Paul Mounts
& Scot Eaton with John Dell and Paul Mounts

ssistant Editor: Michael O'Connor

ditor: Axel Alonso

ollection Editor: Jennifer Grünwald

Assistant Editor: Michael Short

Associate Editor: Mark D. Beazley

Senior Editor, Special Projects: Jeff Youngquist

Senior Vice President of Sales: David Gabriel

Production: Jerron Quality Color & Jerry Kalinowski

Vice President of Creative: Tom Marvelli

Editor in Chief: Joe Quesada

Publisher: Dan Buckley

PREVIOUSLY:

Now that Spider-Man has revealed to the world that he is Peter Parker, our hero's status quo has been shaken up as never before.

Meanwhile, Aunt May faced off against what she believed was a Ben Parker imposter, unaware that she was dismissing a genuine version of her beloved Ben, plucked out of an alternate reality. After encountering a bum in an alley, it appeared as if Ben totally flipped his lid and, in order to remain in this reality, blew away a future Spider-Man from the year 2211. Then again, looks can be deceiving.

Still bewildered over the encounter with the alternate Uncle Ben, Peter now finds himself facing an entirely new situation at the school where he teaches...

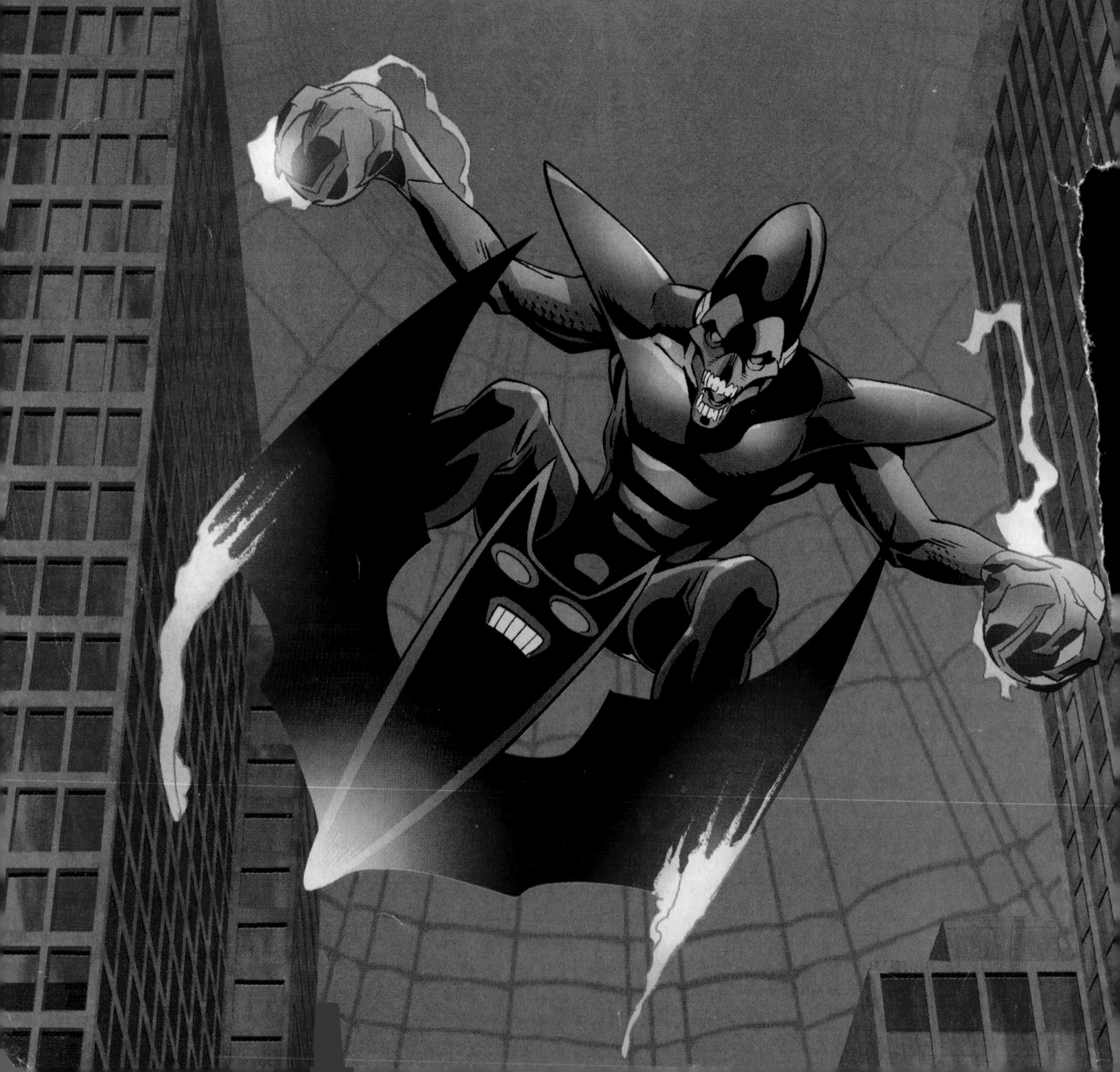

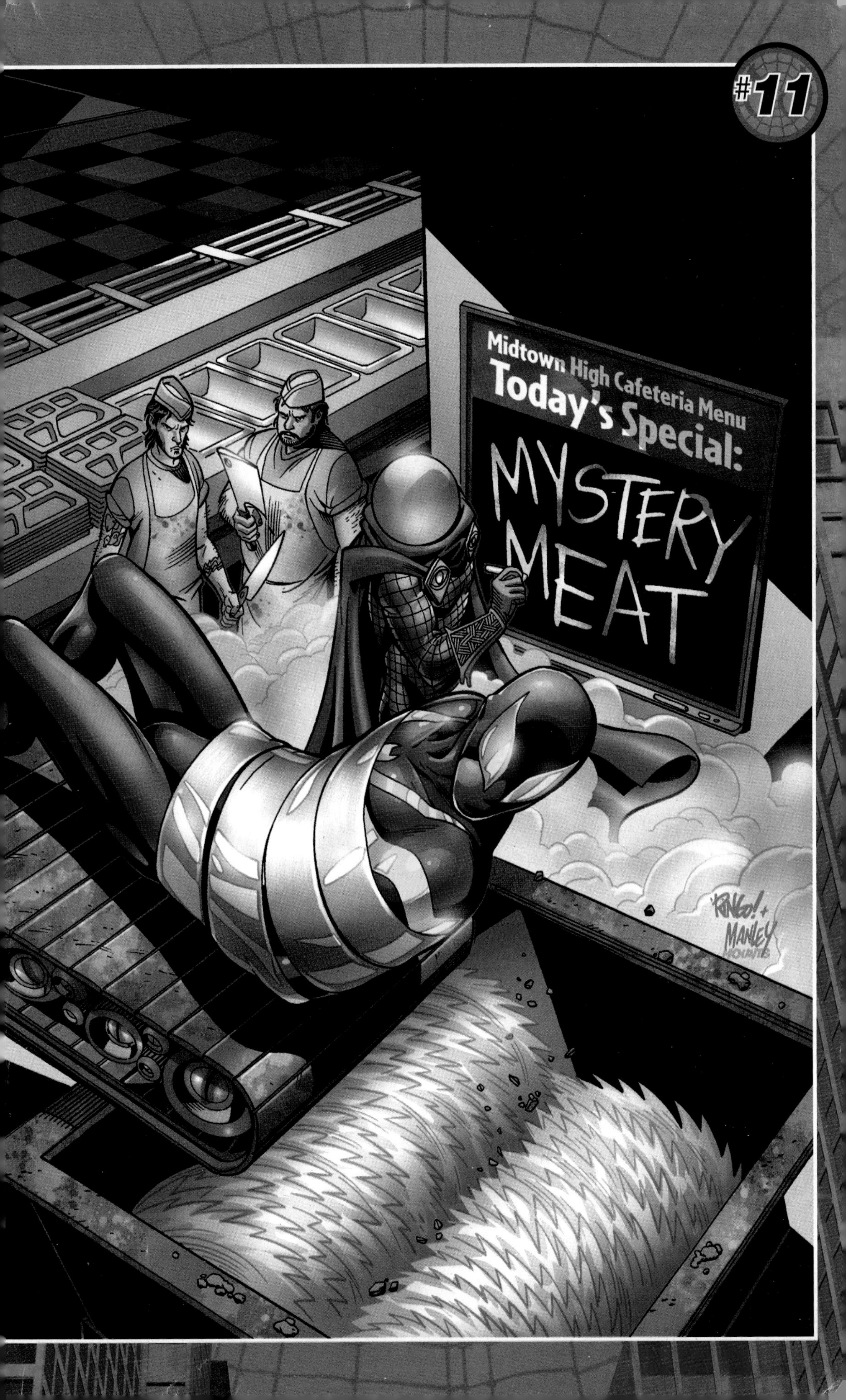

#11
Midtown High Cafeteria Menu
Today's Special:
MYSTERY MEAT

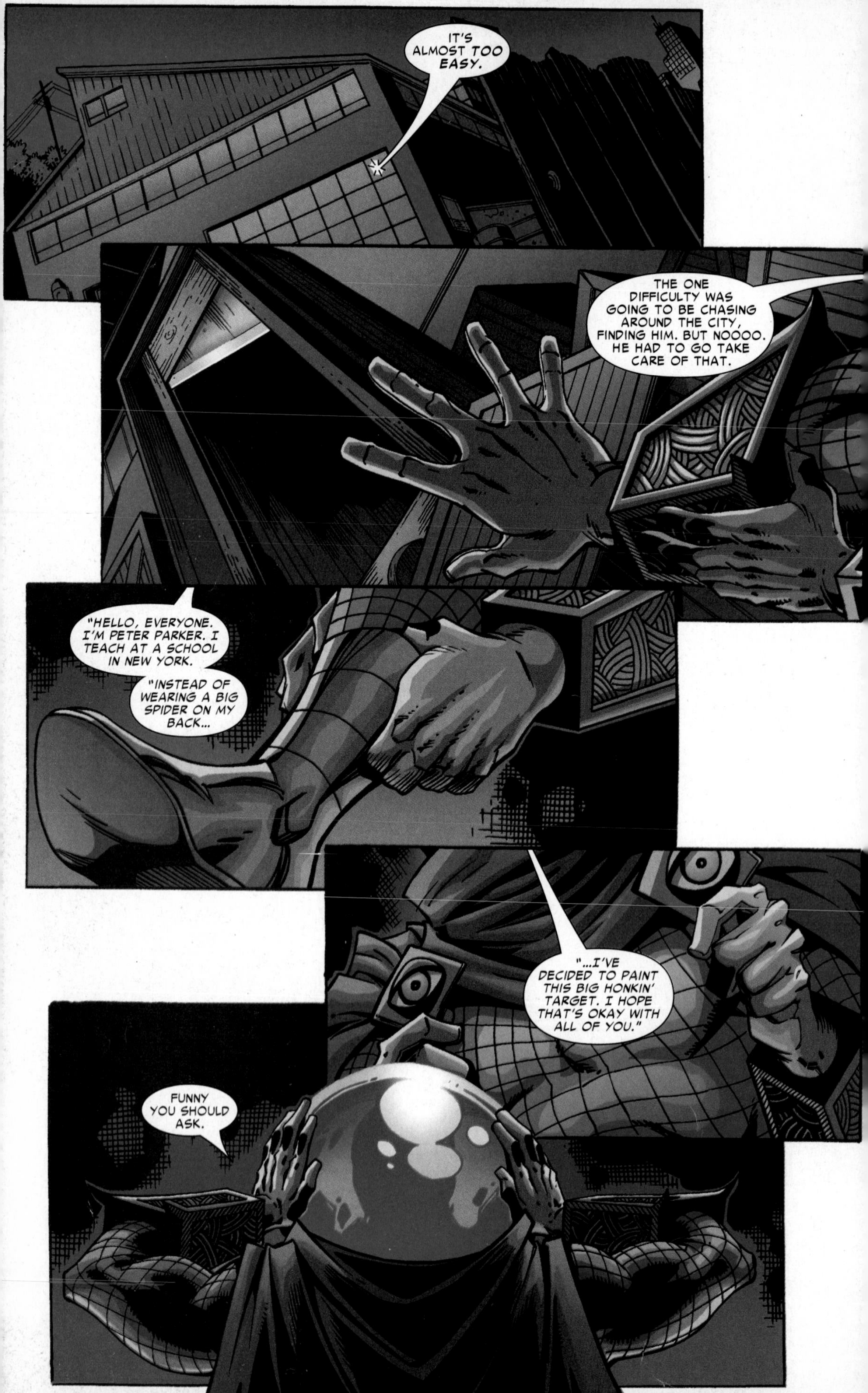
IT'S ALMOST TOO EASY.
THE ONE DIFFICULTY WAS GOING TO BE CHASING AROUND THE CITY, FINDING HIM. BUT NOOOO. HE HAD TO GO TAKE CARE OF THAT.
"HELLO, EVERYONE. I'M PETER PARKER. I TEACH AT A SCHOOL IN NEW YORK.
"INSTEAD OF WEARING A BIG SPIDER ON MY BACK...
"...I'VE DECIDED TO PAINT THIS BIG HONKIN' TARGET. I HOPE THAT'S OKAY WITH ALL OF YOU."
FUNNY YOU SHOULD ASK.

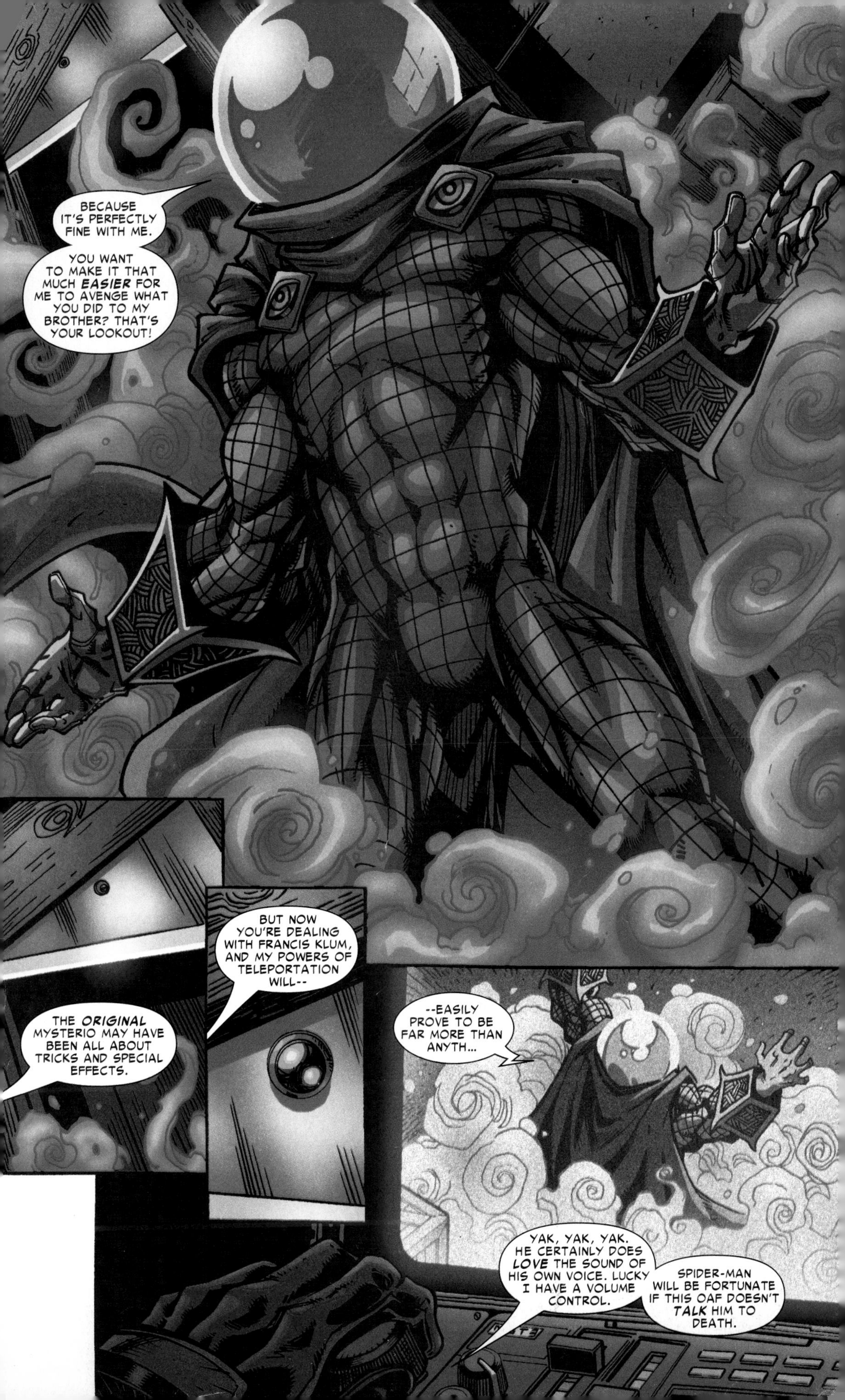
BECAUSE IT'S PERFECTLY FINE WITH ME.
YOU WANT TO MAKE IT THAT MUCH EASIER FOR ME TO AVENGE WHAT YOU DID TO MY BROTHER? THAT'S YOUR LOOKOUT!
THE ORIGINAL MYSTERIO MAY HAVE BEEN ALL ABOUT TRICKS AND SPECIAL EFFECTS.
BUT NOW YOU'RE DEALING WITH FRANCIS KLUM, AND MY POWERS OF TELEPORTATION WILL--
--EASILY PROVE TO BE FAR MORE THAN ANYTH...
YAK, YAK, YAK. HE CERTAINLY DOES LOVE THE SOUND OF HIS OWN VOICE. LUCKY I HAVE A VOLUME CONTROL.
SPIDER-MAN WILL BE FORTUNATE IF THIS OAF DOESN'T TALK HIM TO DEATH.

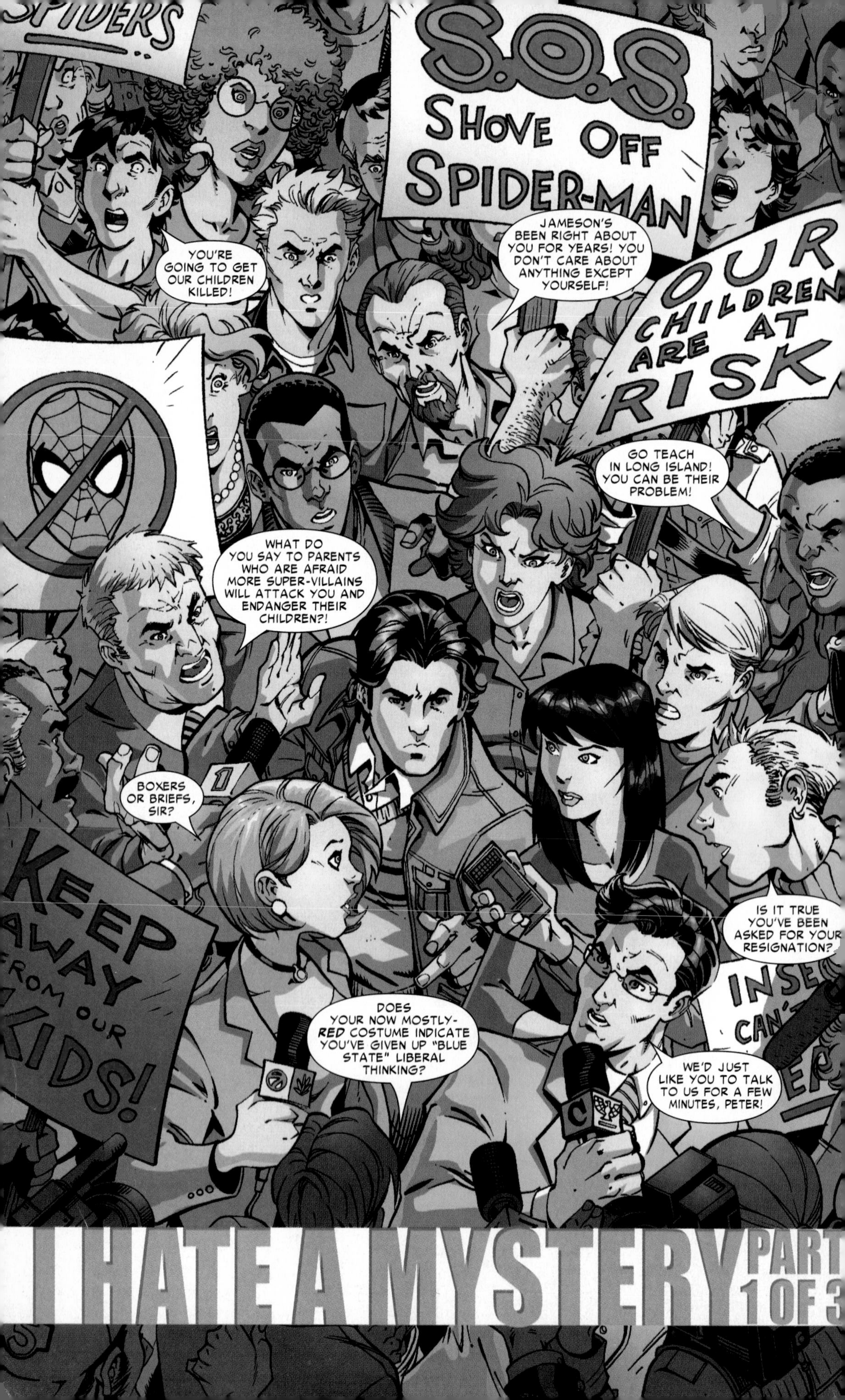
SPIDERS
S.O.S. SHOVE OFF SPIDER-MAN
OUR CHILDREN ARE AT RISK
YOU'RE GOING TO GET OUR CHILDREN KILLED!
JAMESON'S BEEN RIGHT ABOUT YOU FOR YEARS! YOU DON'T CARE ABOUT ANYTHING EXCEPT YOURSELF!
GO TEACH IN LONG ISLAND! YOU CAN BE THEIR PROBLEM!
WHAT DO YOU SAY TO PARENTS WHO ARE AFRAID MORE SUPER-VILLAINS WILL ATTACK YOU AND ENDANGER THEIR CHILDREN?!
BOXERS OR BRIEFS, SIR?
IS IT TRUE YOU'VE BEEN ASKED FOR YOUR RESIGNATION?
KEEP AWAY FROM OUR KIDS!
DOES YOUR NOW MOSTLY-RED COSTUME INDICATE YOU'VE GIVEN UP "BLUE STATE" LIBERAL THINKING?
WE'D JUST LIKE YOU TO TALK TO US FOR A FEW MINUTES, PETER!
I HATE A MYSTERY PART 1 OF 3

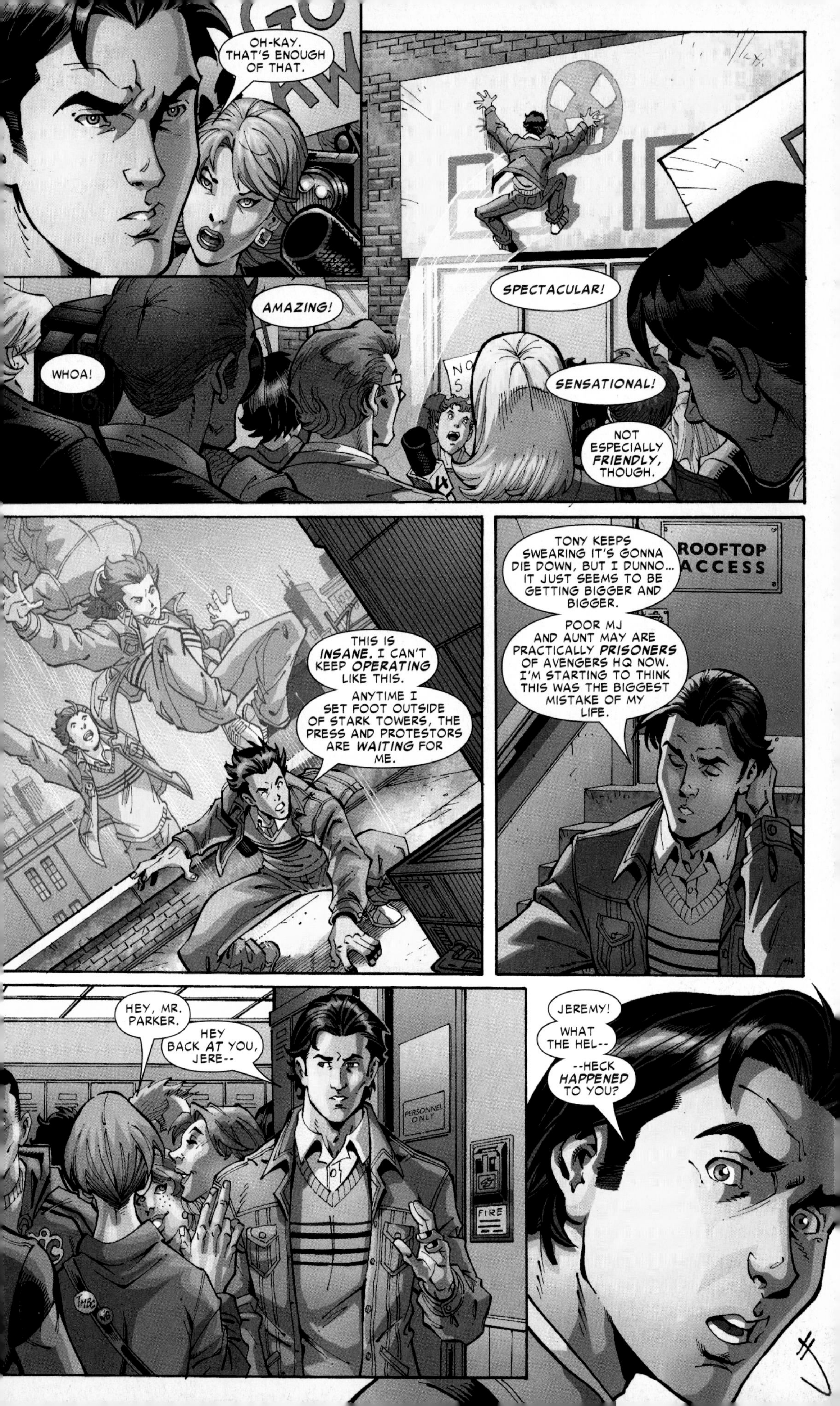

OH-KAY. THAT'S ENOUGH OF THAT.
AMAZING!
SPECTACULAR!
WHOA!
SENSATIONAL!
NOT ESPECIALLY FRIENDLY, THOUGH.
THIS IS INSANE. I CAN'T KEEP OPERATING LIKE THIS.
ANYTIME I SET FOOT OUTSIDE OF STARK TOWERS, THE PRESS AND PROTESTORS ARE WAITING FOR ME.
ROOFTOP ACCESS
TONY KEEPS SWEARING IT'S GONNA DIE DOWN, BUT I DUNNO... IT JUST SEEMS TO BE GETTING BIGGER AND BIGGER.
POOR MJ AND AUNT MAY ARE PRACTICALLY PRISONERS OF AVENGERS HQ NOW. I'M STARTING TO THINK THIS WAS THE BIGGEST MISTAKE OF MY LIFE.
HEY, MR. PARKER.
HEY BACK AT YOU, JERE--
PERSONNEL ONLY
FIRE
JEREMY!
WHAT THE HEL--
--HECK HAPPENED TO YOU?

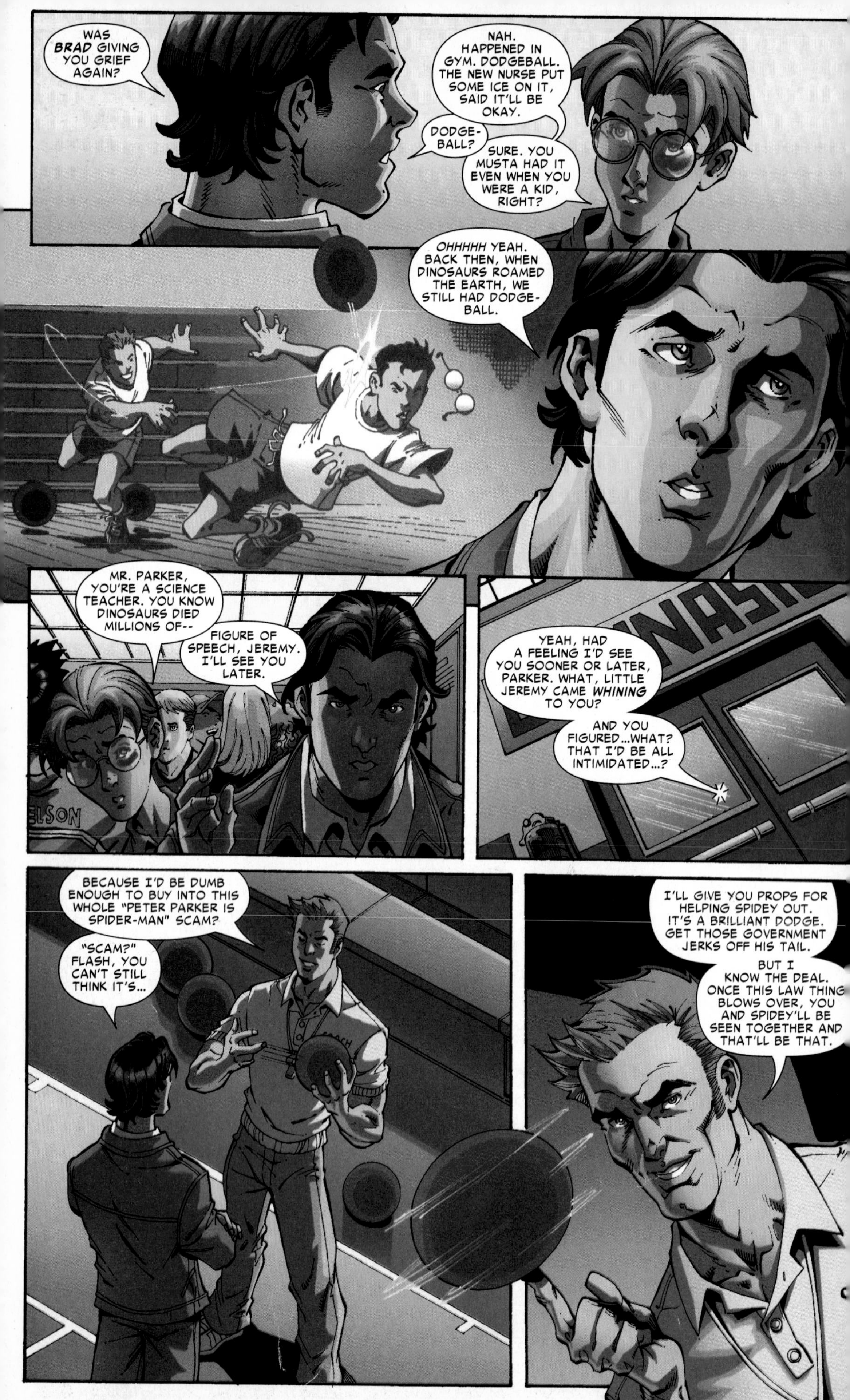
WAS BRAD GIVING YOU GRIEF AGAIN?
NAH. HAPPENED IN GYM. DODGEBALL. THE NEW NURSE PUT SOME ICE ON IT, SAID IT'LL BE OKAY.
DODGE-BALL?
SURE. YOU MUSTA HAD IT EVEN WHEN YOU WERE A KID, RIGHT?
OHHHHH YEAH. BACK THEN, WHEN DINOSAURS ROAMED THE EARTH, WE STILL HAD DODGE-BALL.
MR. PARKER, YOU'RE A SCIENCE TEACHER. YOU KNOW DINOSAURS DIED MILLIONS OF--
FIGURE OF SPEECH, JEREMY. I'LL SEE YOU LATER.
ELSON
YEAH, HAD A FEELING I'D SEE YOU SOONER OR LATER, PARKER. WHAT, LITTLE JEREMY CAME WHINING TO YOU?
AND YOU FIGURED...WHAT? THAT I'D BE ALL INTIMIDATED...?
BECAUSE I'D BE DUMB ENOUGH TO BUY INTO THIS WHOLE "PETER PARKER IS SPIDER-MAN" SCAM?
"SCAM?" FLASH, YOU CAN'T STILL THINK IT'S...
I'LL GIVE YOU PROPS FOR HELPING SPIDEY OUT. IT'S A BRILLIANT DODGE. GET THOSE GOVERNMENT JERKS OFF HIS TAIL.
BUT I KNOW THE DEAL. ONCE THIS LAW THING BLOWS OVER, YOU AND SPIDEY'LL BE SEEN TOGETHER AND THAT'LL BE THAT.

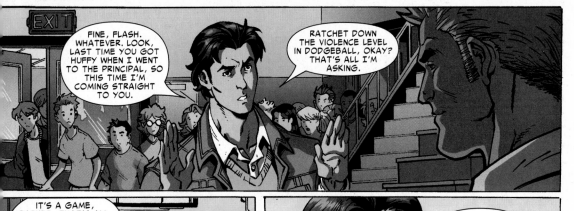

FINE, FLASH. WHATEVER. LOOK, LAST TIME YOU GOT HUFFY WHEN I WENT TO THE PRINCIPAL, SO THIS TIME I'M COMING STRAIGHT TO YOU.

RATCHET DOWN THE VIOLENCE LEVEL IN DODGEBALL, OKAY? THAT'S ALL I'M ASKING.

IT'S A GAME, PARKER, THAT'S ALL. A HARMLESS GAME. NO ONE EXCEPT A WIMP EVER GOT HIMSELF HURT PLAYING DODGEBALL.

BUT THEN, YOU'D KNOW ALL ABOUT THAT, WOULDN'T YOU?

FLASH... YOU'RE LUCKY THAT ONE OF US REMEMBERS WE WERE FRIENDS.

LOOK, THERE'S A LOT ON MY MIND RIGHT NOW, SO JUST--

C'MON. LESSEE WHAT YOU'VE GOT.

WHAT'S THE MATTER, PETEY?

OH, GROW UP, WOULD YOU, PLEA--

AREN'T YOU THE TYPE WHO ALWAYS TELLS KIDS THEY SHOULD STAND UP TO BULLIES?

AFRAID TO PRACTICE WHAT YOU PREACH? TO TAKE SOME RESPONSIBILITY FOR WHAT YOU'RE TELLING THE STUDENTS?

÷SIGH÷ FINE. LET'S GO.

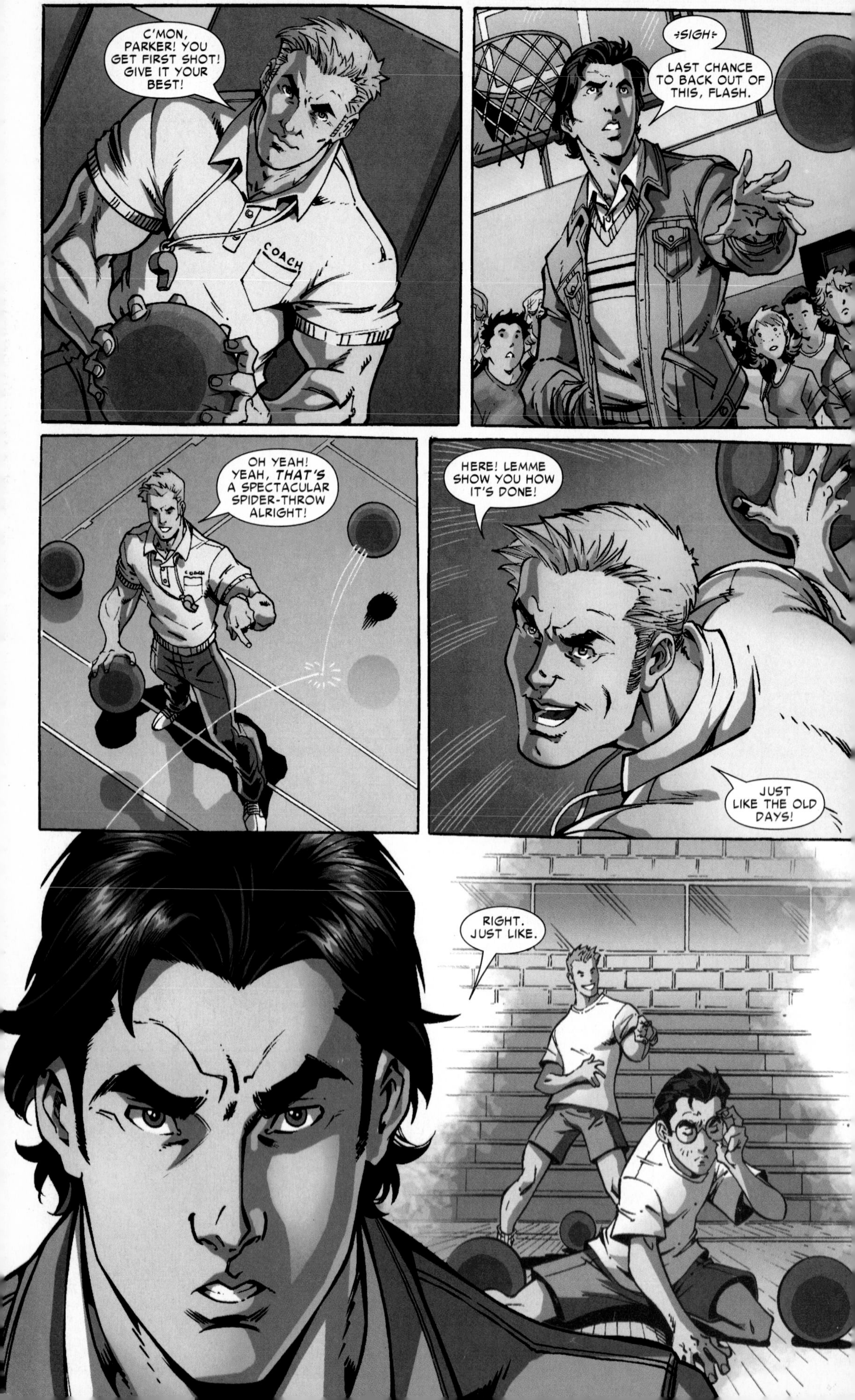
C'MON, PARKER! YOU GET FIRST SHOT! GIVE IT YOUR BEST!
-SIGH-
LAST CHANCE TO BACK OUT OF THIS, FLASH.
COACH
OH YEAH! YEAH, THAT'S A SPECTACULAR SPIDER-THROW ALRIGHT!
HERE! LEMME SHOW YOU HOW IT'S DONE!
JUST LIKE THE OLD DAYS!
RIGHT. JUST LIKE.

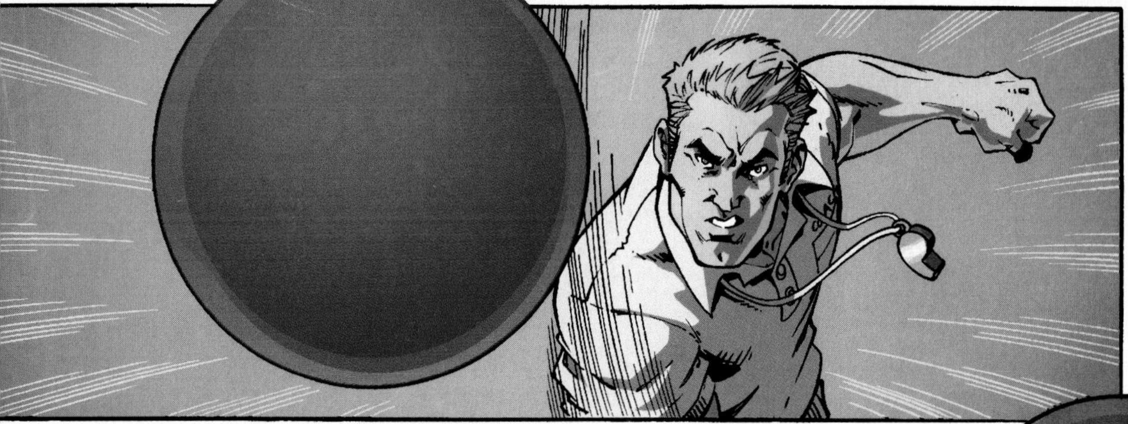
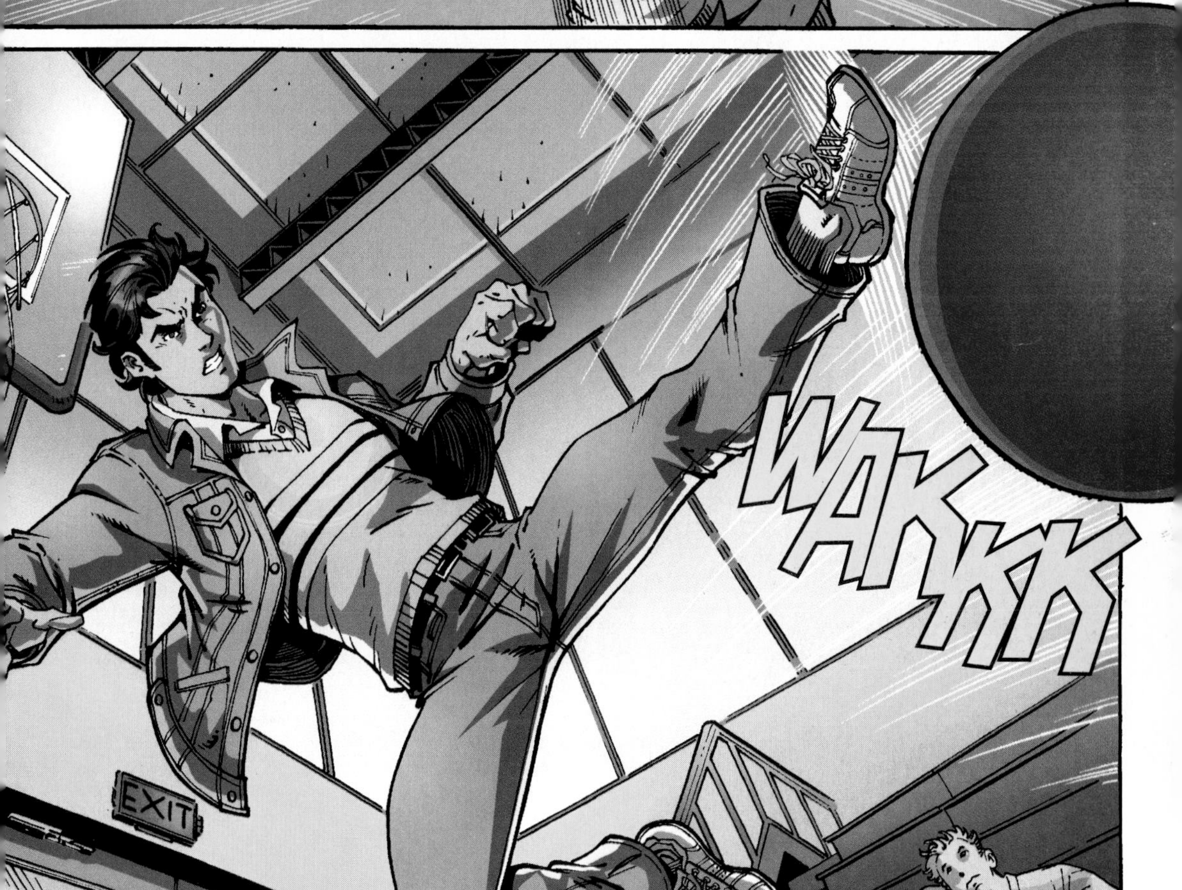
WAKKK
EXIT
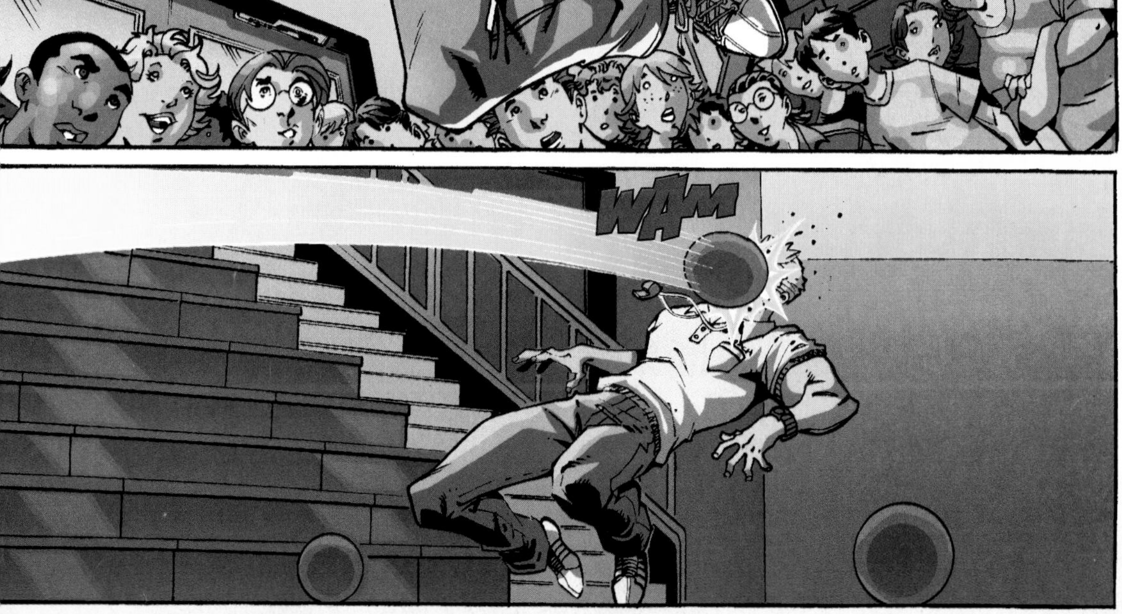
WAM

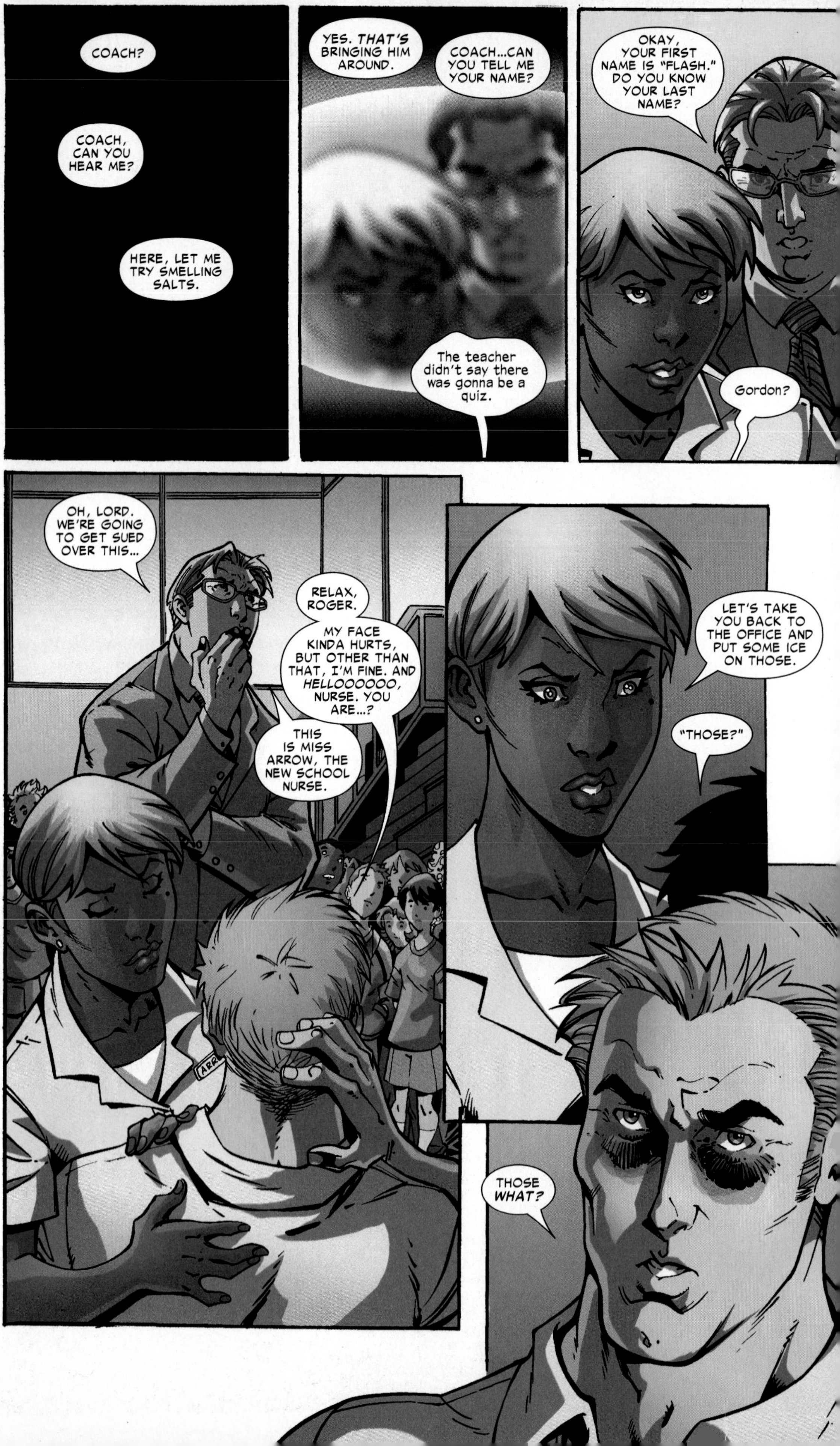

COACH?
COACH, CAN YOU HEAR ME?
HERE, LET ME TRY SMELLING SALTS.
YES. *THAT'S* BRINGING HIM AROUND.
COACH...CAN YOU TELL ME YOUR NAME?
The teacher didn't say there was gonna be a quiz.
OKAY, YOUR FIRST NAME IS "FLASH." DO YOU KNOW YOUR LAST NAME?
Gordon?
OH, LORD. WE'RE GOING TO GET SUED OVER THIS...
RELAX, ROGER.
MY FACE KINDA HURTS, BUT OTHER THAN THAT, I'M FINE. AND *HELLOOOOOO,* NURSE. YOU ARE...?
THIS IS MISS ARROW, THE NEW SCHOOL NURSE.
LET'S TAKE YOU BACK TO THE OFFICE AND PUT SOME ICE ON THOSE.
"THOSE?"
THOSE *WHAT?*

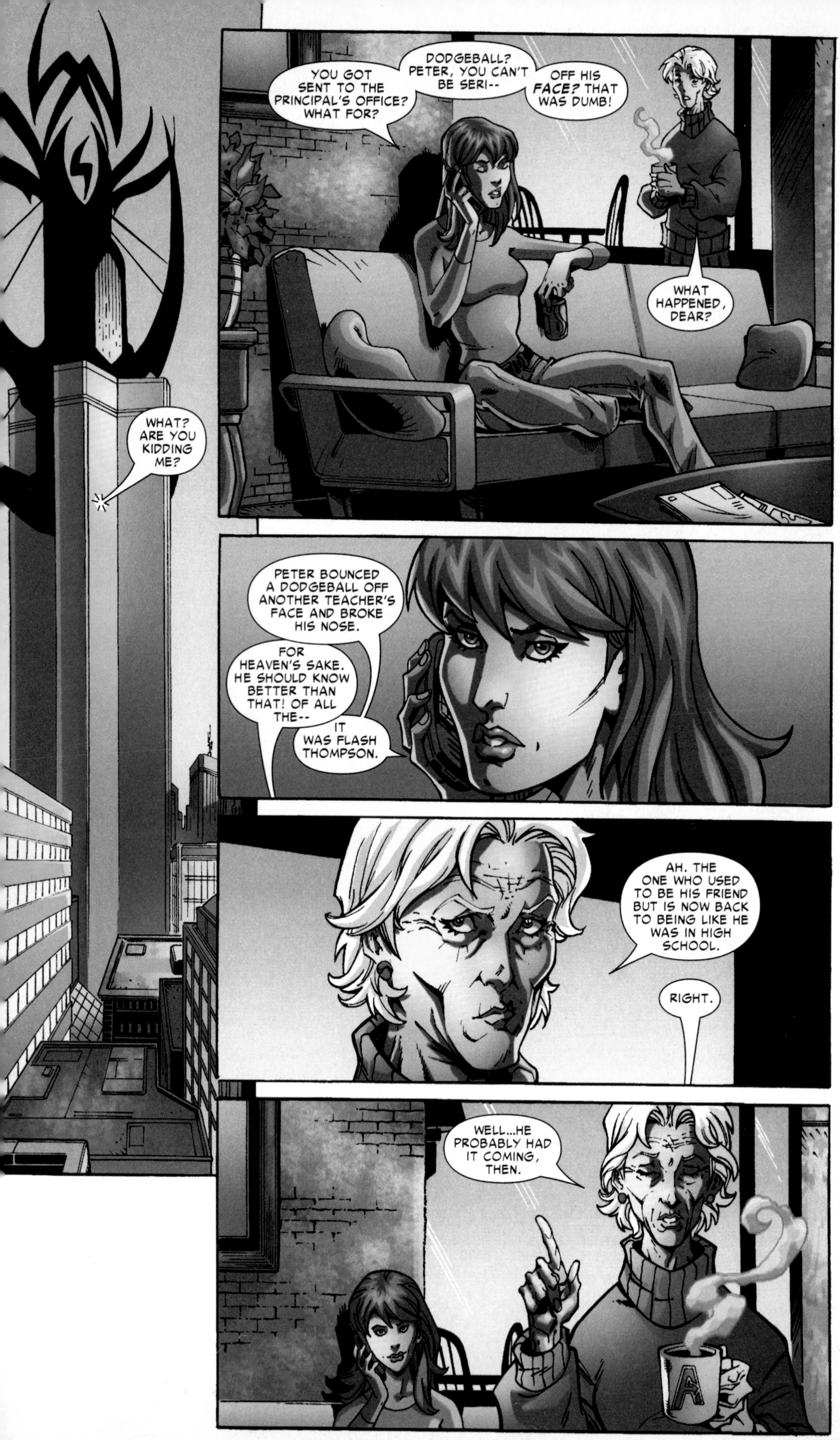
WHAT? ARE YOU KIDDING ME?
YOU GOT SENT TO THE PRINCIPAL'S OFFICE? WHAT FOR?
DODGEBALL? PETER, YOU CAN'T BE SERI--
OFF HIS *FACE?* THAT WAS DUMB!
WHAT HAPPENED, DEAR?
PETER BOUNCED A DODGEBALL OFF ANOTHER TEACHER'S FACE AND BROKE HIS NOSE.
FOR HEAVEN'S SAKE. HE SHOULD KNOW BETTER THAN THAT! OF ALL THE--
IT WAS FLASH THOMPSON.
AH. THE ONE WHO USED TO BE HIS FRIEND BUT IS NOW BACK TO BEING LIKE HE WAS IN HIGH SCHOOL.
RIGHT.
WELL...HE PROBABLY HAD IT COMING, THEN.

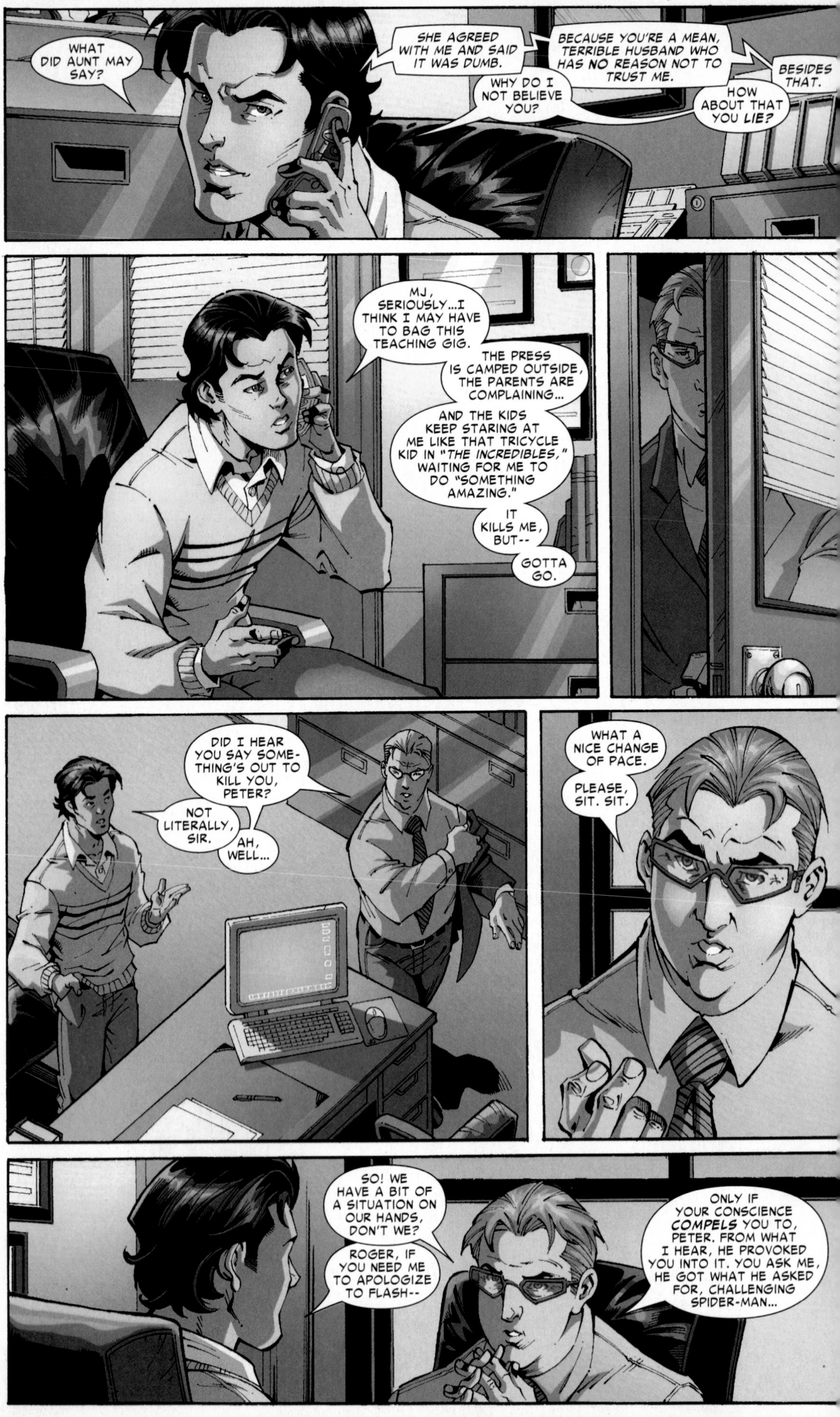

WHAT DID AUNT MAY SAY?
SHE AGREED WITH ME AND SAID IT WAS DUMB.
WHY DO I NOT BELIEVE YOU?
BECAUSE YOU'RE A MEAN, TERRIBLE HUSBAND WHO HAS NO REASON NOT TO TRUST ME.
BESIDES THAT.
HOW ABOUT THAT YOU LIE?
MJ, SERIOUSLY...I THINK I MAY HAVE TO BAG THIS TEACHING GIG.
THE PRESS IS CAMPED OUTSIDE, THE PARENTS ARE COMPLAINING...
AND THE KIDS KEEP STARING AT ME LIKE THAT TRICYCLE KID IN "THE INCREDIBLES," WAITING FOR ME TO DO "SOMETHING AMAZING."
IT KILLS ME, BUT--
GOTTA GO.
DID I HEAR YOU SAY SOMETHING'S OUT TO KILL YOU, PETER?
NOT LITERALLY, SIR.
AH, WELL...
WHAT A NICE CHANGE OF PACE.
PLEASE, SIT. SIT.
SO! WE HAVE A BIT OF A SITUATION ON OUR HANDS, DON'T WE?
ROGER, IF YOU NEED ME TO APOLOGIZE TO FLASH--
ONLY IF YOUR CONSCIENCE COMPELS YOU TO, PETER. FROM WHAT I HEAR, HE PROVOKED YOU INTO IT. YOU ASK ME, HE GOT WHAT HE ASKED FOR, CHALLENGING SPIDER-MAN...

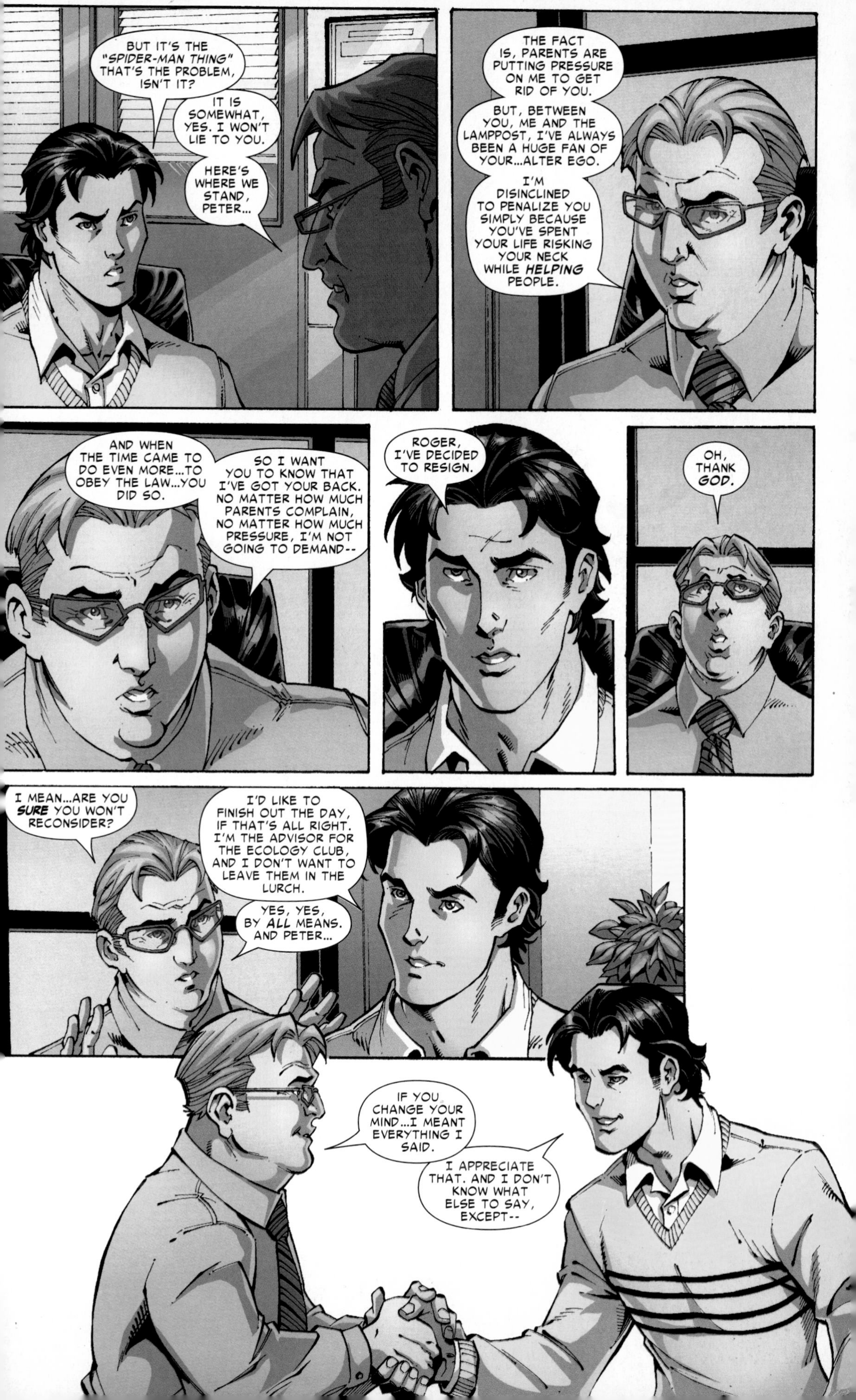
BUT IT'S THE "SPIDER-MAN THING" THAT'S THE PROBLEM, ISN'T IT?
IT IS SOMEWHAT, YES. I WON'T LIE TO YOU.
HERE'S WHERE WE STAND, PETER...
THE FACT IS, PARENTS ARE PUTTING PRESSURE ON ME TO GET RID OF YOU.
BUT, BETWEEN YOU, ME AND THE LAMPPOST, I'VE ALWAYS BEEN A HUGE FAN OF YOUR...ALTER EGO.
I'M DISINCLINED TO PENALIZE YOU SIMPLY BECAUSE YOU'VE SPENT YOUR LIFE RISKING YOUR NECK WHILE HELPING PEOPLE.
AND WHEN THE TIME CAME TO DO EVEN MORE...TO OBEY THE LAW...YOU DID SO.
SO I WANT YOU TO KNOW THAT I'VE GOT YOUR BACK. NO MATTER HOW MUCH PARENTS COMPLAIN, NO MATTER HOW MUCH PRESSURE, I'M NOT GOING TO DEMAND--
ROGER, I'VE DECIDED TO RESIGN.
OH, THANK GOD.
I MEAN...ARE YOU SURE YOU WON'T RECONSIDER?
I'D LIKE TO FINISH OUT THE DAY, IF THAT'S ALL RIGHT. I'M THE ADVISOR FOR THE ECOLOGY CLUB, AND I DON'T WANT TO LEAVE THEM IN THE LURCH.
YES, YES, BY ALL MEANS. AND PETER...
IF YOU CHANGE YOUR MIND...I MEANT EVERYTHING I SAID.
I APPRECIATE THAT. AND I DON'T KNOW WHAT ELSE TO SAY, EXCEPT--

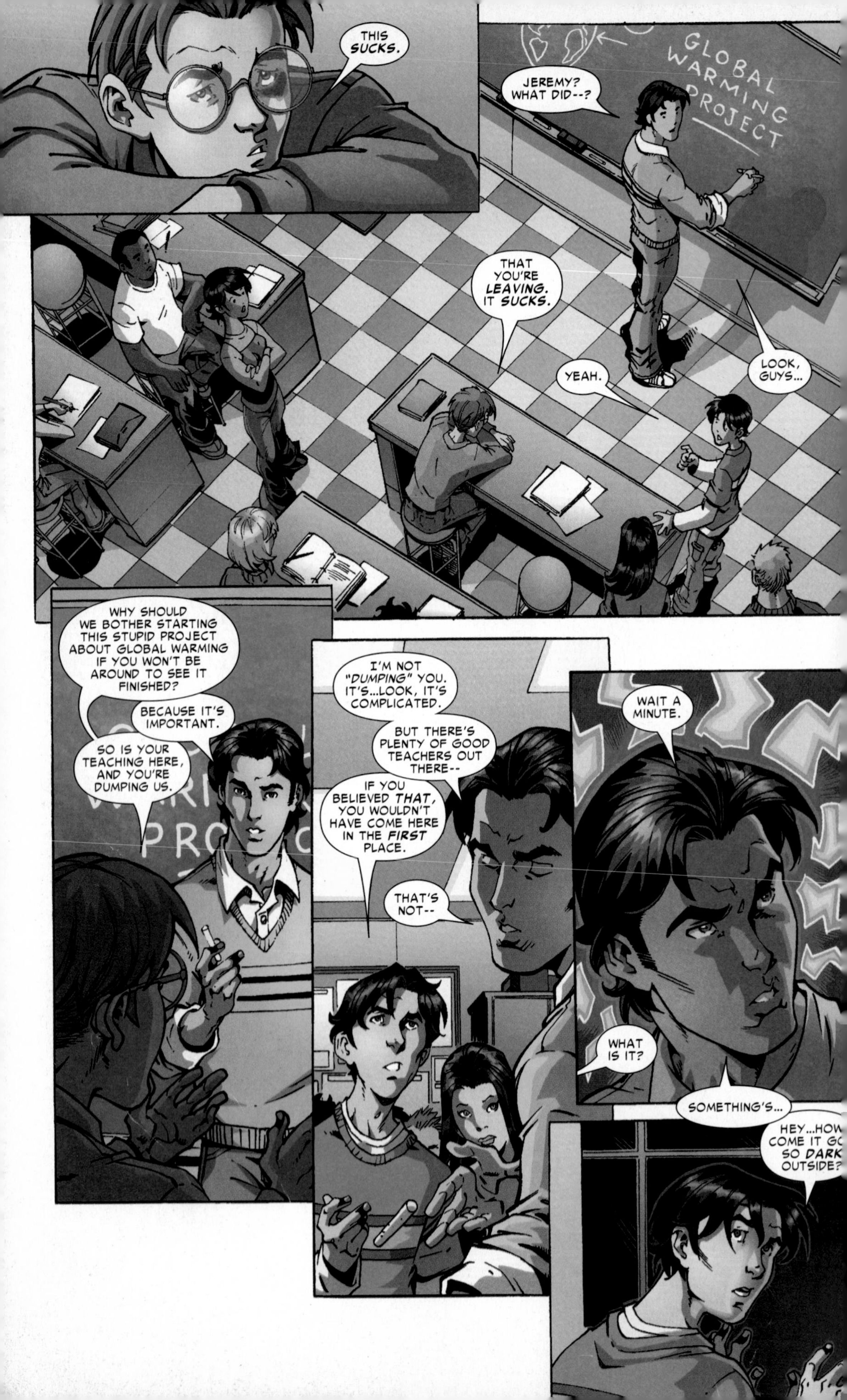
THIS SUCKS.
GLOBAL WARMING PROJECT
JEREMY? WHAT DID--?
THAT YOU'RE LEAVING. IT SUCKS.
YEAH.
LOOK, GUYS...
WHY SHOULD WE BOTHER STARTING THIS STUPID PROJECT ABOUT GLOBAL WARMING IF YOU WON'T BE AROUND TO SEE IT FINISHED?
BECAUSE IT'S IMPORTANT.
SO IS YOUR TEACHING HERE, AND YOU'RE DUMPING US.
I'M NOT "DUMPING" YOU. IT'S...LOOK, IT'S COMPLICATED.
BUT THERE'S PLENTY OF GOOD TEACHERS OUT THERE--
IF YOU BELIEVED THAT, YOU WOULDN'T HAVE COME HERE IN THE FIRST PLACE.
THAT'S NOT--
WAIT A MINUTE.
WHAT IS IT?
SOMETHING'S...
HEY...HOW COME IT GO SO DARK OUTSIDE?

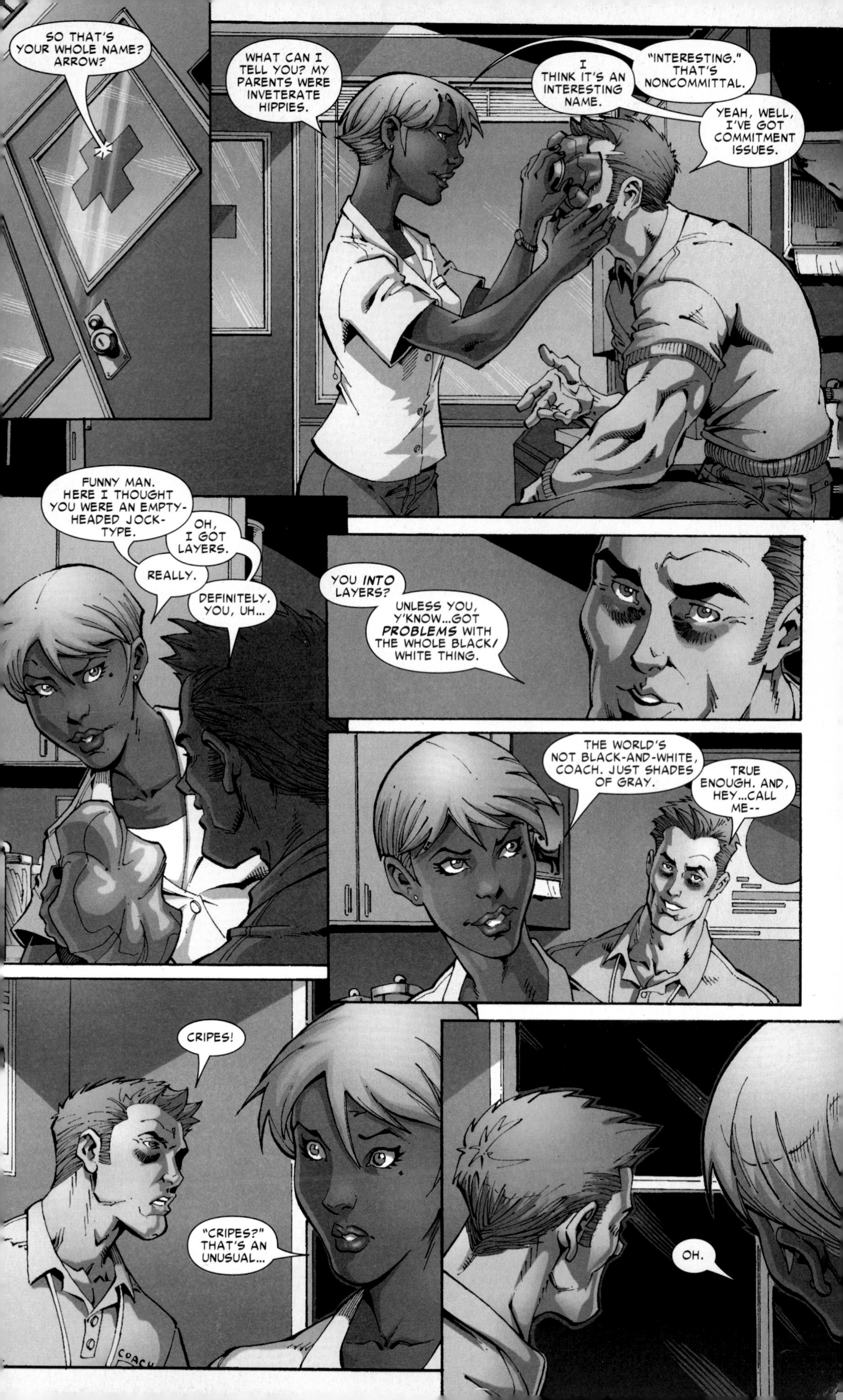
SO THAT'S YOUR WHOLE NAME? ARROW?
WHAT CAN I TELL YOU? MY PARENTS WERE INVETERATE HIPPIES.
I THINK IT'S AN INTERESTING NAME.
"INTERESTING." THAT'S NONCOMMITTAL.
YEAH, WELL, I'VE GOT COMMITMENT ISSUES.
FUNNY MAN. HERE I THOUGHT YOU WERE AN EMPTY-HEADED JOCK-TYPE.
OH, I GOT LAYERS.
REALLY.
DEFINITELY. YOU, UH...
YOU INTO LAYERS?
UNLESS YOU, Y'KNOW...GOT PROBLEMS WITH THE WHOLE BLACK/ WHITE THING.
THE WORLD'S NOT BLACK-AND-WHITE, COACH. JUST SHADES OF GRAY.
TRUE ENOUGH. AND, HEY...CALL ME--
CRIPES!
"CRIPES?" THAT'S AN UNUSUAL...
OH.

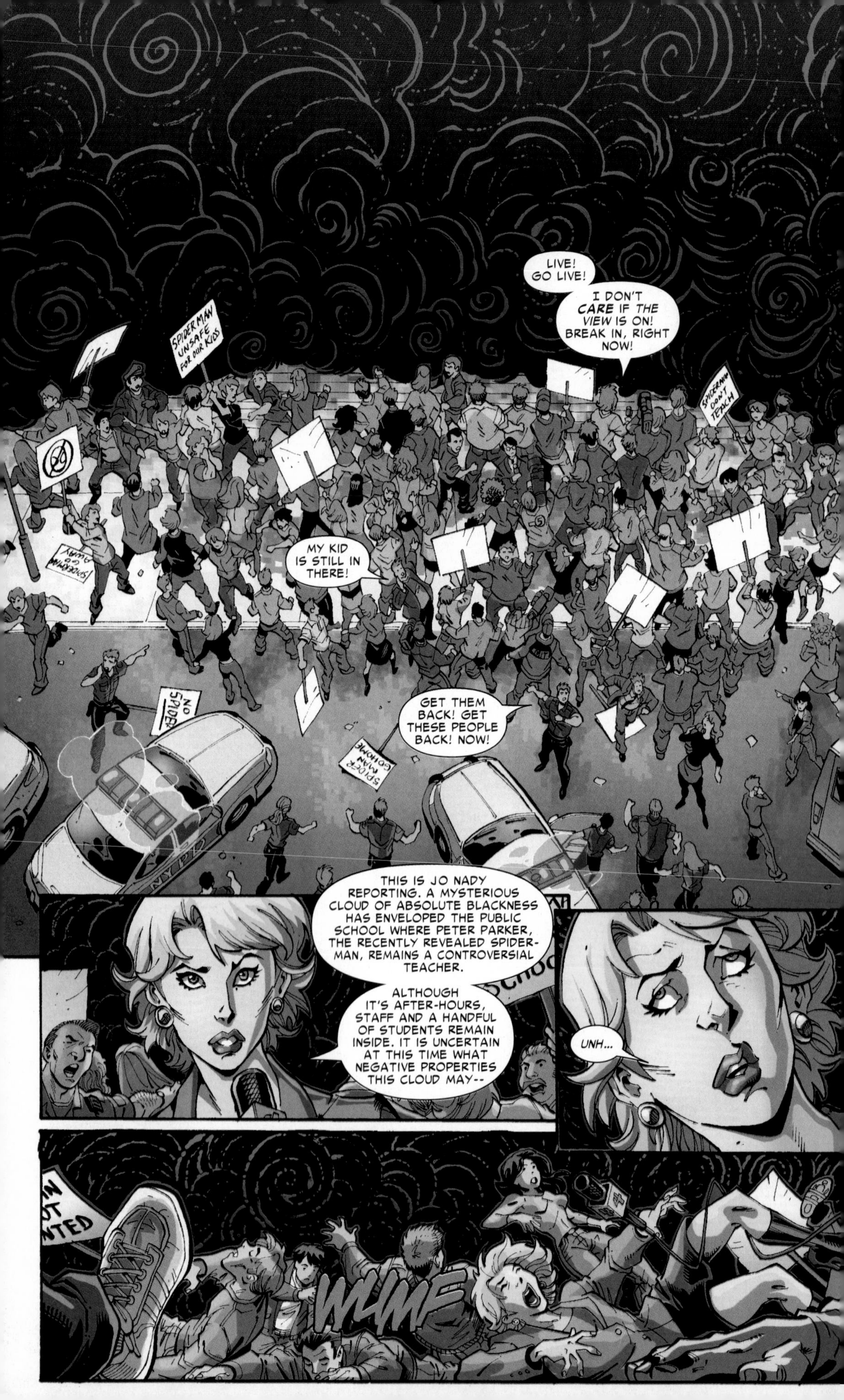
SPIDERMAN UNSAFE FOR OUR KIDS
LIVE! GO LIVE!
I DON'T CARE IF THE VIEW IS ON! BREAK IN, RIGHT NOW!
MY KID IS STILL IN THERE!
GET THEM BACK! GET THESE PEOPLE BACK! NOW!
THIS IS JO NADY REPORTING. A MYSTERIOUS CLOUD OF ABSOLUTE BLACKNESS HAS ENVELOPED THE PUBLIC SCHOOL WHERE PETER PARKER, THE RECENTLY REVEALED SPIDER-MAN, REMAINS A CONTROVERSIAL TEACHER.
ALTHOUGH IT'S AFTER-HOURS, STAFF AND A HANDFUL OF STUDENTS REMAIN INSIDE. IT IS UNCERTAIN AT THIS TIME WHAT NEGATIVE PROPERTIES THIS CLOUD MAY--
UNH...
WUMF

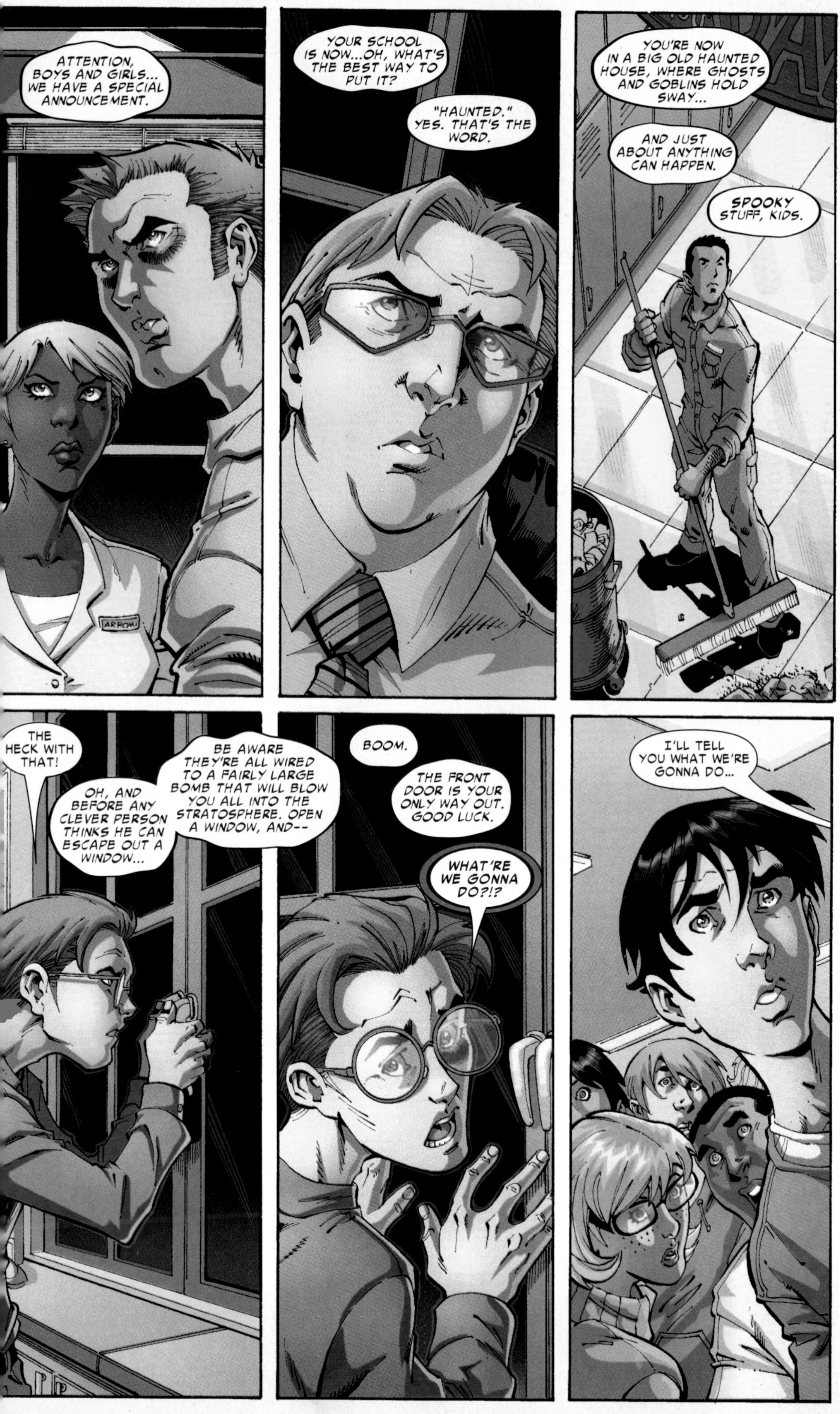

ATTENTION, BOYS AND GIRLS... WE HAVE A SPECIAL ANNOUNCEMENT.
YOUR SCHOOL IS NOW...OH, WHAT'S THE BEST WAY TO PUT IT?
"HAUNTED." YES. THAT'S THE WORD.
YOU'RE NOW IN A BIG OLD HAUNTED HOUSE, WHERE GHOSTS AND GOBLINS HOLD SWAY...
AND JUST ABOUT ANYTHING CAN HAPPEN.
SPOOKY STUFF, KIDS.
THE HECK WITH THAT!
OH, AND BEFORE ANY CLEVER PERSON THINKS HE CAN ESCAPE OUT A WINDOW...
BE AWARE THEY'RE ALL WIRED TO A FAIRLY LARGE BOMB THAT WILL BLOW YOU ALL INTO THE STRATOSPHERE. OPEN A WINDOW, AND--
BOOM.
THE FRONT DOOR IS YOUR ONLY WAY OUT. GOOD LUCK.
WHAT'RE WE GONNA DO?!?
I'LL TELL YOU WHAT WE'RE GONNA DO...

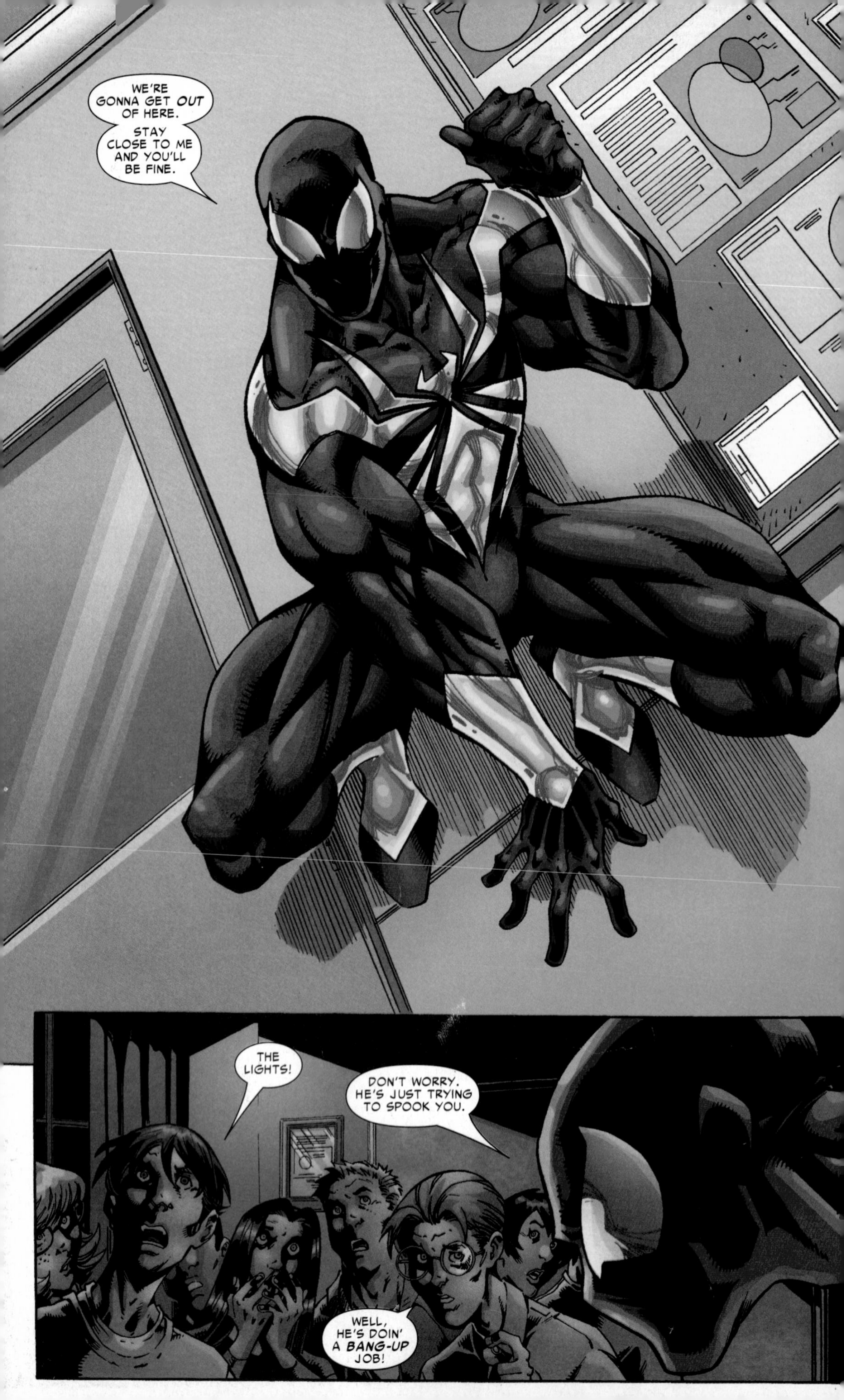
WE'RE GONNA GET OUT OF HERE.
STAY CLOSE TO ME AND YOU'LL BE FINE.
THE LIGHTS!
DON'T WORRY. HE'S JUST TRYING TO SPOOK YOU.
WELL, HE'S DOIN' A BANG-UP JOB!

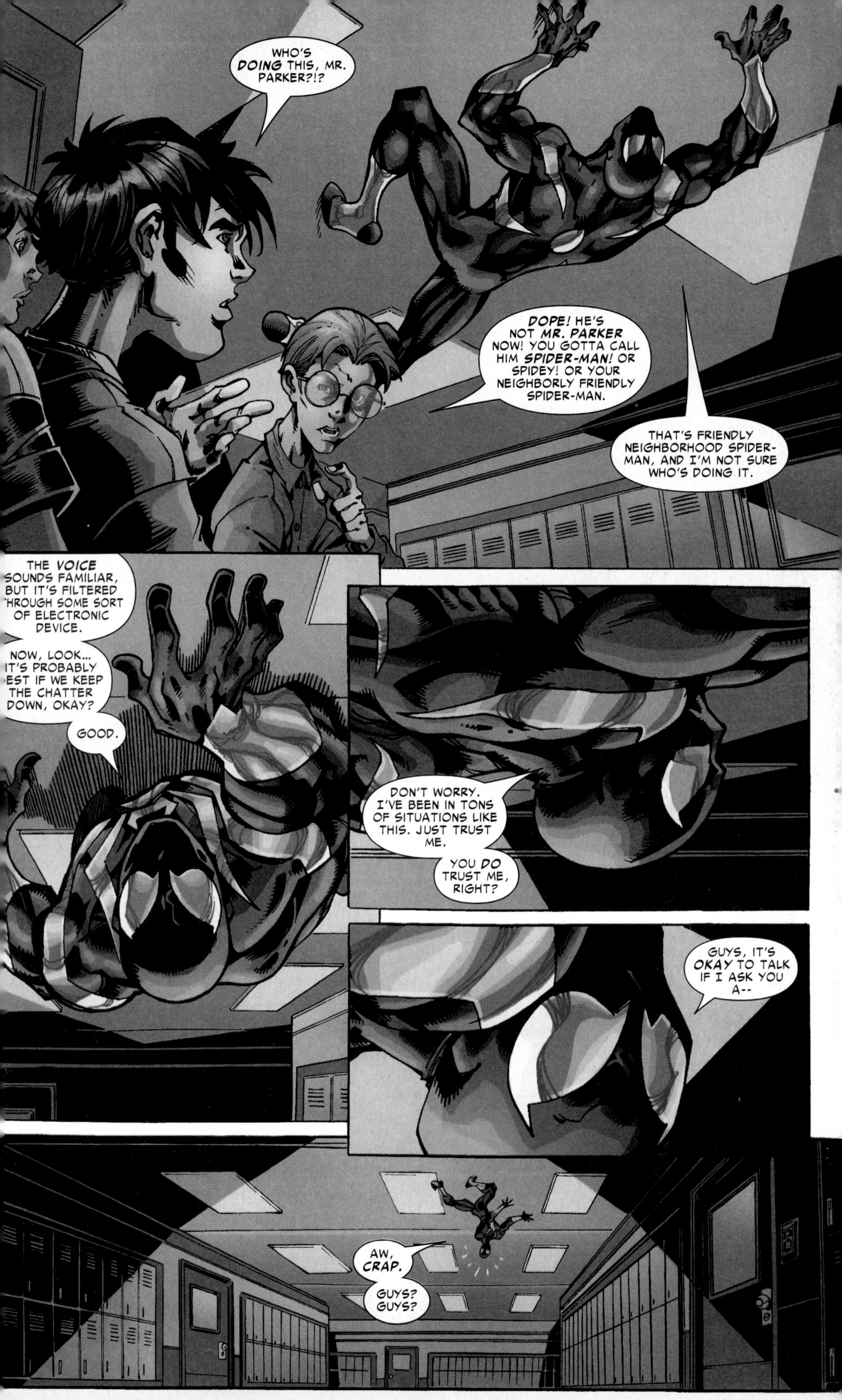

WHO'S DOING THIS, MR. PARKER?!?
DOPE! HE'S NOT MR. PARKER NOW! YOU GOTTA CALL HIM SPIDER-MAN! OR SPIDEY! OR YOUR NEIGHBORLY FRIENDLY SPIDER-MAN.
THAT'S FRIENDLY NEIGHBORHOOD SPIDER-MAN, AND I'M NOT SURE WHO'S DOING IT.
THE VOICE SOUNDS FAMILIAR, BUT IT'S FILTERED THROUGH SOME SORT OF ELECTRONIC DEVICE.
NOW, LOOK... IT'S PROBABLY BEST IF WE KEEP THE CHATTER DOWN, OKAY?
GOOD.
DON'T WORRY. I'VE BEEN IN TONS OF SITUATIONS LIKE THIS. JUST TRUST ME.
YOU DO TRUST ME, RIGHT?
GUYS, IT'S OKAY TO TALK IF I ASK YOU A--
AW, CRAP.
GUYS? GUYS?

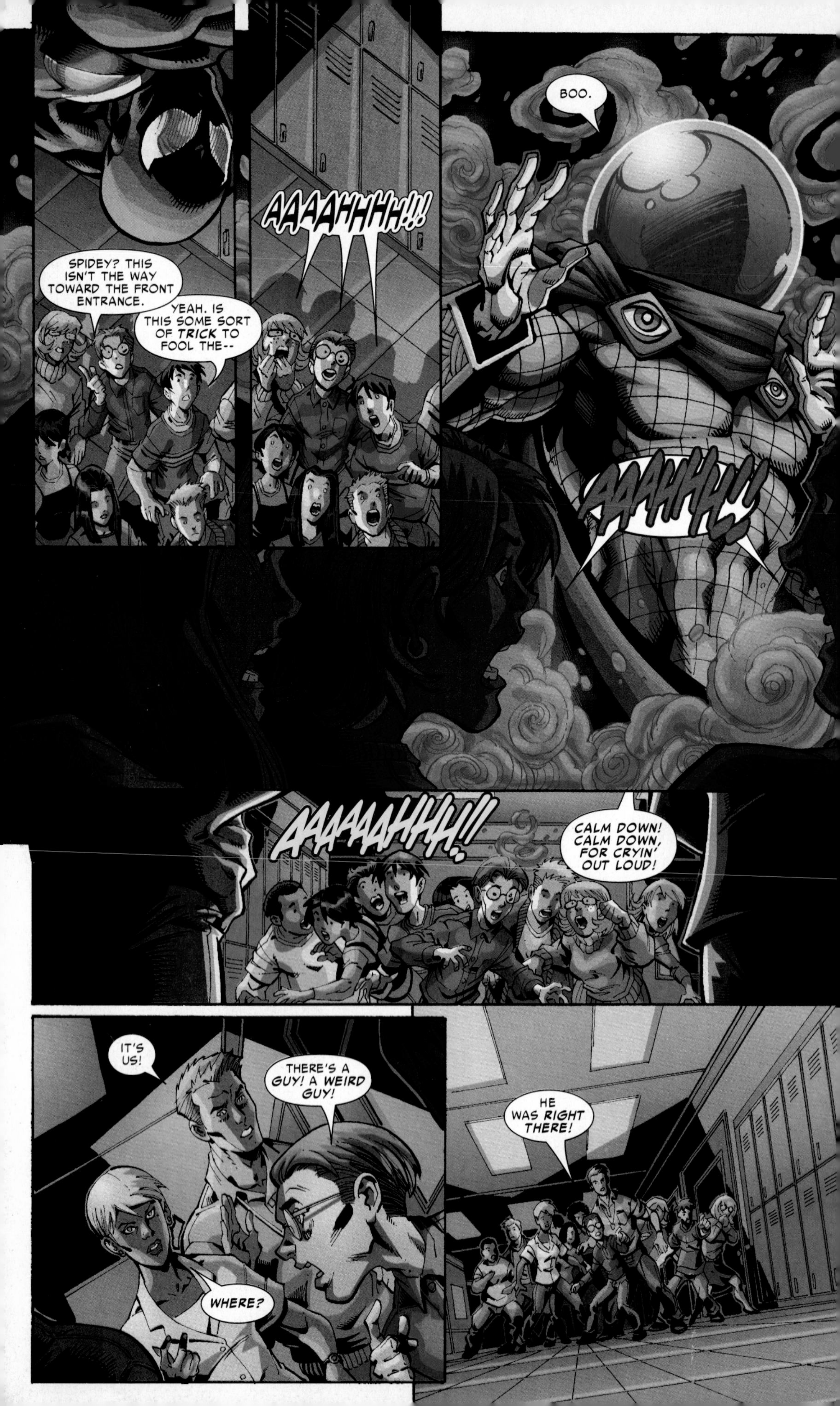
SPIDEY? THIS ISN'T THE WAY TOWARD THE FRONT ENTRANCE.
YEAH. IS THIS SOME SORT OF TRICK TO FOOL THE--
AAAAHHHH!!!
BOO.
AAAHHH!!
AAAAAAHHHH!!
CALM DOWN! CALM DOWN, FOR CRYIN' OUT LOUD!
IT'S US!
THERE'S A GUY! A WEIRD GUY!
WHERE?
HE WAS RIGHT THERE!

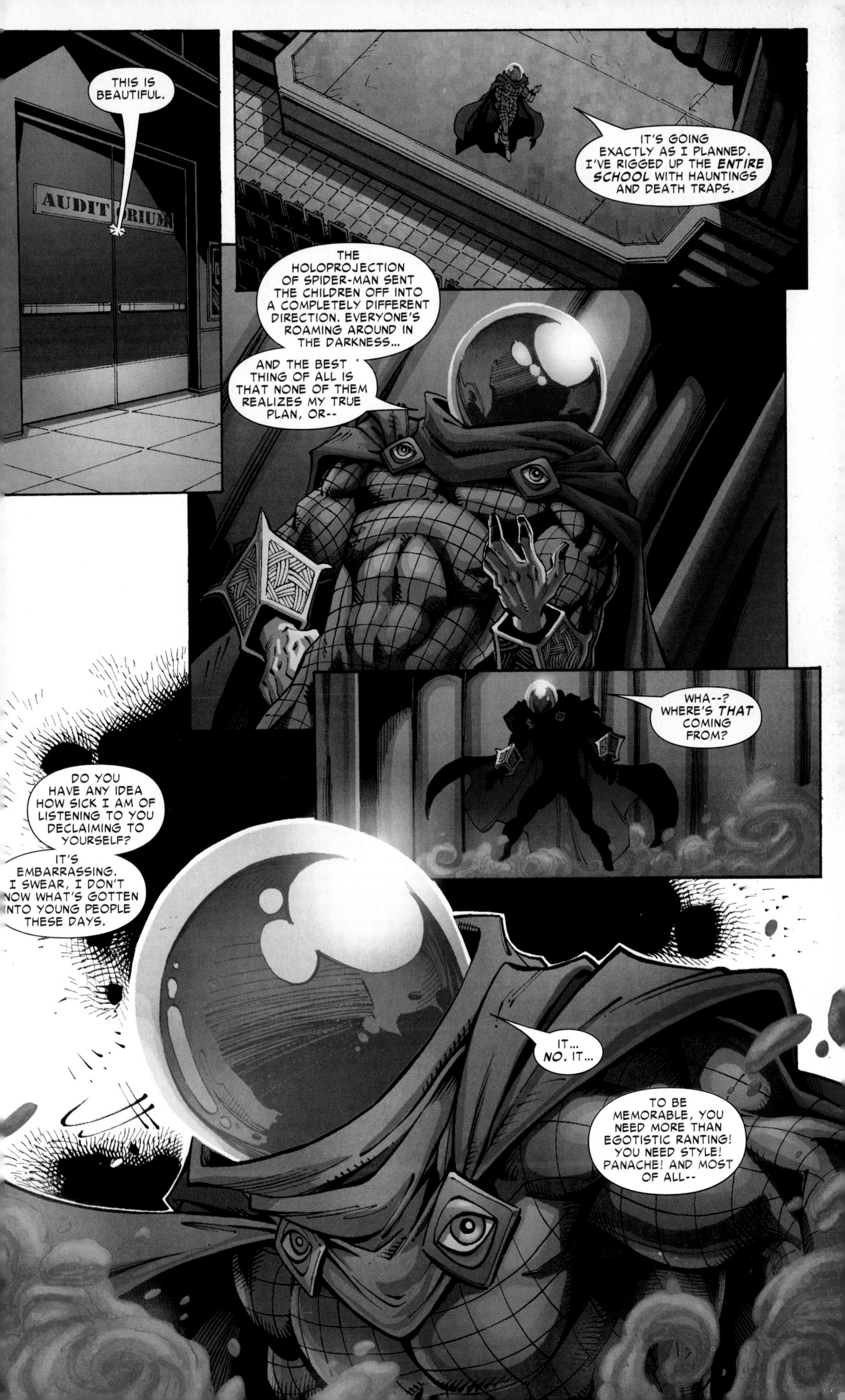
THIS IS BEAUTIFUL.
AUDITORIUM
IT'S GOING EXACTLY AS I PLANNED. I'VE RIGGED UP THE ENTIRE SCHOOL WITH HAUNTINGS AND DEATH TRAPS.
THE HOLOPROJECTION OF SPIDER-MAN SENT THE CHILDREN OFF INTO A COMPLETELY DIFFERENT DIRECTION. EVERYONE'S ROAMING AROUND IN THE DARKNESS...
AND THE BEST THING OF ALL IS THAT NONE OF THEM REALIZES MY TRUE PLAN, OR--
WHA--? WHERE'S THAT COMING FROM?
DO YOU HAVE ANY IDEA HOW SICK I AM OF LISTENING TO YOU DECLAIMING TO YOURSELF?
IT'S EMBARRASSING. I SWEAR, I DON'T NOW WHAT'S GOTTEN INTO YOUNG PEOPLE THESE DAYS.
IT... NO. IT...
TO BE MEMORABLE, YOU NEED MORE THAN EGOTISTIC RANTING! YOU NEED STYLE! PANACHE! AND MOST OF ALL--

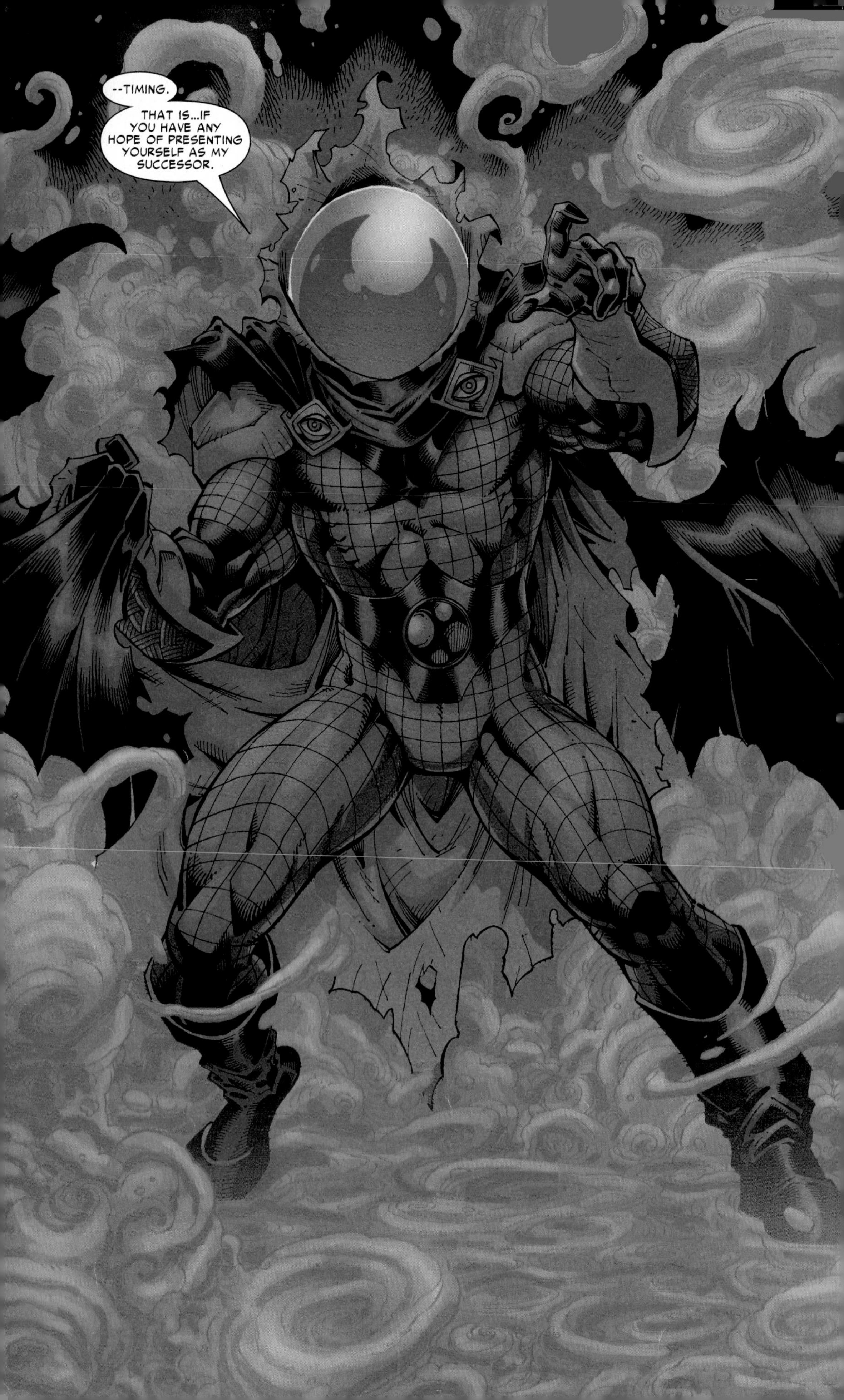
--TIMING.
THAT IS...IF YOU HAVE ANY HOPE OF PRESENTING YOURSELF AS MY SUCCESSOR.

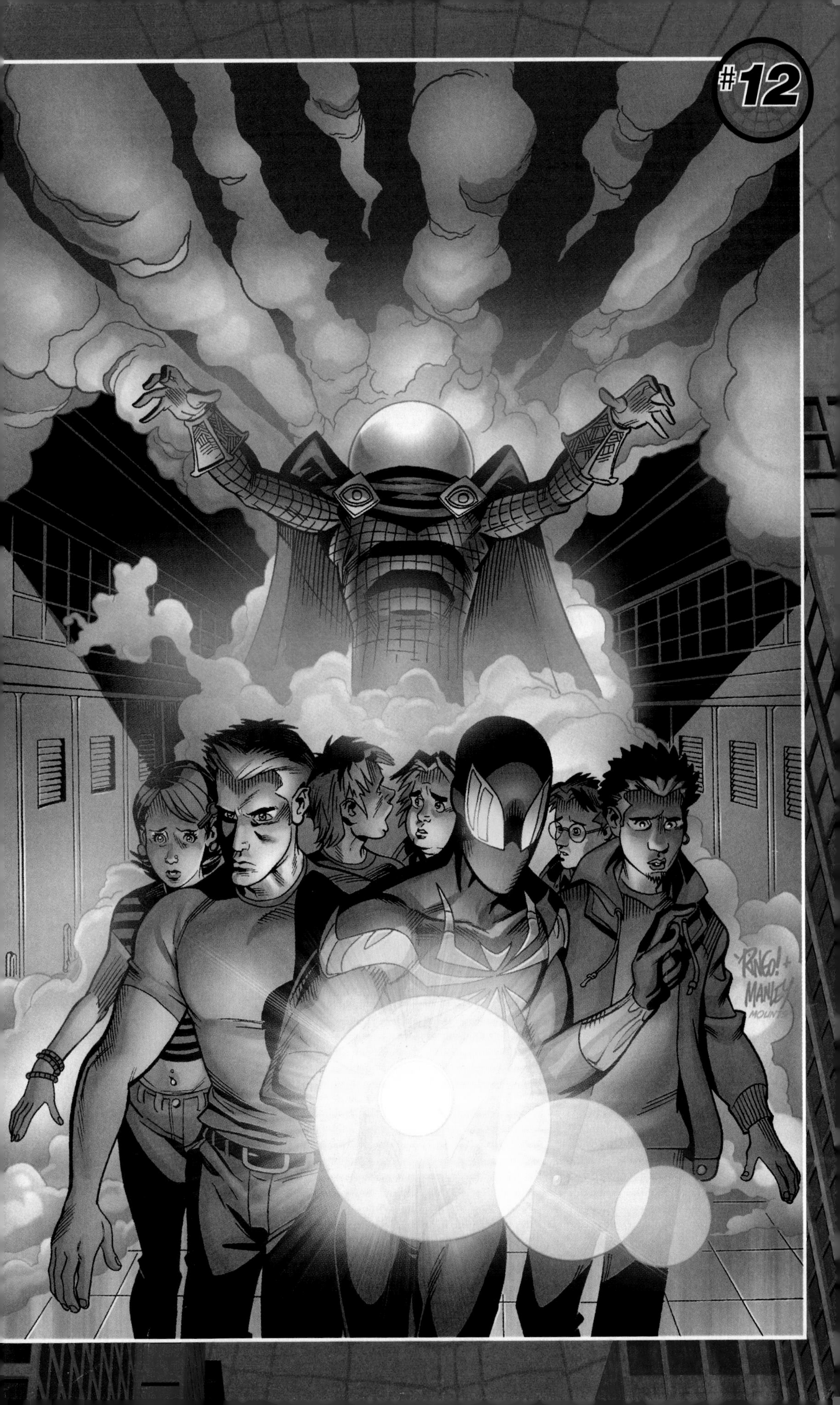
#12
RINGO! +
MANLEY
MOUNTS

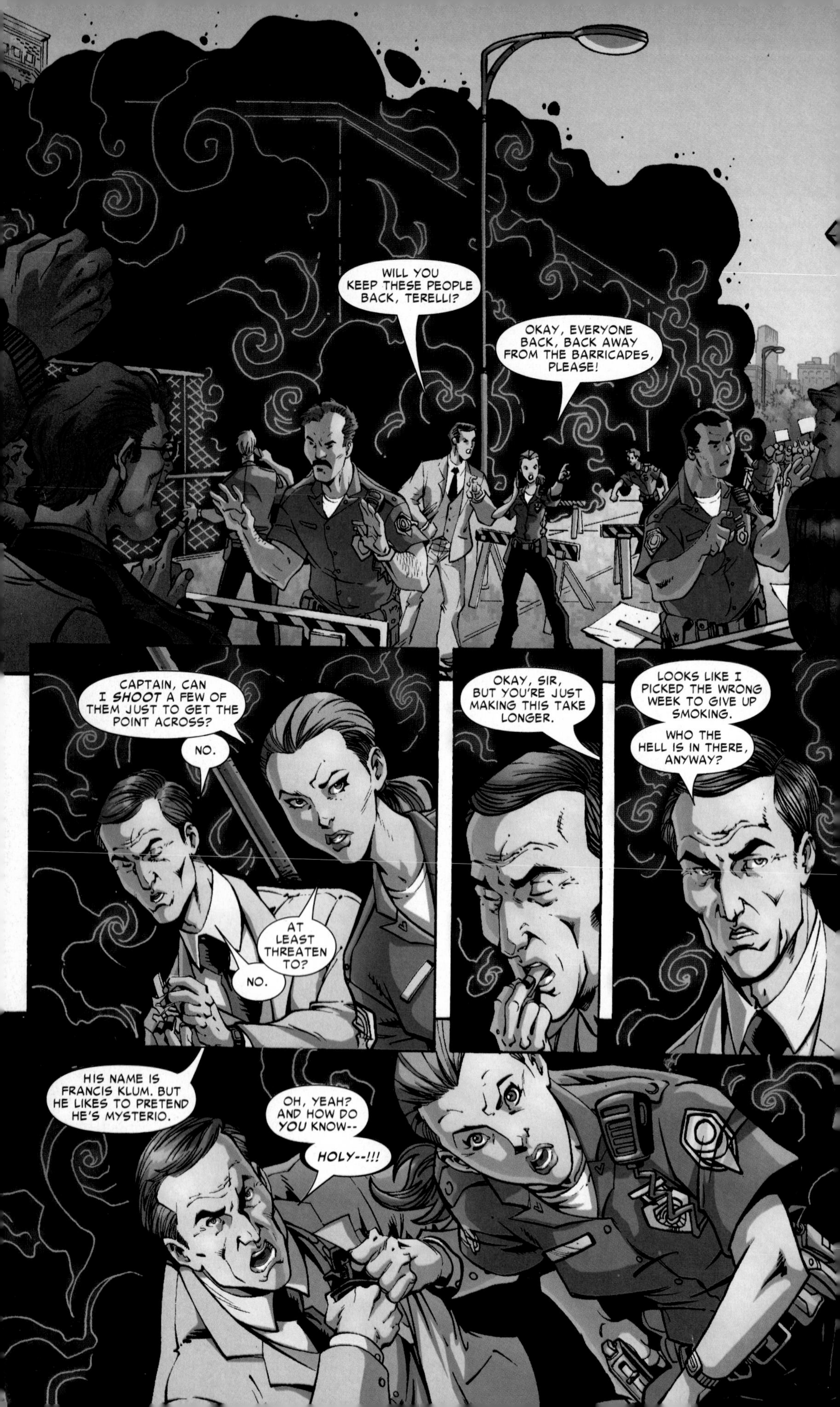

WILL YOU KEEP THESE PEOPLE BACK, TERELLI?
OKAY, EVERYONE BACK, BACK AWAY FROM THE BARRICADES, PLEASE!
CAPTAIN, CAN I *SHOOT* A FEW OF THEM JUST TO GET THE POINT ACROSS?
NO.
AT LEAST THREATEN TO?
NO.
OKAY, SIR, BUT YOU'RE JUST MAKING THIS TAKE LONGER.
LOOKS LIKE I PICKED THE WRONG WEEK TO GIVE UP SMOKING.
WHO THE HELL IS IN THERE, ANYWAY?
HIS NAME IS FRANCIS KLUM. BUT HE LIKES TO PRETEND HE'S MYSTERIO.
OH, YEAH? AND HOW DO *YOU* KNOW--
HOLY--!!!

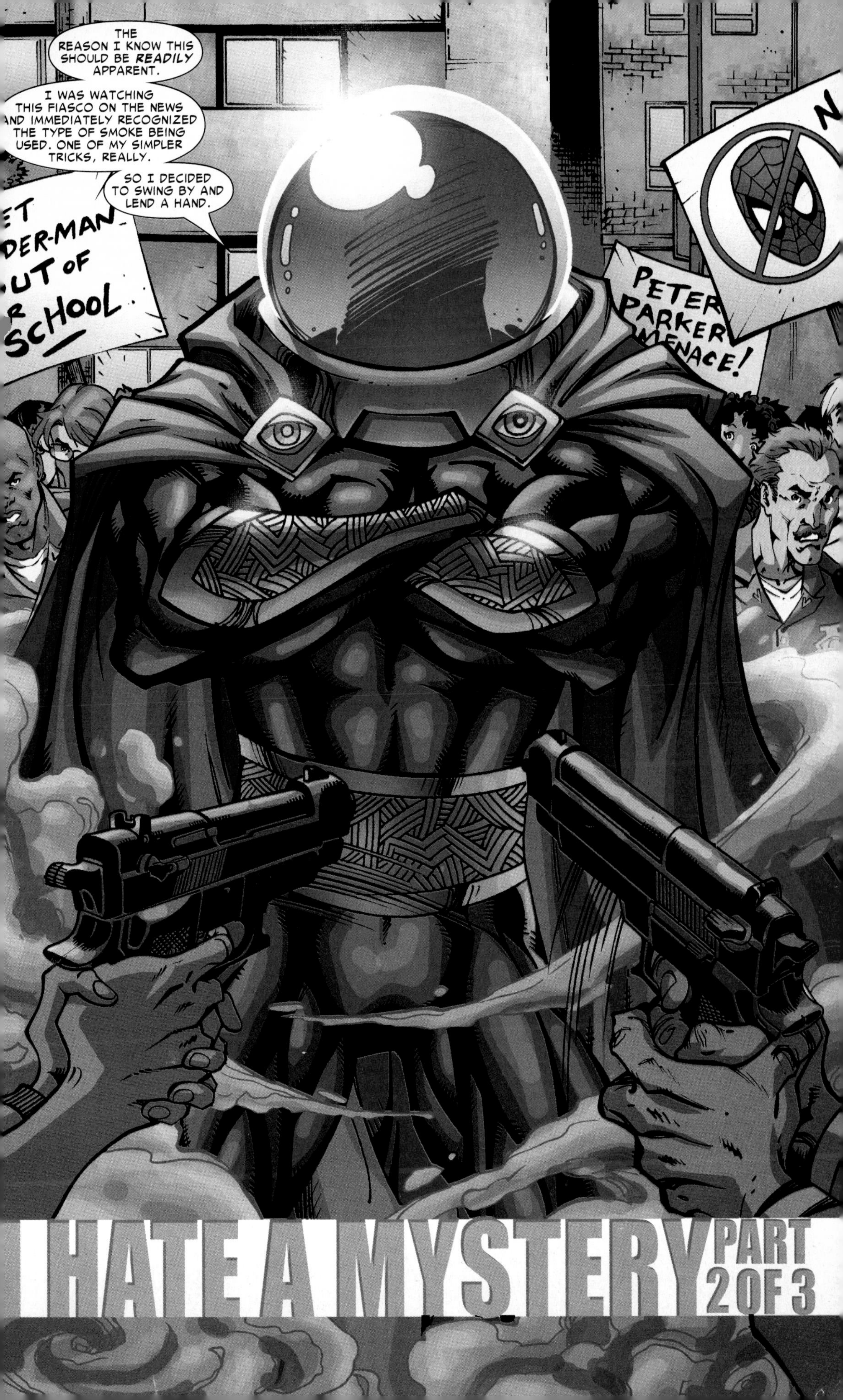

THE REASON I KNOW THIS SHOULD BE *READILY* APPARENT.
I WAS WATCHING THIS FIASCO ON THE NEWS AND IMMEDIATELY RECOGNIZED THE TYPE OF SMOKE BEING USED. ONE OF MY SIMPLER TRICKS, REALLY.
SO I DECIDED TO SWING BY AND LEND A HAND.
PETER PARKER MENACE!
I HATE A MYSTERY PART 2 OF 3

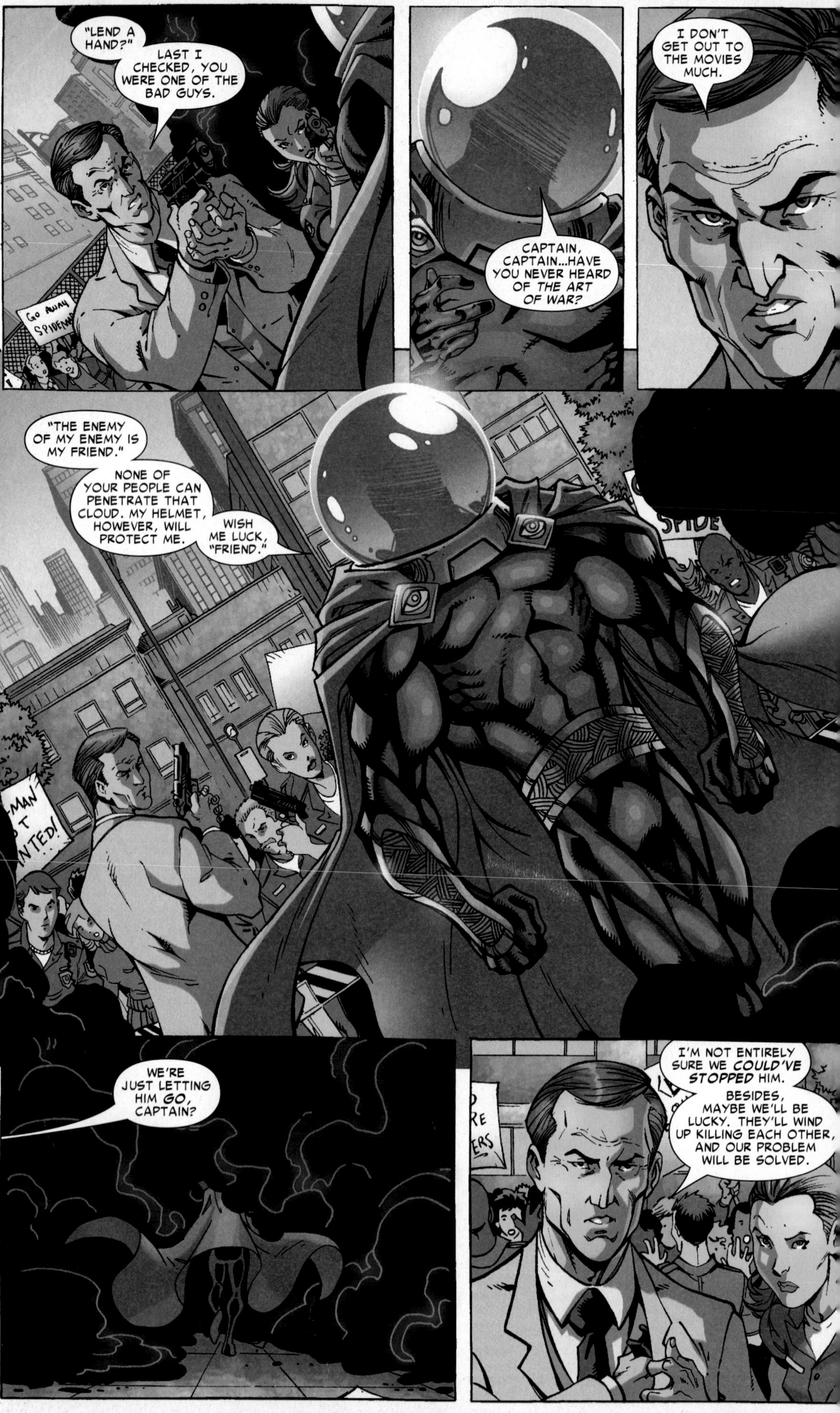
"LEND A HAND?"
LAST I CHECKED, YOU WERE ONE OF THE BAD GUYS.
CAPTAIN, CAPTAIN...HAVE YOU NEVER HEARD OF THE ART OF WAR?
I DON'T GET OUT TO THE MOVIES MUCH.
"THE ENEMY OF MY ENEMY IS MY FRIEND."
NONE OF YOUR PEOPLE CAN PENETRATE THAT CLOUD. MY HELMET, HOWEVER, WILL PROTECT ME.
WISH ME LUCK, "FRIEND."
WE'RE JUST LETTING HIM GO, CAPTAIN?
I'M NOT ENTIRELY SURE WE COULD'VE STOPPED HIM.
BESIDES, MAYBE WE'LL BE LUCKY. THEY'LL WIND UP KILLING EACH OTHER, AND OUR PROBLEM WILL BE SOLVED.

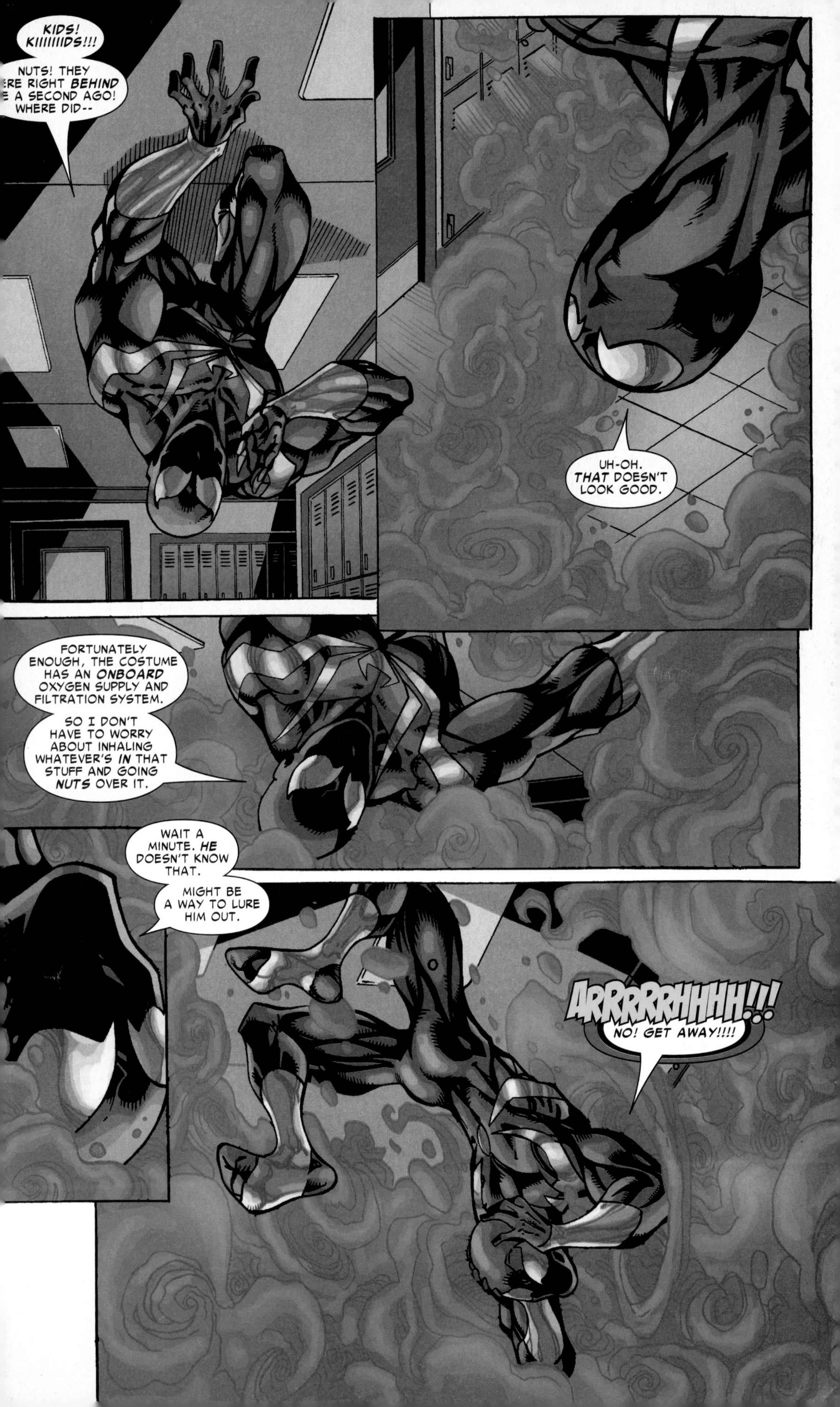
KIDS! KIIIIIIDS!!!
NUTS! THEY ERE RIGHT BEHIND E A SECOND AGO! WHERE DID--
UH-OH. THAT DOESN'T LOOK GOOD.
FORTUNATELY ENOUGH, THE COSTUME HAS AN ONBOARD OXYGEN SUPPLY AND FILTRATION SYSTEM.
SO I DON'T HAVE TO WORRY ABOUT INHALING WHATEVER'S IN THAT STUFF AND GOING NUTS OVER IT.
WAIT A MINUTE. HE DOESN'T KNOW THAT.
MIGHT BE A WAY TO LURE HIM OUT.
ARRRRRHHHH!!!
NO! GET AWAY!!!!

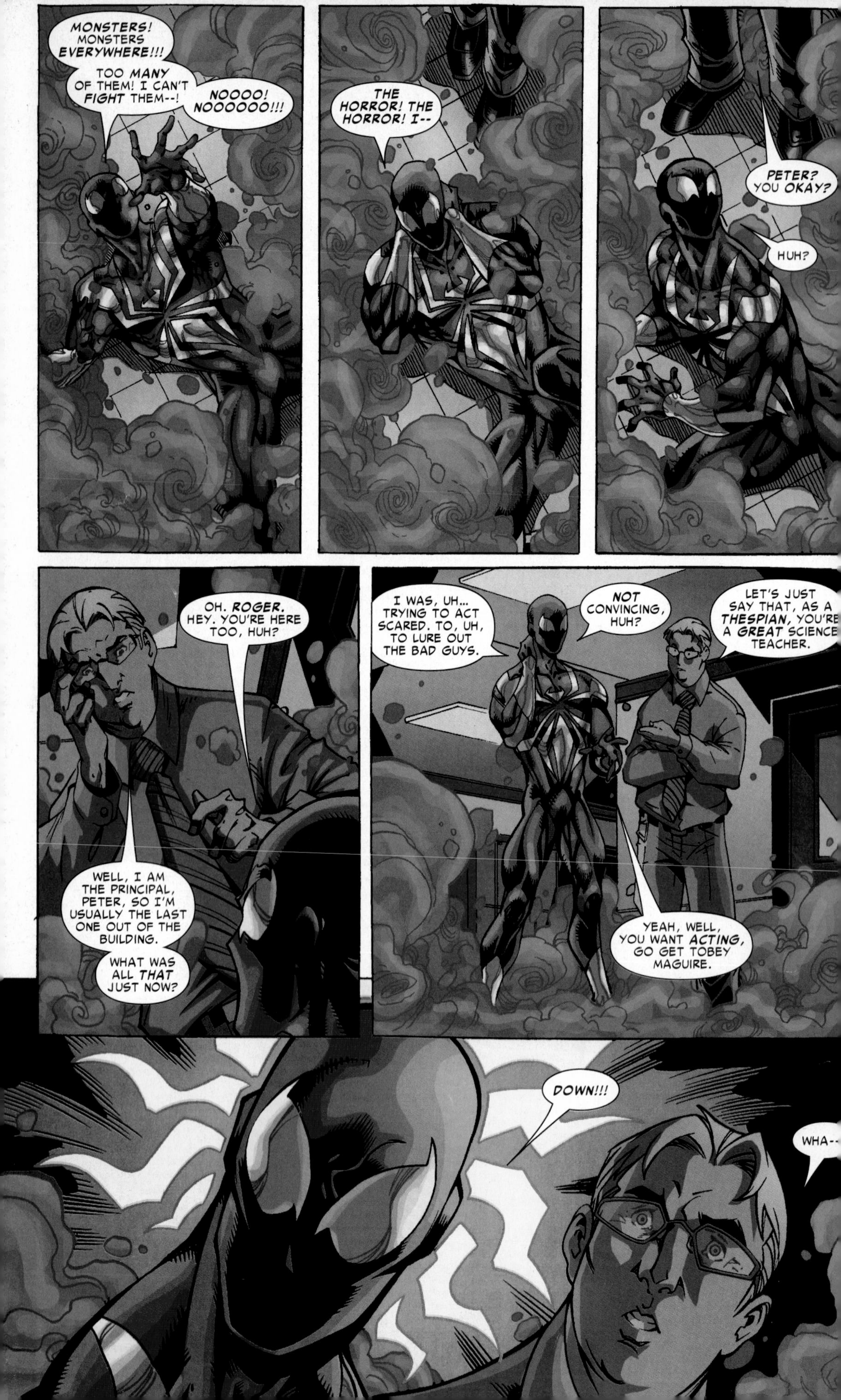

MONSTERS! MONSTERS EVERYWHERE!!!
TOO MANY OF THEM! I CAN'T FIGHT THEM--!
NOOOO! NOOOOOO!!!
THE HORROR! THE HORROR! I--
PETER? YOU OKAY?
HUH?
OH. ROGER. HEY. YOU'RE HERE TOO, HUH?
WELL, I AM THE PRINCIPAL, PETER, SO I'M USUALLY THE LAST ONE OUT OF THE BUILDING.
WHAT WAS ALL THAT JUST NOW?
I WAS, UH... TRYING TO ACT SCARED. TO, UH, TO LURE OUT THE BAD GUYS.
NOT CONVINCING, HUH?
LET'S JUST SAY THAT, AS A THESPIAN, YOU'RE A GREAT SCIENCE TEACHER.
YEAH, WELL, YOU WANT ACTING, GO GET TOBEY MAGUIRE.
DOWN!!!
WHA--

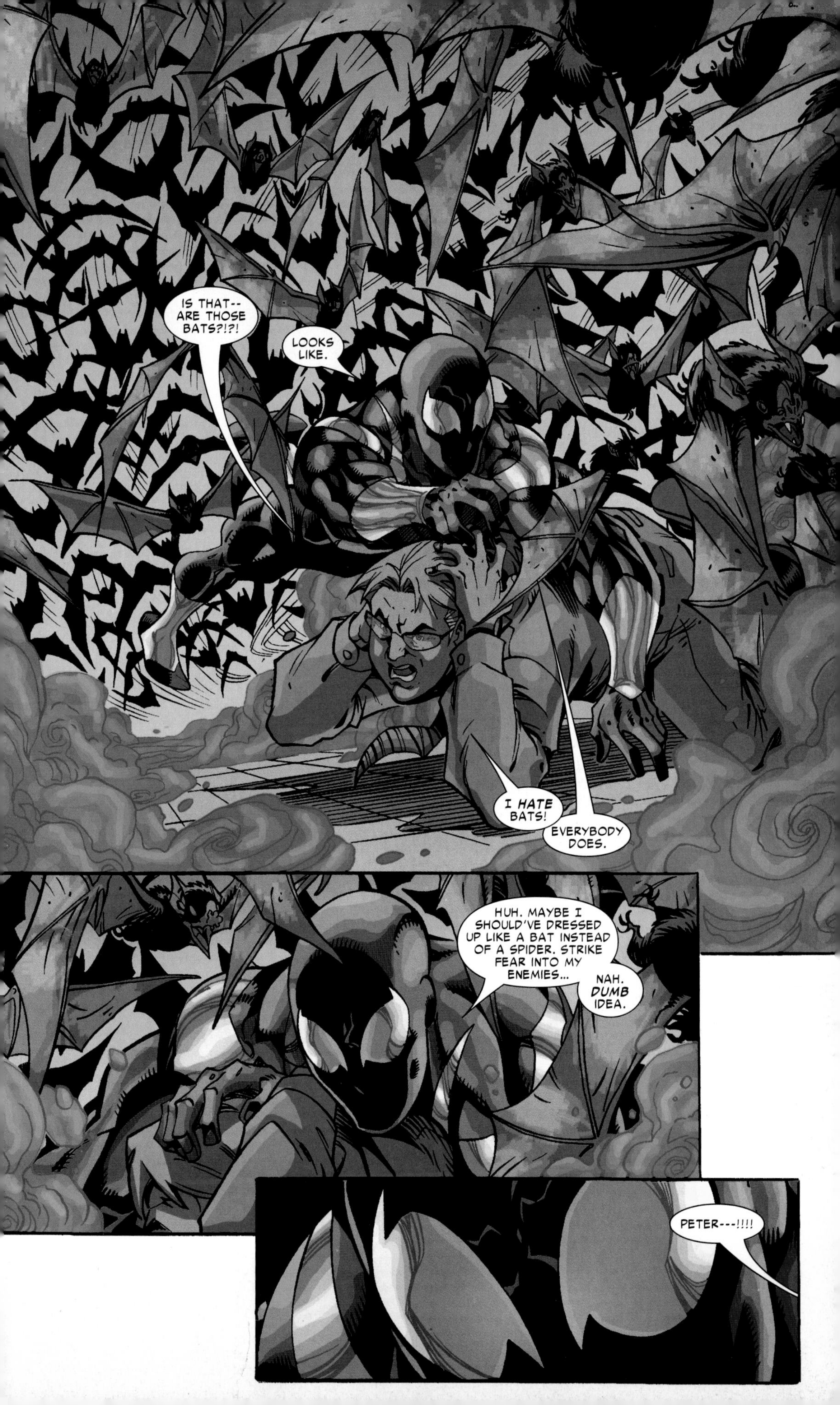
IS THAT-- ARE THOSE BATS?!?!
LOOKS LIKE.
I HATE BATS!
EVERYBODY DOES.
HUH. MAYBE I SHOULD'VE DRESSED UP LIKE A BAT INSTEAD OF A SPIDER. STRIKE FEAR INTO MY ENEMIES...
NAH. DUMB IDEA.
PETER---!!!!

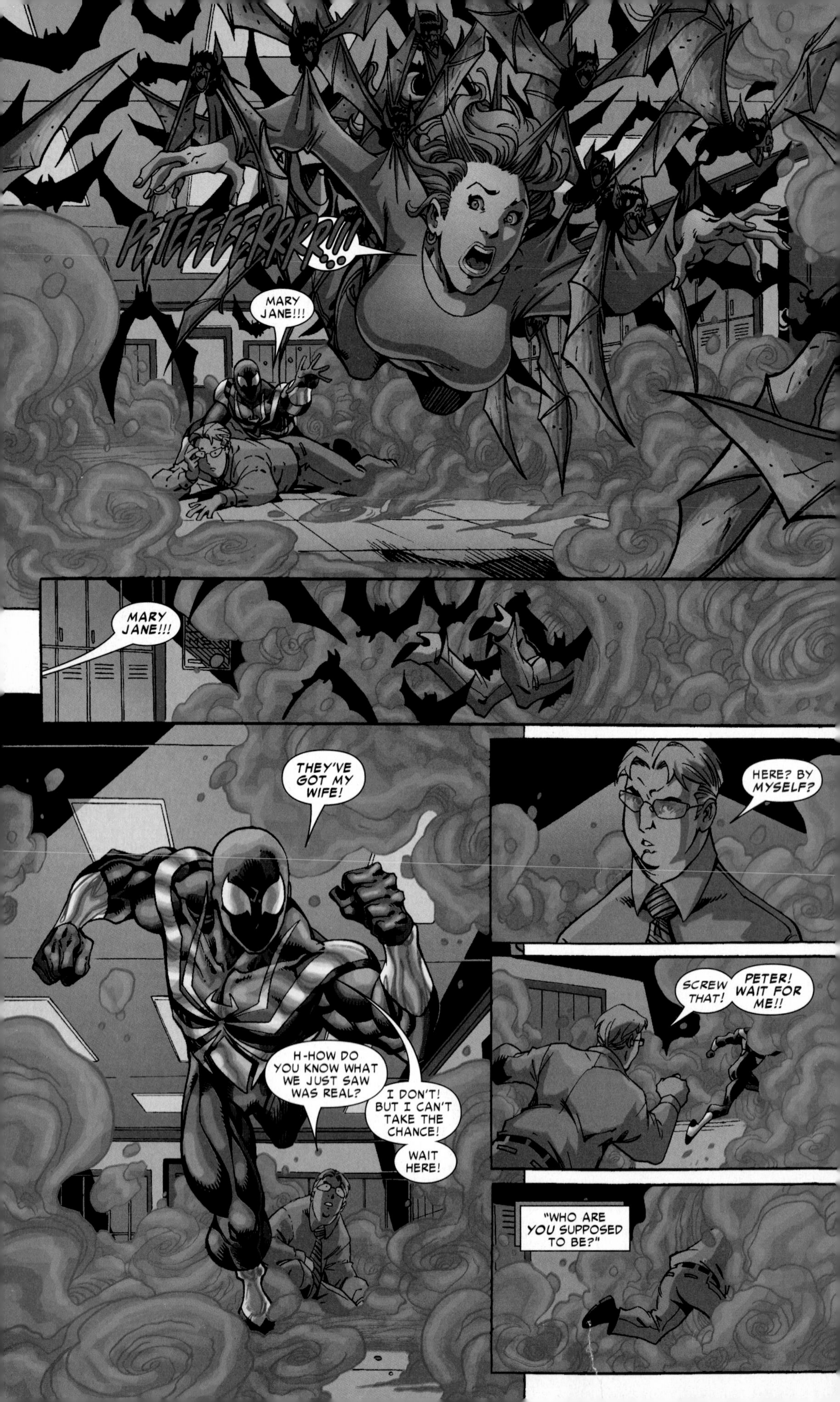
PETEEEEERRRR!!!
MARY JANE!!!
MARY JANE!!!
THEY'VE GOT MY WIFE!
H-HOW DO YOU KNOW WHAT WE JUST SAW WAS REAL?
I DON'T! BUT I CAN'T TAKE THE CHANCE!
WAIT HERE!
HERE? BY MYSELF?
SCREW THAT!
PETER! WAIT FOR ME!!
"WHO ARE YOU SUPPOSED TO BE?"

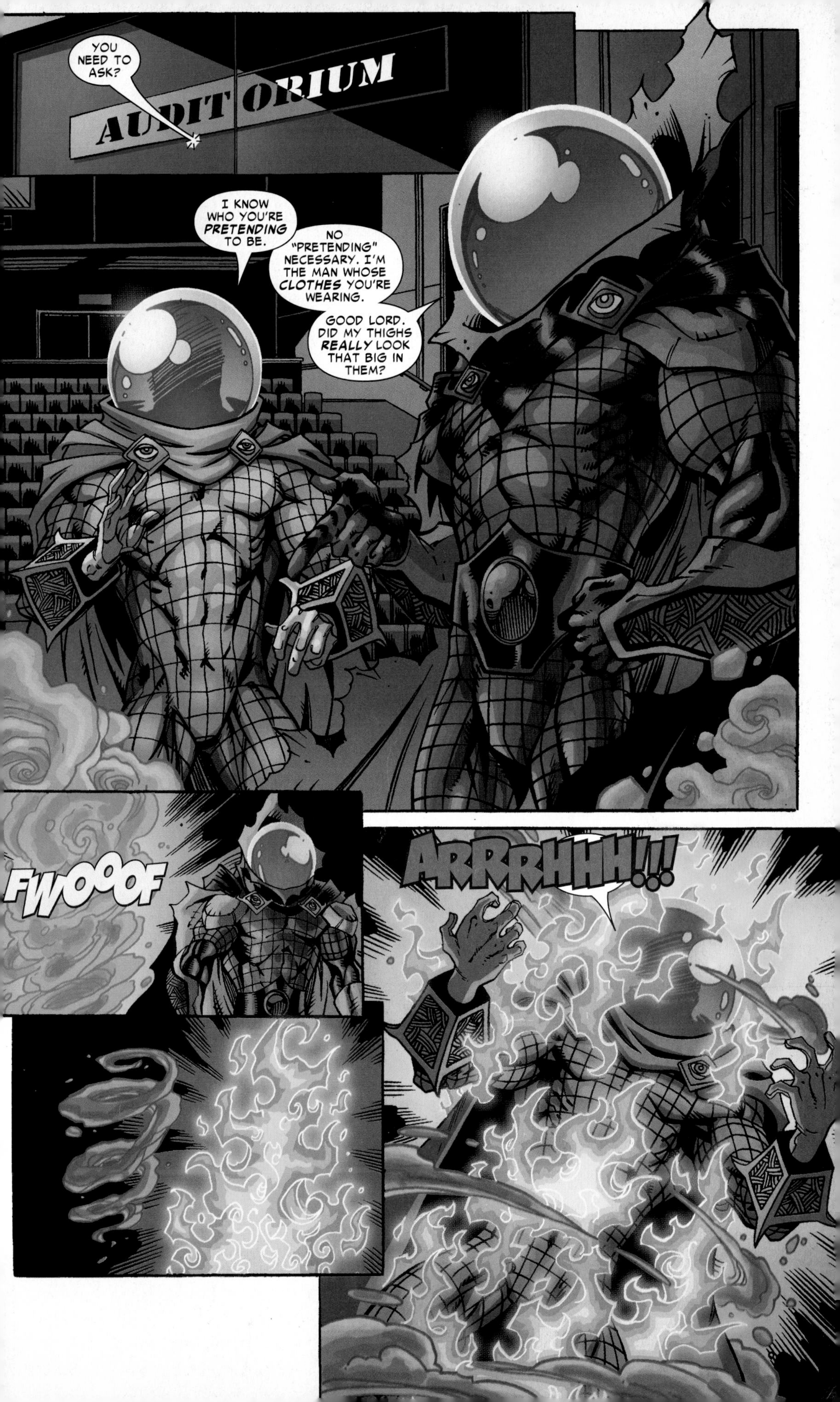
YOU NEED TO ASK?
AUDITORIUM
I KNOW WHO YOU'RE PRETENDING TO BE.
NO "PRETENDING" NECESSARY. I'M THE MAN WHOSE CLOTHES YOU'RE WEARING.
GOOD LORD. DID MY THIGHS REALLY LOOK THAT BIG IN THEM?
FWOOOF
ARRRHHH!!!

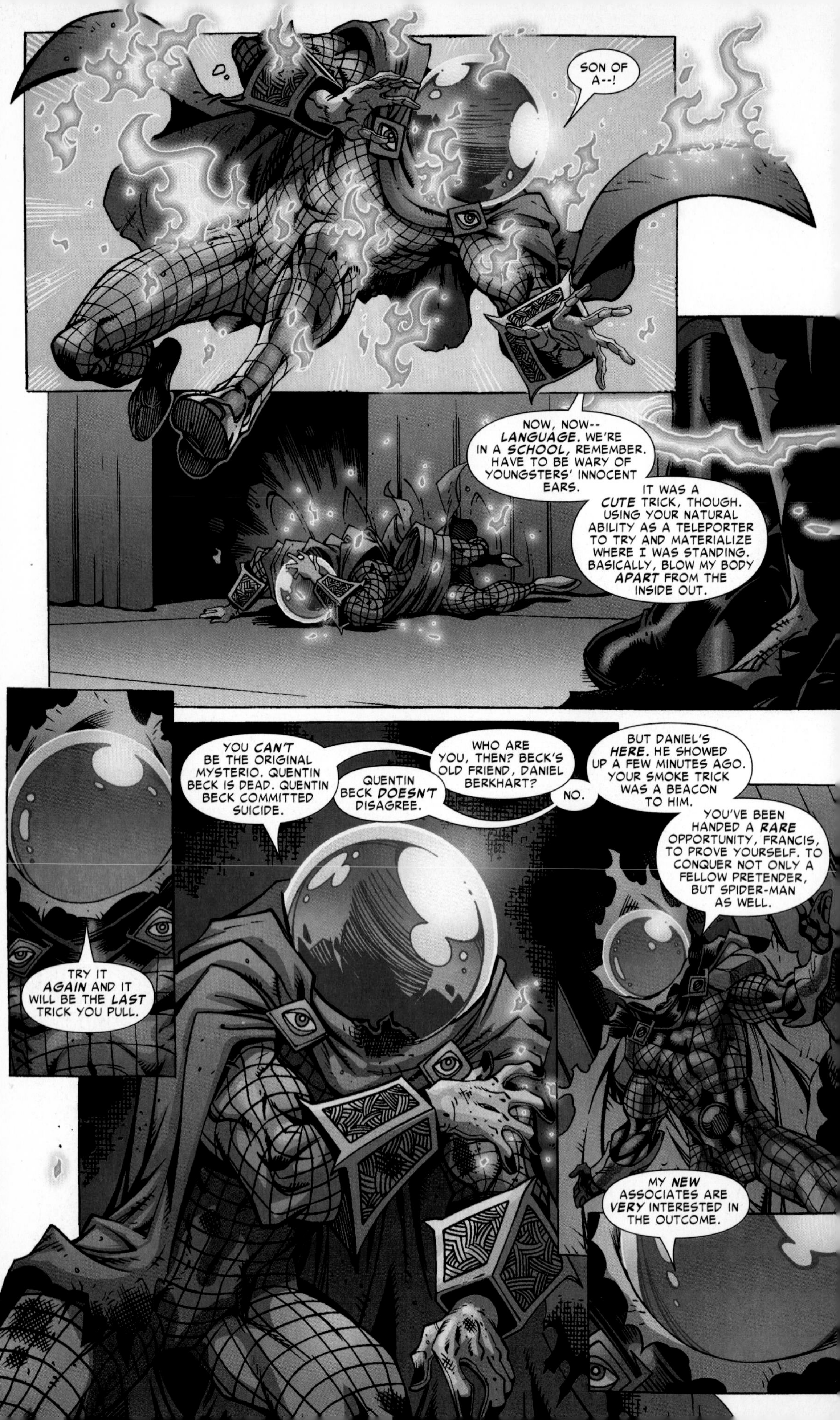

SON OF A--!
NOW, NOW-- LANGUAGE. WE'RE IN A SCHOOL, REMEMBER. HAVE TO BE WARY OF YOUNGSTERS' INNOCENT EARS.
IT WAS A CUTE TRICK, THOUGH. USING YOUR NATURAL ABILITY AS A TELEPORTER TO TRY AND MATERIALIZE WHERE I WAS STANDING. BASICALLY, BLOW MY BODY APART FROM THE INSIDE OUT.
TRY IT AGAIN AND IT WILL BE THE LAST TRICK YOU PULL.
YOU CAN'T BE THE ORIGINAL MYSTERIO. QUENTIN BECK IS DEAD. QUENTIN BECK COMMITTED SUICIDE.
QUENTIN BECK DOESN'T DISAGREE.
WHO ARE YOU, THEN? BECK'S OLD FRIEND, DANIEL BERKHART?
NO.
BUT DANIEL'S HERE. HE SHOWED UP A FEW MINUTES AGO. YOUR SMOKE TRICK WAS A BEACON TO HIM.
YOU'VE BEEN HANDED A RARE OPPORTUNITY, FRANCIS, TO PROVE YOURSELF. TO CONQUER NOT ONLY A FELLOW PRETENDER, BUT SPIDER-MAN AS WELL.
MY NEW ASSOCIATES ARE VERY INTERESTED IN THE OUTCOME.

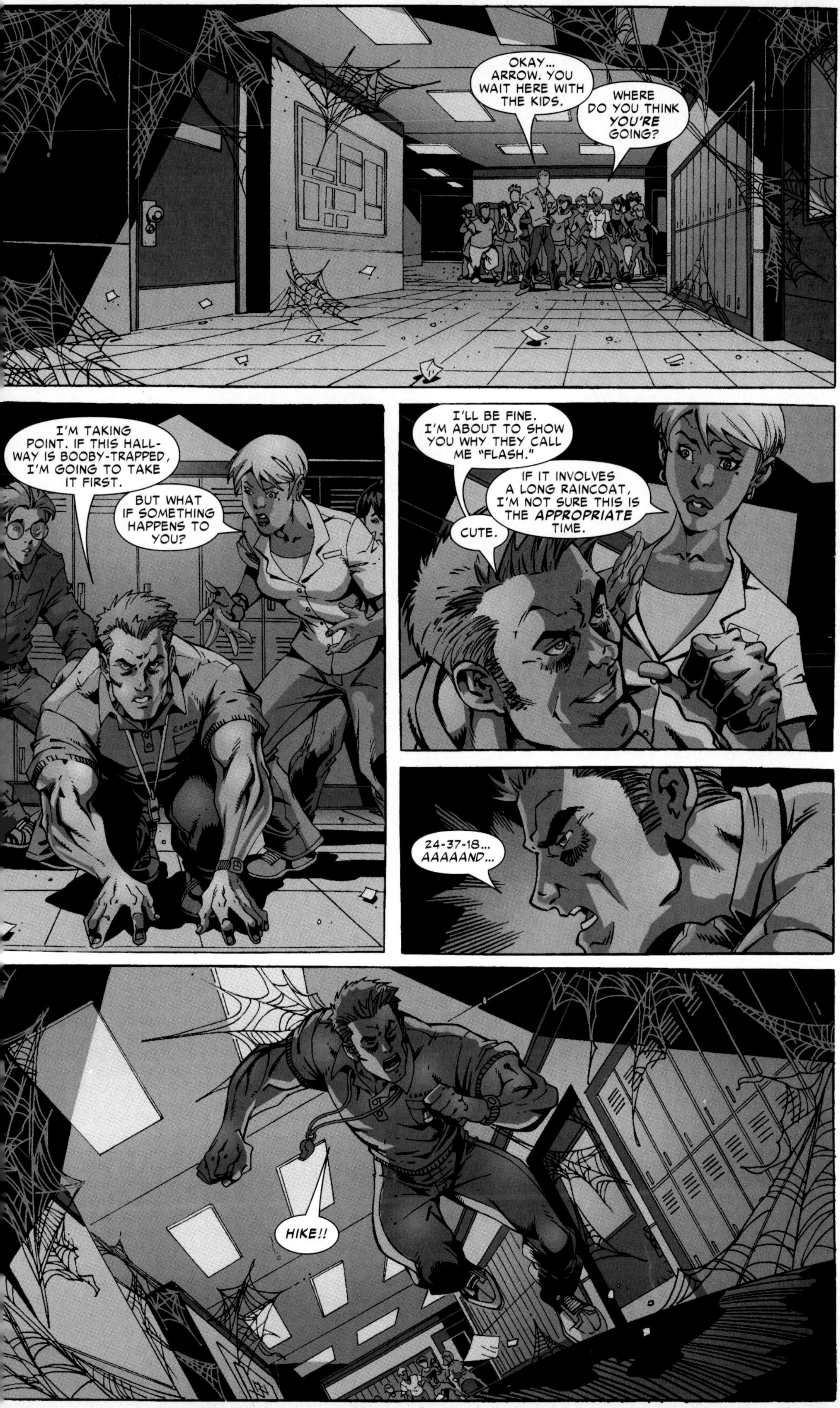
OKAY... ARROW. YOU WAIT HERE WITH THE KIDS.
WHERE DO YOU THINK *YOU'RE* GOING?
I'M TAKING POINT. IF THIS HALLWAY IS BOOBY-TRAPPED, I'M GOING TO TAKE IT FIRST.
BUT WHAT IF SOMETHING HAPPENS TO YOU?
I'LL BE FINE. I'M ABOUT TO SHOW YOU WHY THEY CALL ME "FLASH."
IF IT INVOLVES A LONG RAINCOAT, I'M NOT SURE THIS IS THE *APPROPRIATE* TIME.
CUTE.
24-37-18... AAAAAND...
HIKE!!

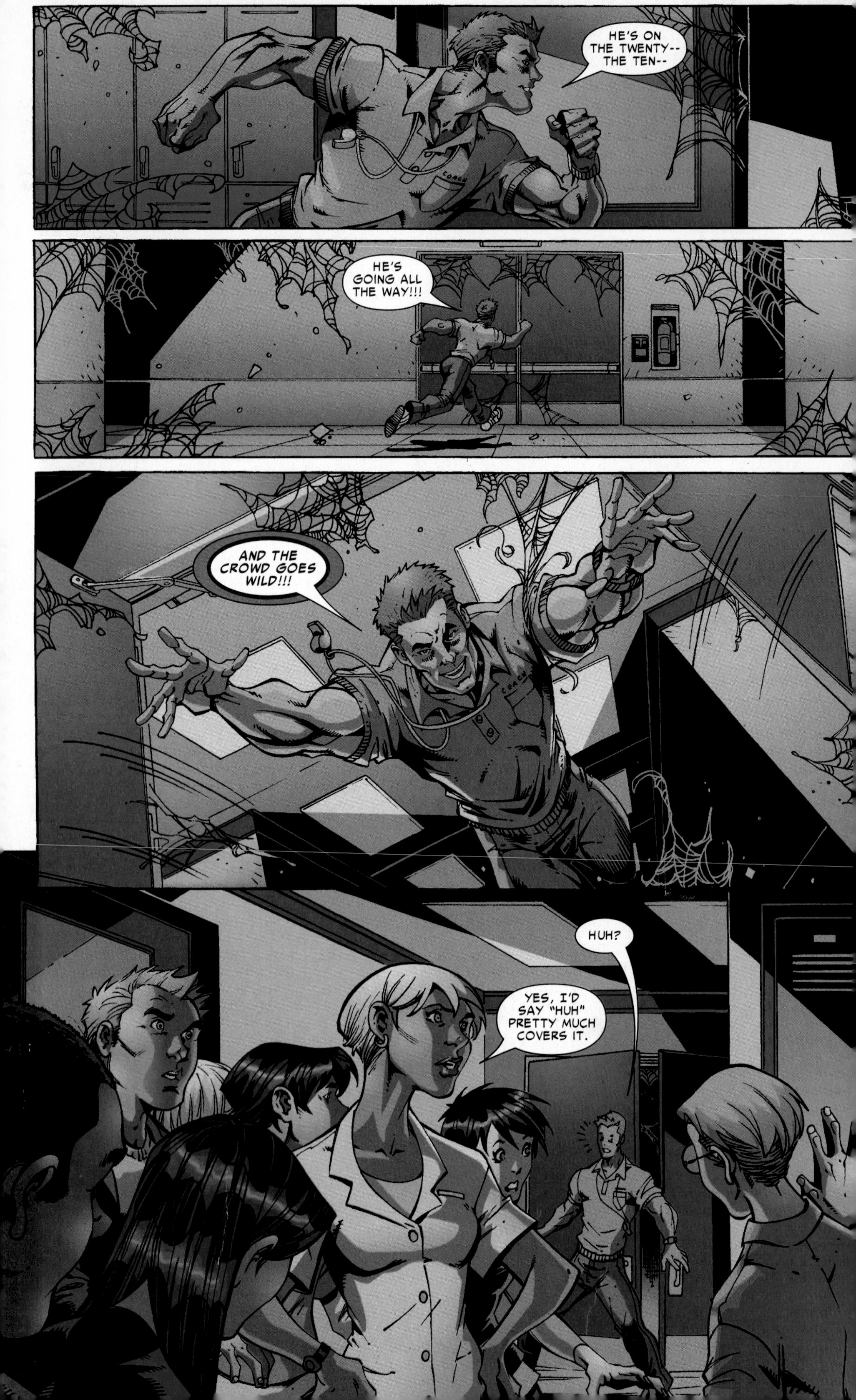
HE'S ON THE TWENTY-- THE TEN--
HE'S GOING ALL THE WAY!!!
AND THE CROWD GOES WILD!!!
HUH?
YES, I'D SAY "HUH" PRETTY MUCH COVERS IT.

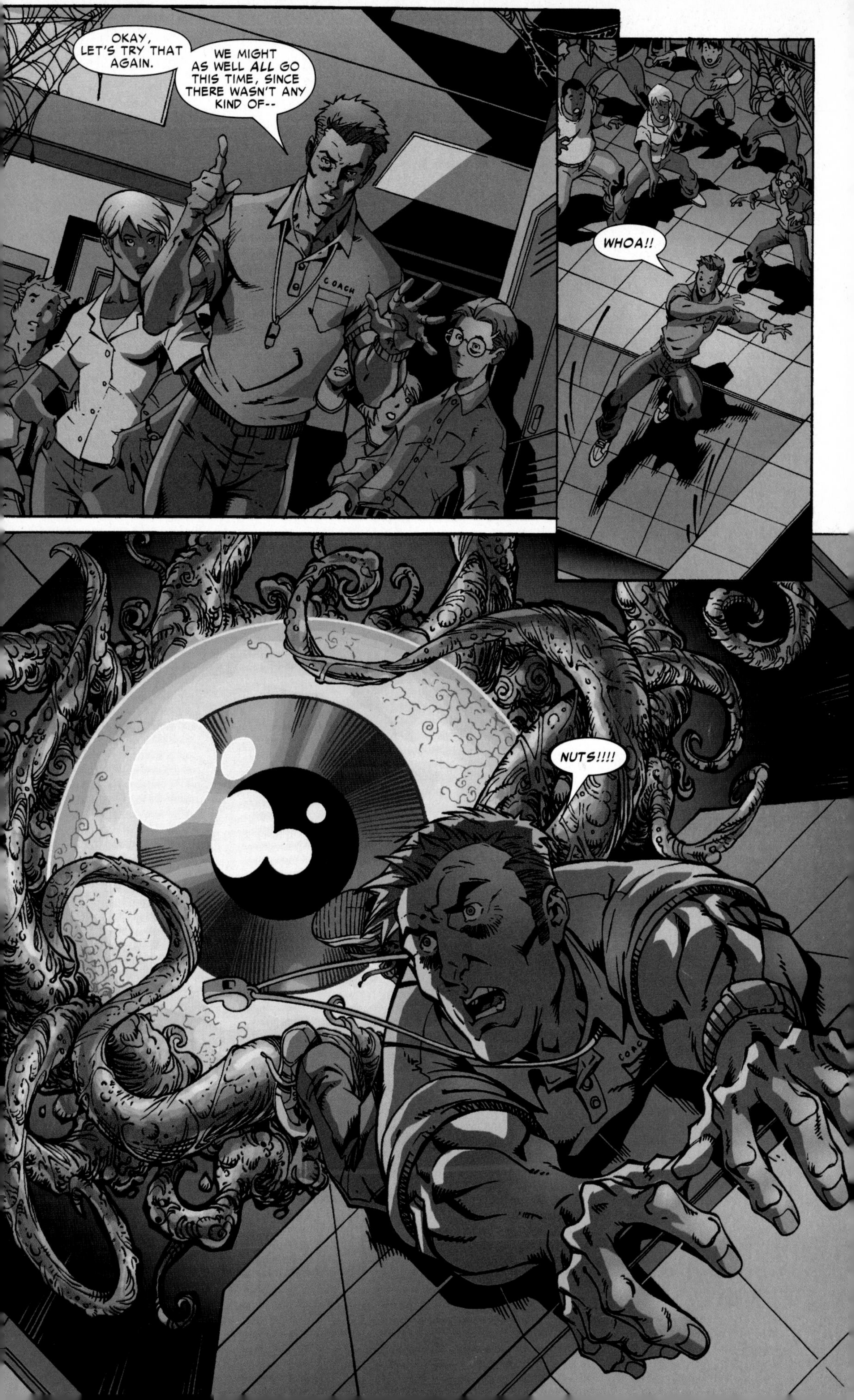
OKAY, LET'S TRY THAT AGAIN.
WE MIGHT AS WELL ALL GO THIS TIME, SINCE THERE WASN'T ANY KIND OF--
WHOA!!
NUTS!!!!

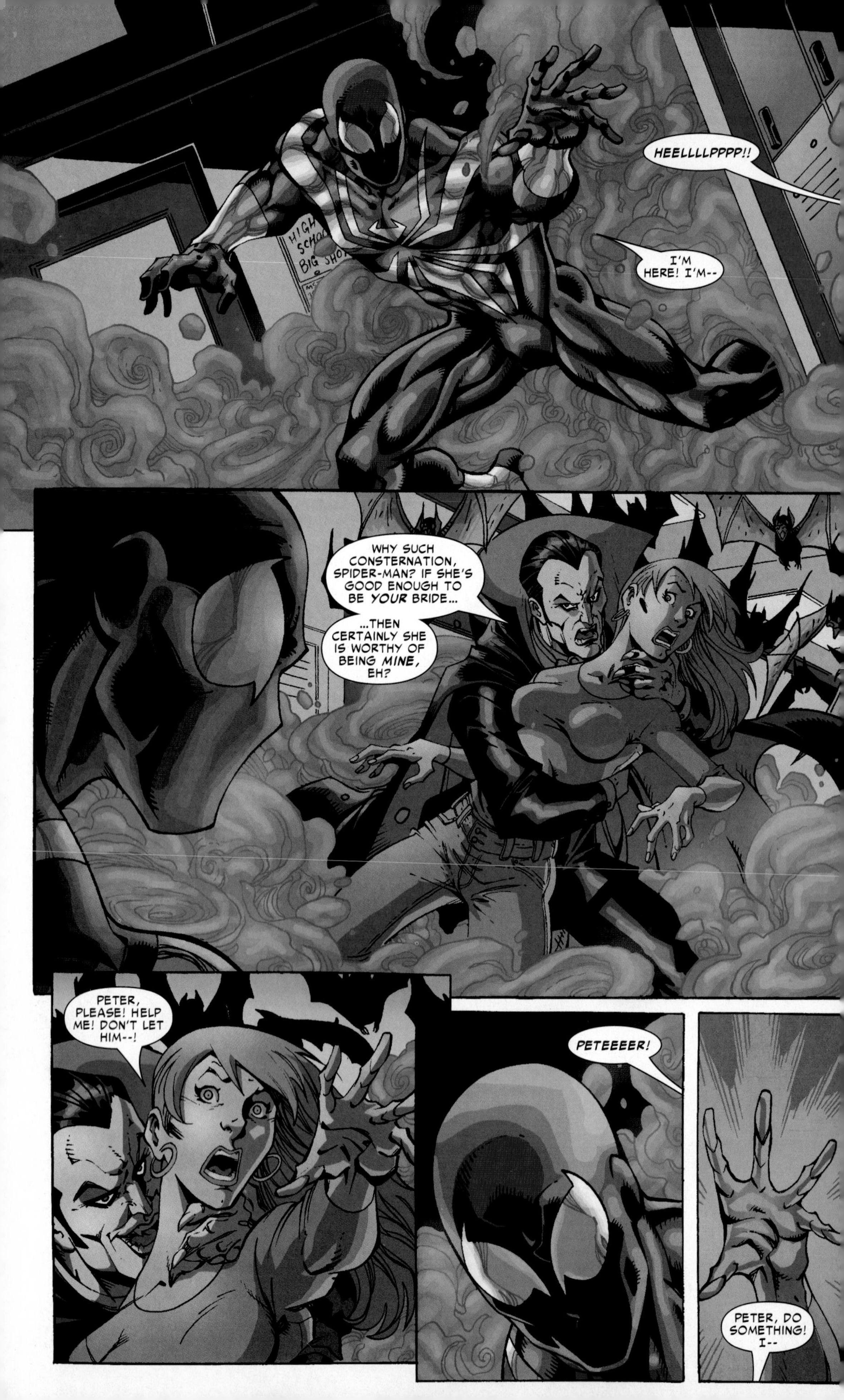
HEELLLLPPPP!!
I'M HERE! I'M--
WHY SUCH CONSTERNATION, SPIDER-MAN? IF SHE'S GOOD ENOUGH TO BE YOUR BRIDE...
...THEN CERTAINLY SHE IS WORTHY OF BEING MINE, EH?
PETER, PLEASE! HELP ME! DON'T LET HIM--!
PETEEEER!
PETER, DO SOMETHING! I--

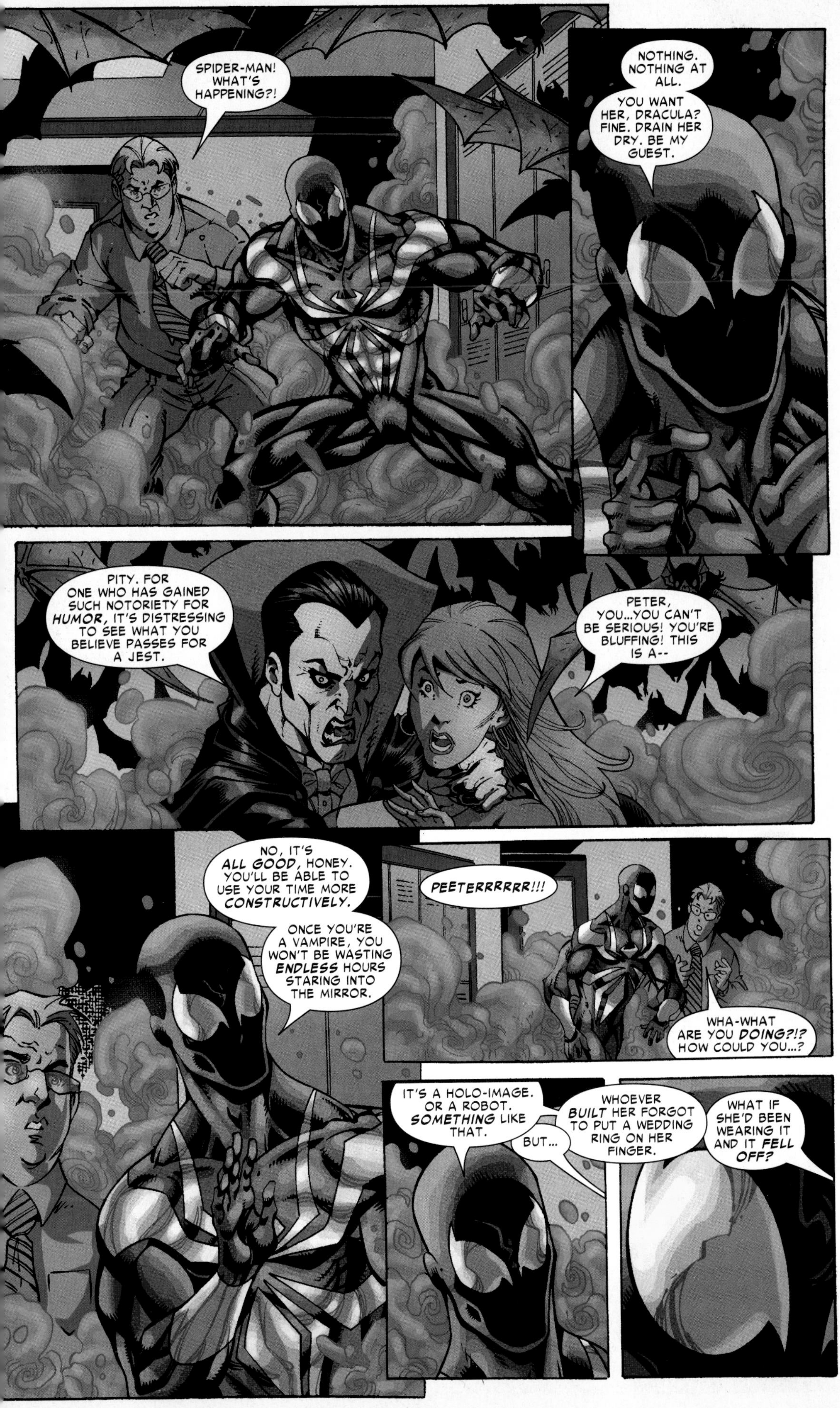
SPIDER-MAN! WHAT'S HAPPENING?!
NOTHING. NOTHING AT ALL.
YOU WANT HER, DRACULA? FINE. DRAIN HER DRY. BE MY GUEST.
PITY. FOR ONE WHO HAS GAINED SUCH NOTORIETY FOR HUMOR, IT'S DISTRESSING TO SEE WHAT YOU BELIEVE PASSES FOR A JEST.
PETER, YOU...YOU CAN'T BE SERIOUS! YOU'RE BLUFFING! THIS IS A--
NO, IT'S ALL GOOD, HONEY. YOU'LL BE ABLE TO USE YOUR TIME MORE CONSTRUCTIVELY.
ONCE YOU'RE A VAMPIRE, YOU WON'T BE WASTING ENDLESS HOURS STARING INTO THE MIRROR.
PEETERRRRRR!!!
WHA-WHAT ARE YOU DOING?!? HOW COULD YOU...?
IT'S A HOLO-IMAGE. OR A ROBOT. SOMETHING LIKE THAT.
BUT...
WHOEVER BUILT HER FORGOT TO PUT A WEDDING RING ON HER FINGER.
WHAT IF SHE'D BEEN WEARING IT AND IT FELL OFF?

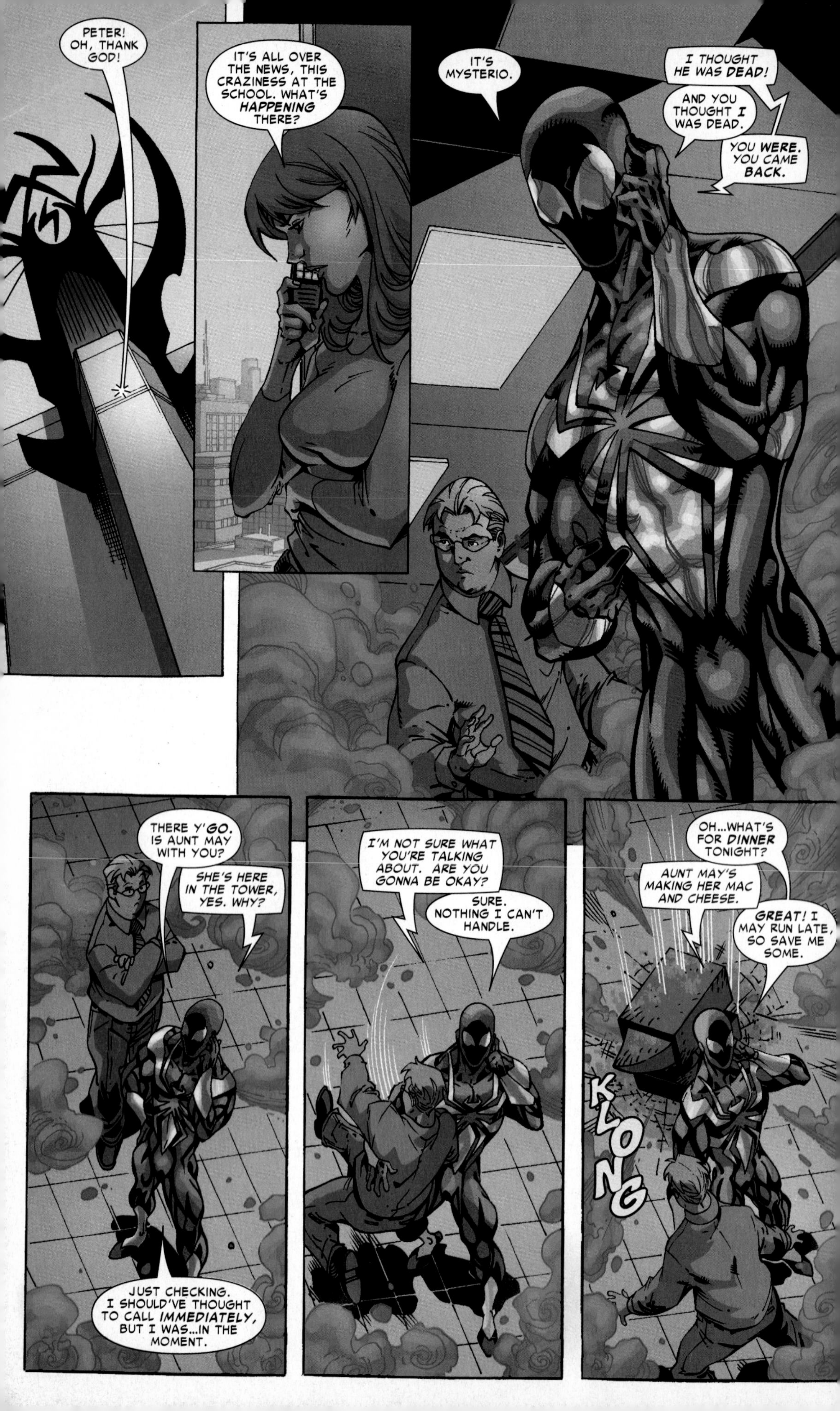
PETER! OH, THANK GOD!
IT'S ALL OVER THE NEWS, THIS CRAZINESS AT THE SCHOOL. WHAT'S HAPPENING THERE?
IT'S MYSTERIO.
I THOUGHT HE WAS DEAD!
AND YOU THOUGHT I WAS DEAD.
YOU WERE. YOU CAME BACK.
THERE Y'GO. IS AUNT MAY WITH YOU?
SHE'S HERE IN THE TOWER, YES. WHY?
JUST CHECKING. I SHOULD'VE THOUGHT TO CALL IMMEDIATELY, BUT I WAS...IN THE MOMENT.
I'M NOT SURE WHAT YOU'RE TALKING ABOUT. ARE YOU GONNA BE OKAY?
SURE. NOTHING I CAN'T HANDLE.
OH...WHAT'S FOR DINNER TONIGHT?
AUNT MAY'S MAKING HER MAC AND CHEESE.
GREAT! I MAY RUN LATE, SO SAVE ME SOME.
KLONG

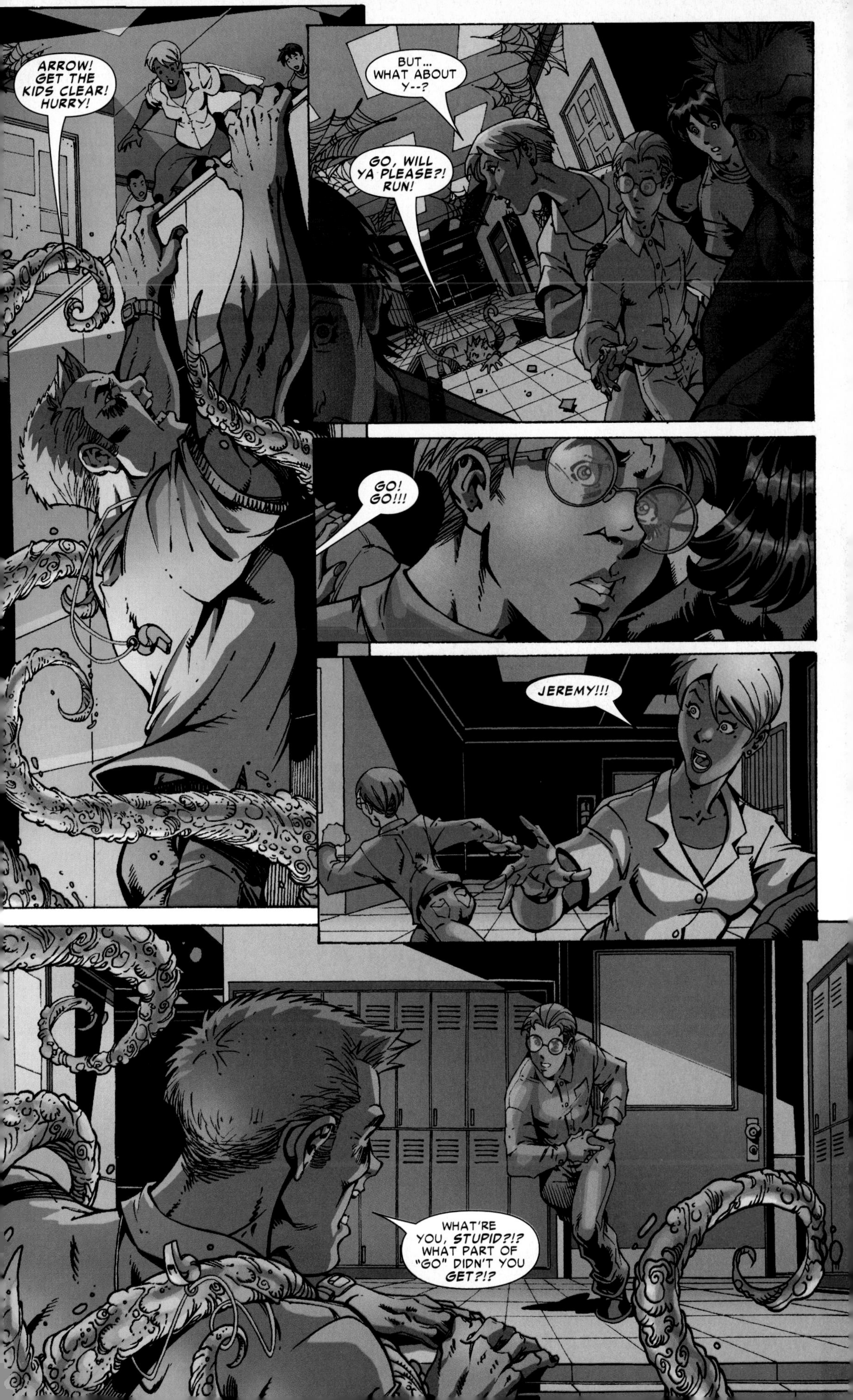
ARROW! GET THE KIDS CLEAR! HURRY!
BUT... WHAT ABOUT Y--?
GO, WILL YA PLEASE?! RUN!
GO! GO!!!
JEREMY!!!
WHAT'RE YOU, STUPID?!? WHAT PART OF "GO" DIDN'T YOU GET?!?

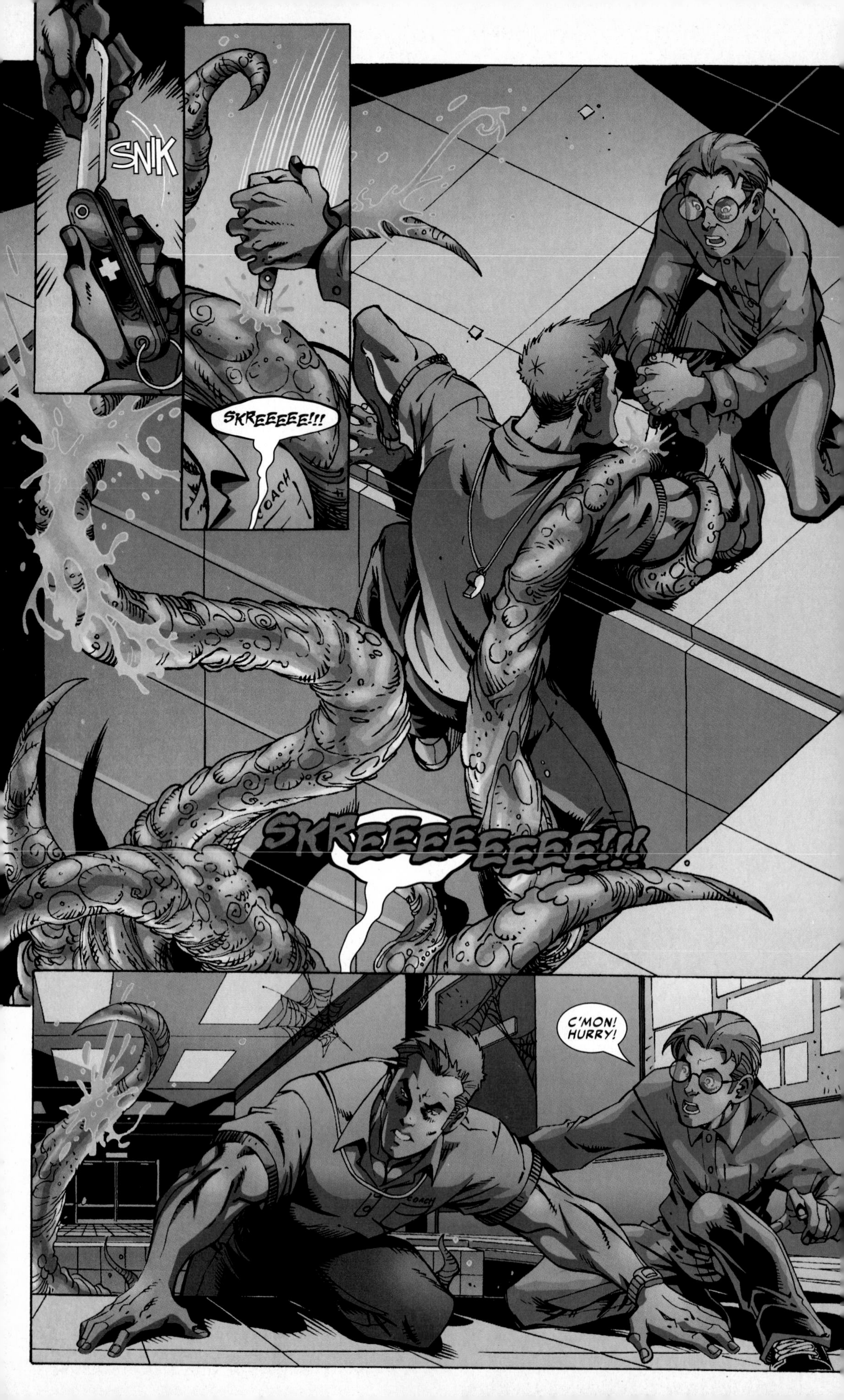
SNIK
SKREEEEE!!!
COACH
SKREEEEEEEEEE!!!
C'MON! HURRY!
COACH

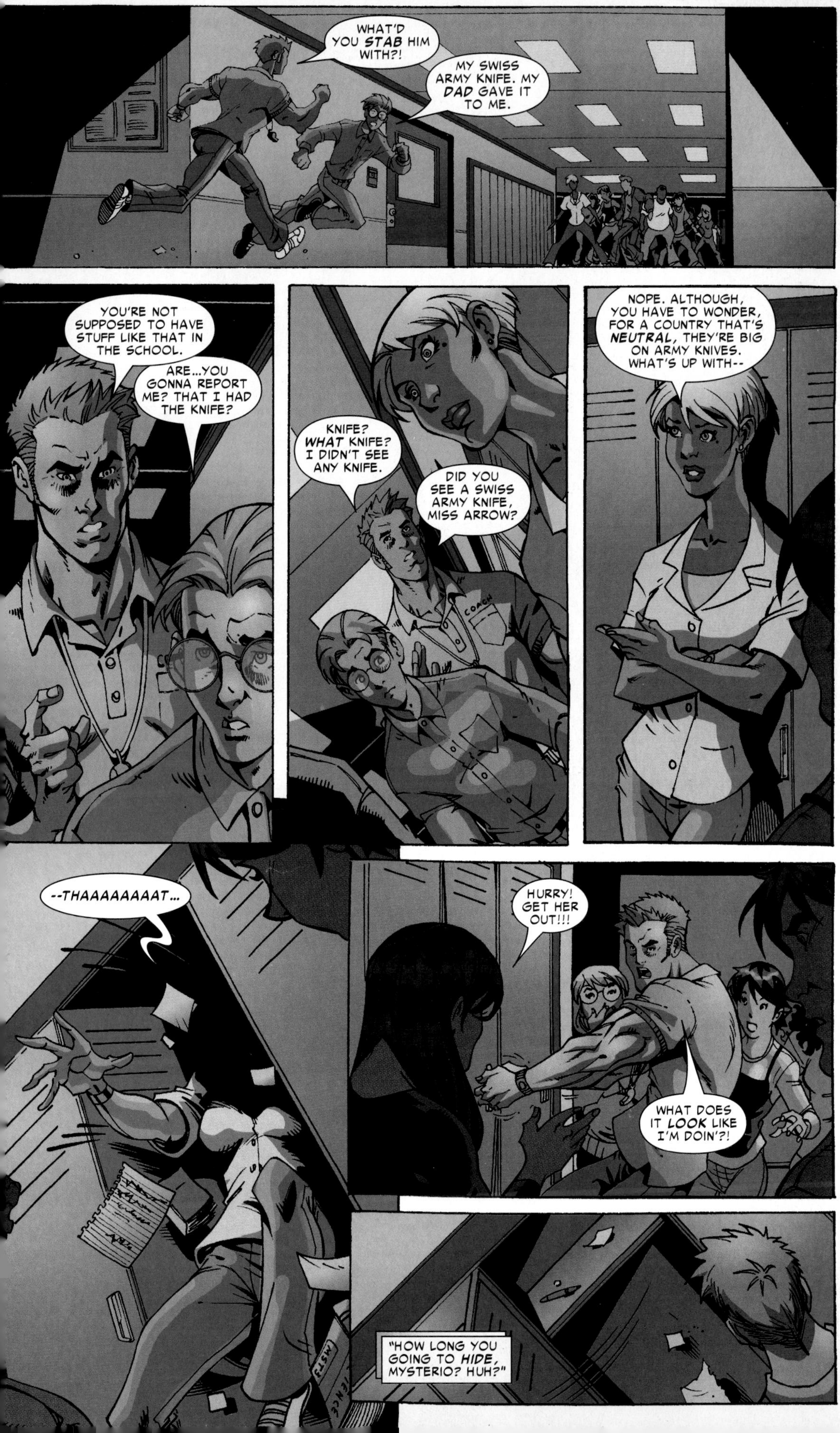
WHAT'D YOU STAB HIM WITH?!
MY SWISS ARMY KNIFE. MY DAD GAVE IT TO ME.
YOU'RE NOT SUPPOSED TO HAVE STUFF LIKE THAT IN THE SCHOOL.
ARE...YOU GONNA REPORT ME? THAT I HAD THE KNIFE?
KNIFE? WHAT KNIFE? I DIDN'T SEE ANY KNIFE.
DID YOU SEE A SWISS ARMY KNIFE, MISS ARROW?
COACH
NOPE. ALTHOUGH, YOU HAVE TO WONDER, FOR A COUNTRY THAT'S NEUTRAL, THEY'RE BIG ON ARMY KNIVES. WHAT'S UP WITH--
--THAAAAAAAAT...
HURRY! GET HER OUT!!!
WHAT DOES IT LOOK LIKE I'M DOIN'?!
"HOW LONG YOU GOING TO HIDE, MYSTERIO? HUH?"

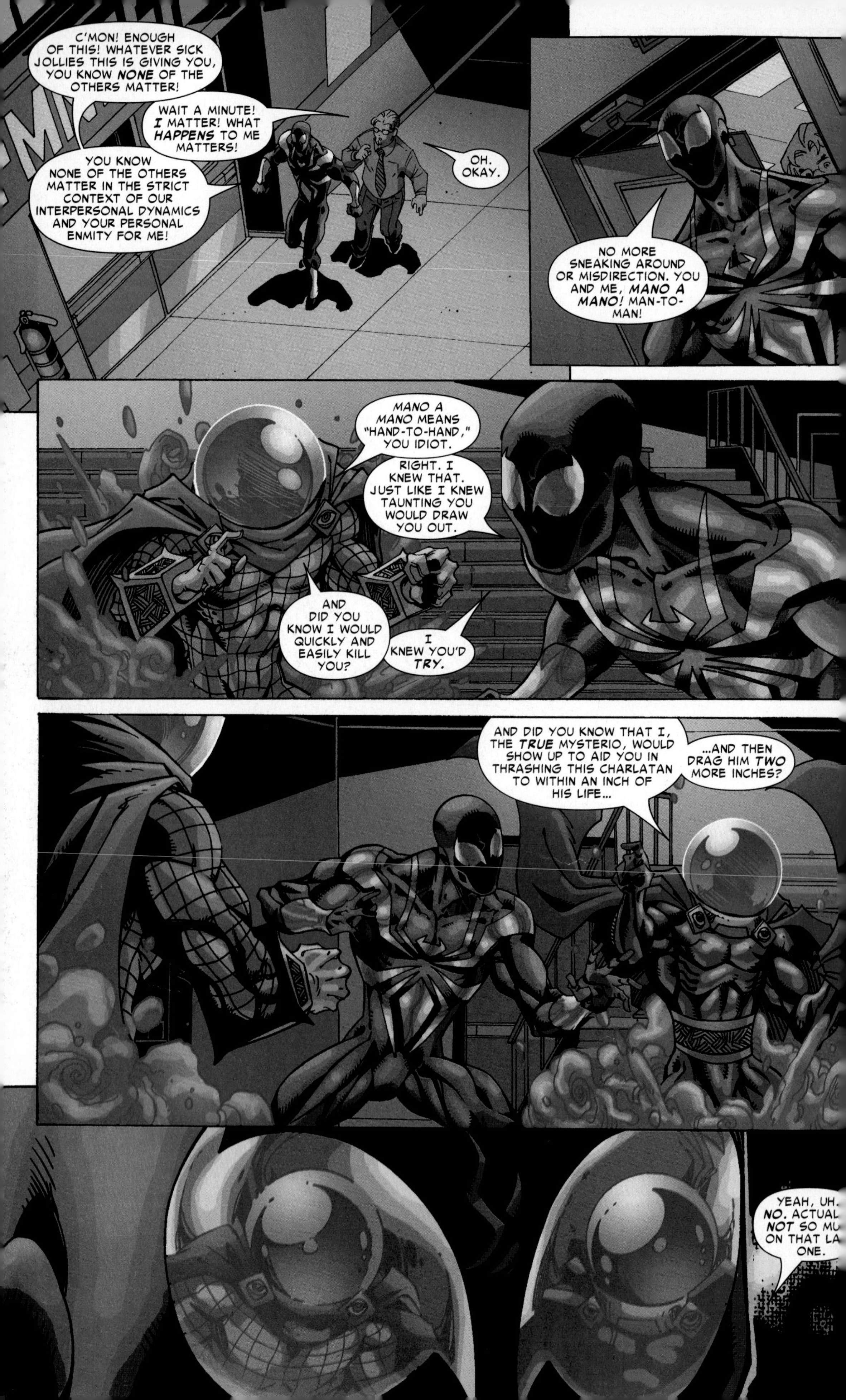
C'MON! ENOUGH OF THIS! WHATEVER SICK JOLLIES THIS IS GIVING YOU, YOU KNOW NONE OF THE OTHERS MATTER!
WAIT A MINUTE! I MATTER! WHAT HAPPENS TO ME MATTERS!
YOU KNOW NONE OF THE OTHERS MATTER IN THE STRICT CONTEXT OF OUR INTERPERSONAL DYNAMICS AND YOUR PERSONAL ENMITY FOR ME!
OH. OKAY.
NO MORE SNEAKING AROUND OR MISDIRECTION. YOU AND ME, MANO A MANO! MAN-TO-MAN!
MANO A MANO MEANS "HAND-TO-HAND," YOU IDIOT.
RIGHT. I KNEW THAT. JUST LIKE I KNEW TAUNTING YOU WOULD DRAW YOU OUT.
AND DID YOU KNOW I WOULD QUICKLY AND EASILY KILL YOU?
I KNEW YOU'D TRY.
AND DID YOU KNOW THAT I, THE TRUE MYSTERIO, WOULD SHOW UP TO AID YOU IN THRASHING THIS CHARLATAN TO WITHIN AN INCH OF HIS LIFE...
...AND THEN DRAG HIM TWO MORE INCHES?
YEAH, UH. NO. ACTUAL NOT SO MU ON THAT LA ONE.

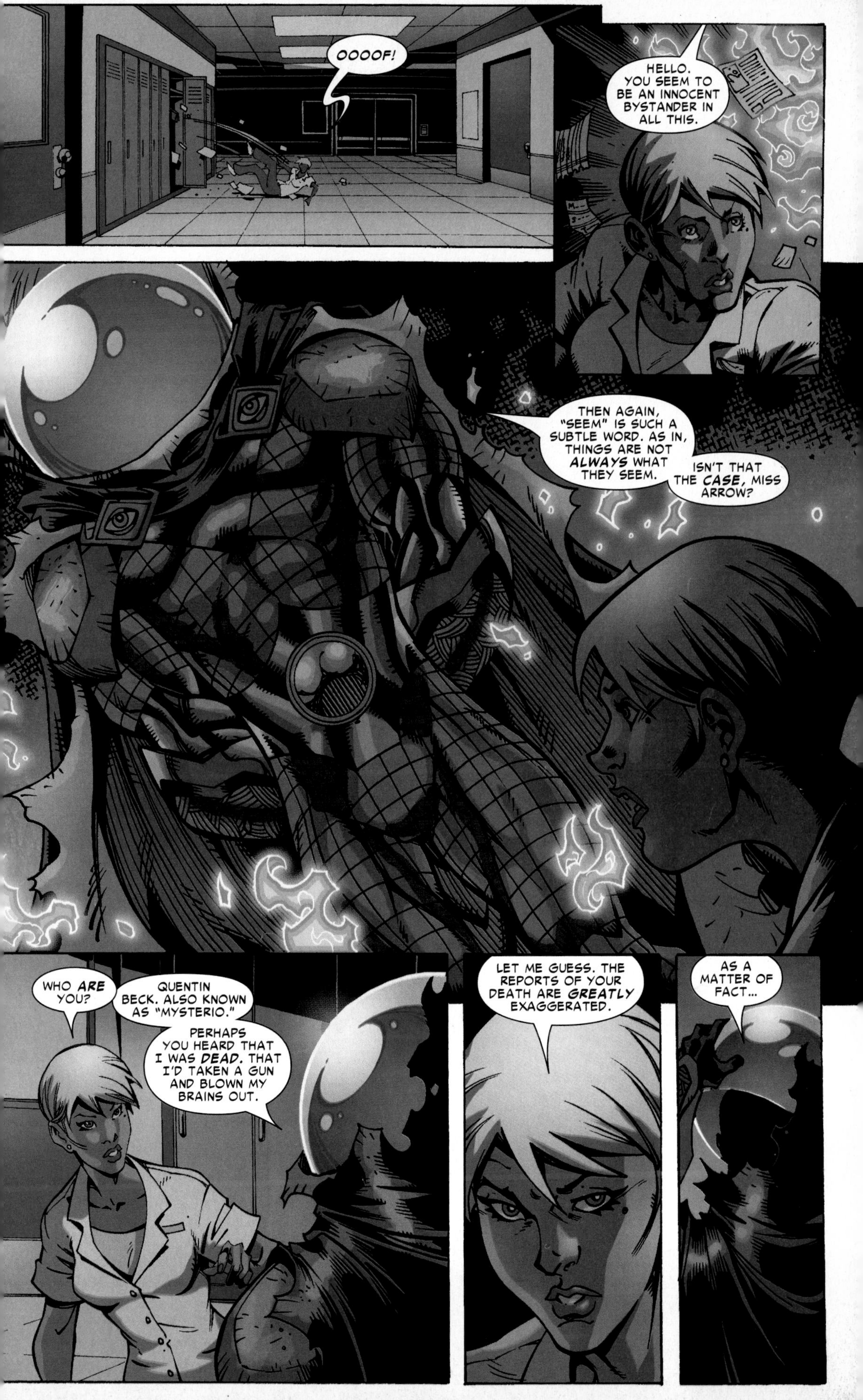

OOOOF!
HELLO. YOU SEEM TO BE AN INNOCENT BYSTANDER IN ALL THIS.
THEN AGAIN, "SEEM" IS SUCH A SUBTLE WORD. AS IN, THINGS ARE NOT ALWAYS WHAT THEY SEEM.
ISN'T THAT THE CASE, MISS ARROW?
WHO ARE YOU?
QUENTIN BECK. ALSO KNOWN AS "MYSTERIO."
PERHAPS YOU HEARD THAT I WAS DEAD. THAT I'D TAKEN A GUN AND BLOWN MY BRAINS OUT.
LET ME GUESS. THE REPORTS OF YOUR DEATH ARE GREATLY EXAGGERATED.
AS A MATTER OF FACT...

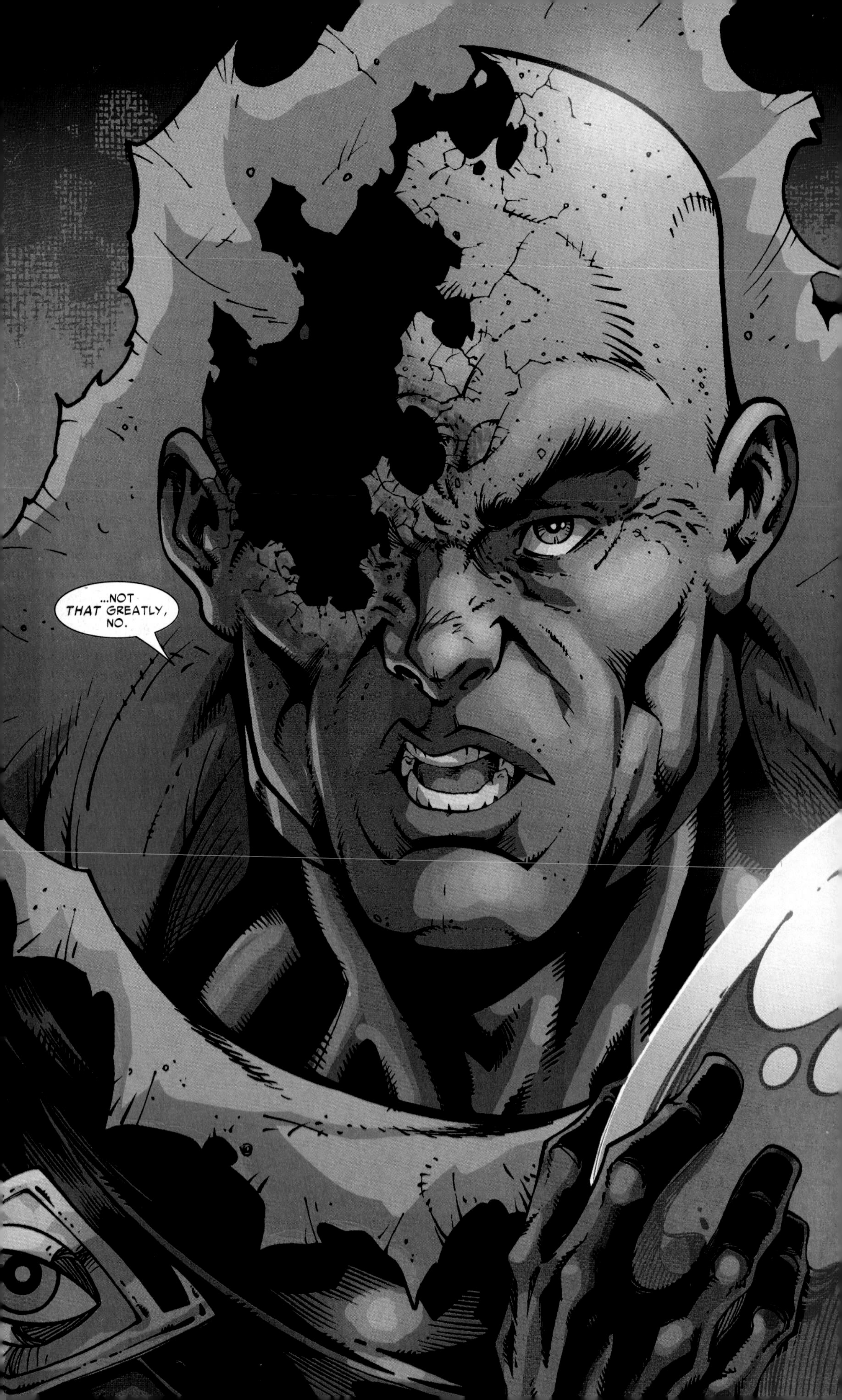
...NOT THAT GREATLY, NO.

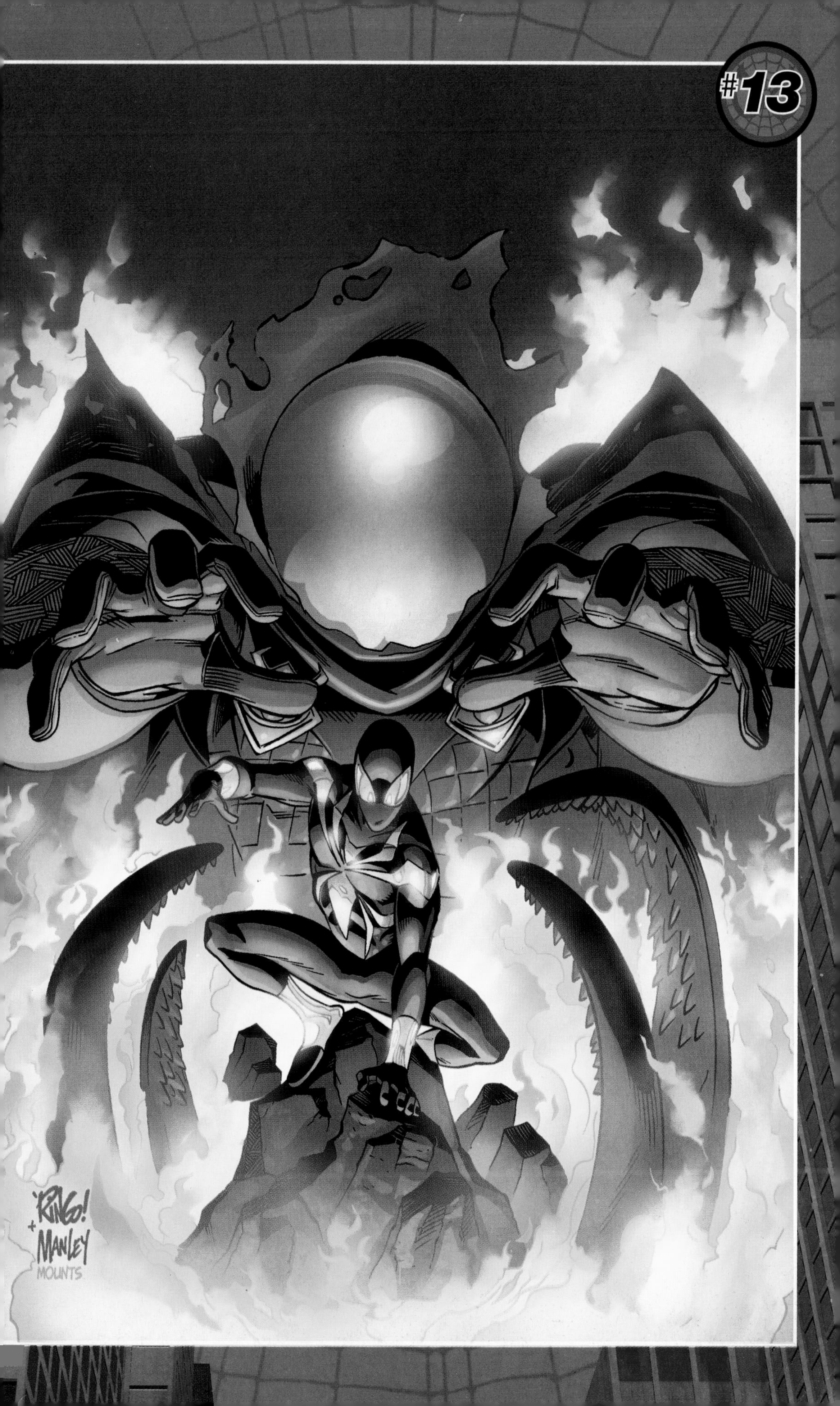

#13
RINGO!
+
MANLEY
MOUNTS

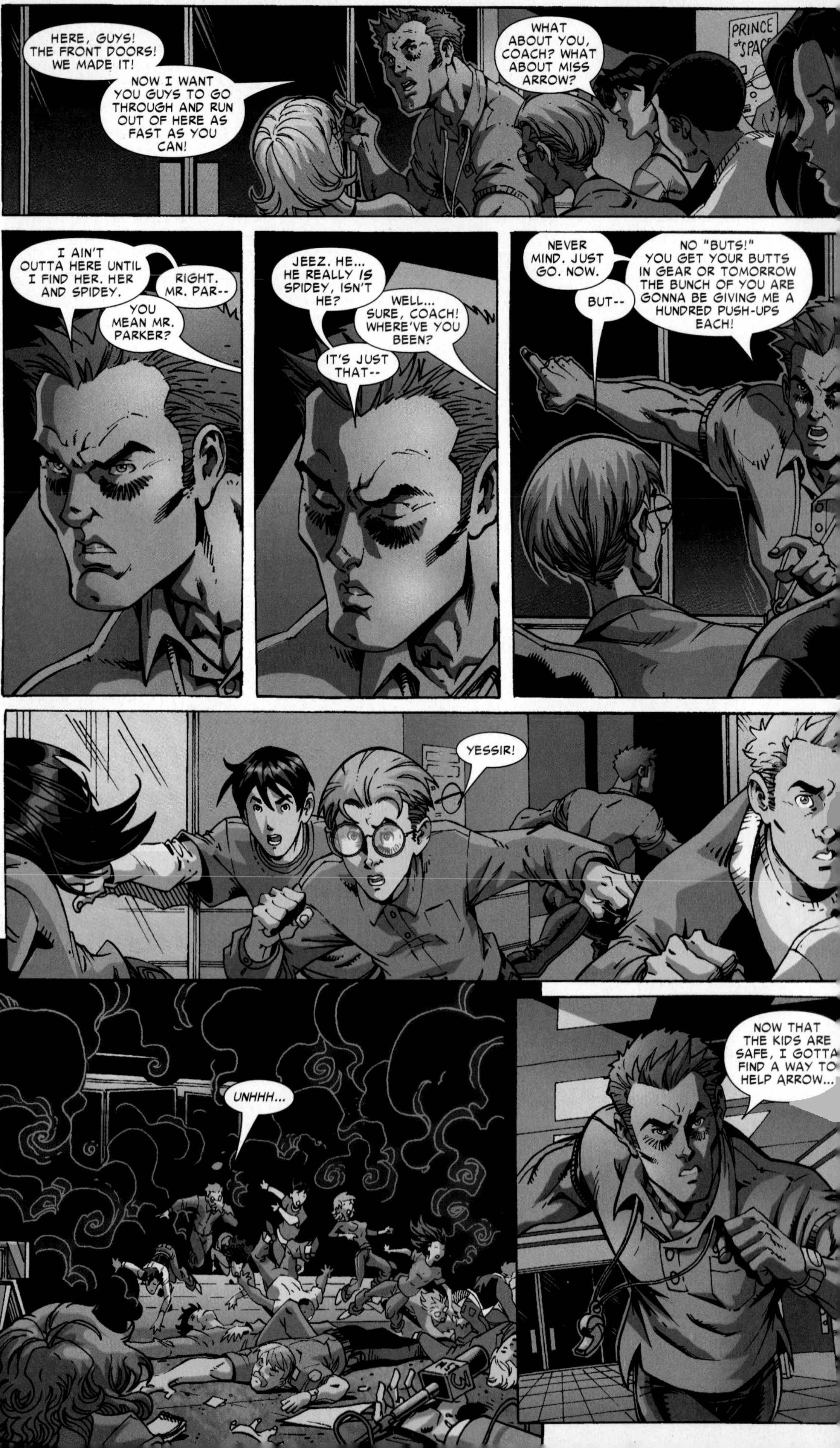
HERE, GUYS! THE FRONT DOORS! WE MADE IT!
NOW I WANT YOU GUYS TO GO THROUGH AND RUN OUT OF HERE AS FAST AS YOU CAN!
WHAT ABOUT YOU, COACH? WHAT ABOUT MISS ARROW?
PRINCE of SPAC
I AIN'T OUTTA HERE UNTIL I FIND HER. HER AND SPIDEY.
RIGHT. MR. PAR--
YOU MEAN MR. PARKER?
JEEZ. HE... HE REALLY IS SPIDEY, ISN'T HE?
WELL... SURE, COACH! WHERE'VE YOU BEEN?
IT'S JUST THAT--
NEVER MIND. JUST GO. NOW.
BUT--
NO "BUTS!" YOU GET YOUR BUTTS IN GEAR OR TOMORROW THE BUNCH OF YOU ARE GONNA BE GIVING ME A HUNDRED PUSH-UPS EACH!
YESSIR!
UNHHH...
NOW THAT THE KIDS ARE SAFE, I GOTTA FIND A WAY TO HELP ARROW...

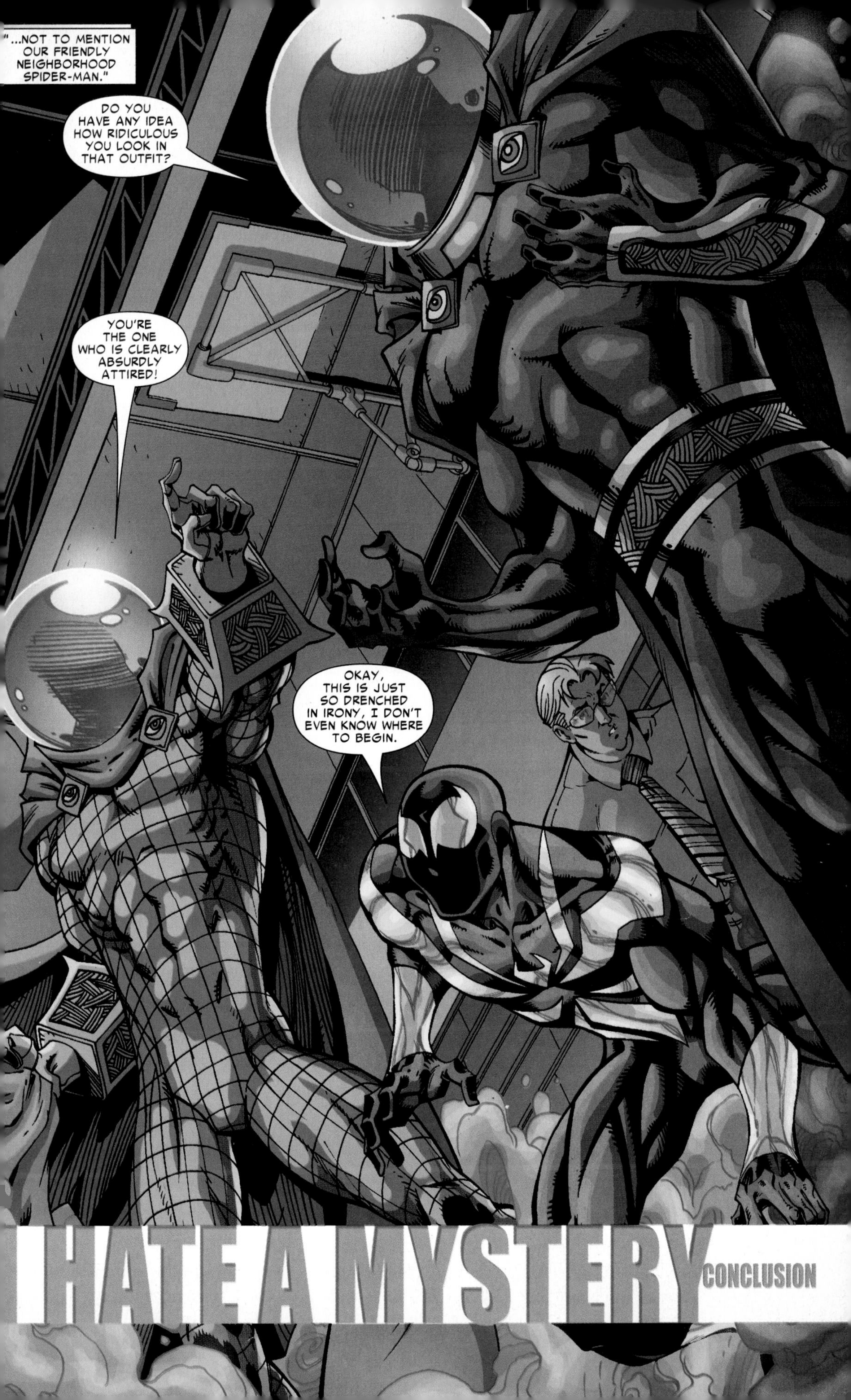
"...NOT TO MENTION OUR FRIENDLY NEIGHBORHOOD SPIDER-MAN."
DO YOU HAVE ANY IDEA HOW RIDICULOUS YOU LOOK IN THAT OUTFIT?
YOU'RE THE ONE WHO IS CLEARLY ABSURDLY ATTIRED!
OKAY, THIS IS JUST SO DRENCHED IN IRONY, I DON'T EVEN KNOW WHERE TO BEGIN.
I HATE A MYSTERY CONCLUSION

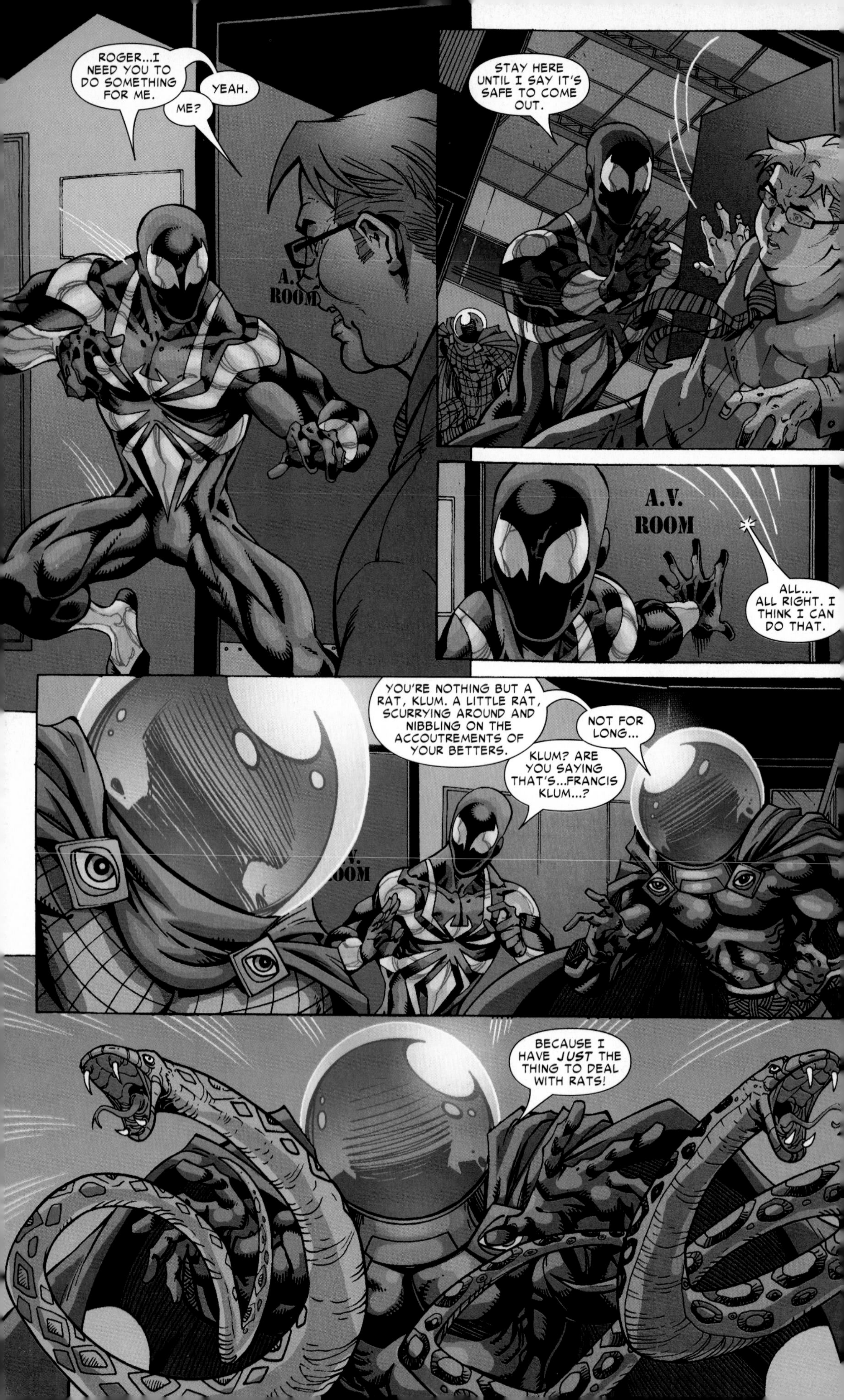
ROGER...I NEED YOU TO DO SOMETHING FOR ME.
ME?
YEAH.
STAY HERE UNTIL I SAY IT'S SAFE TO COME OUT.
A.V. ROOM
ALL... ALL RIGHT. I THINK I CAN DO THAT.
YOU'RE NOTHING BUT A RAT, KLUM. A LITTLE RAT, SCURRYING AROUND AND NIBBLING ON THE ACCOUTREMENTS OF YOUR BETTERS.
KLUM? ARE YOU SAYING THAT'S...FRANCIS KLUM...?
NOT FOR LONG...
BECAUSE I HAVE JUST THE THING TO DEAL WITH RATS!

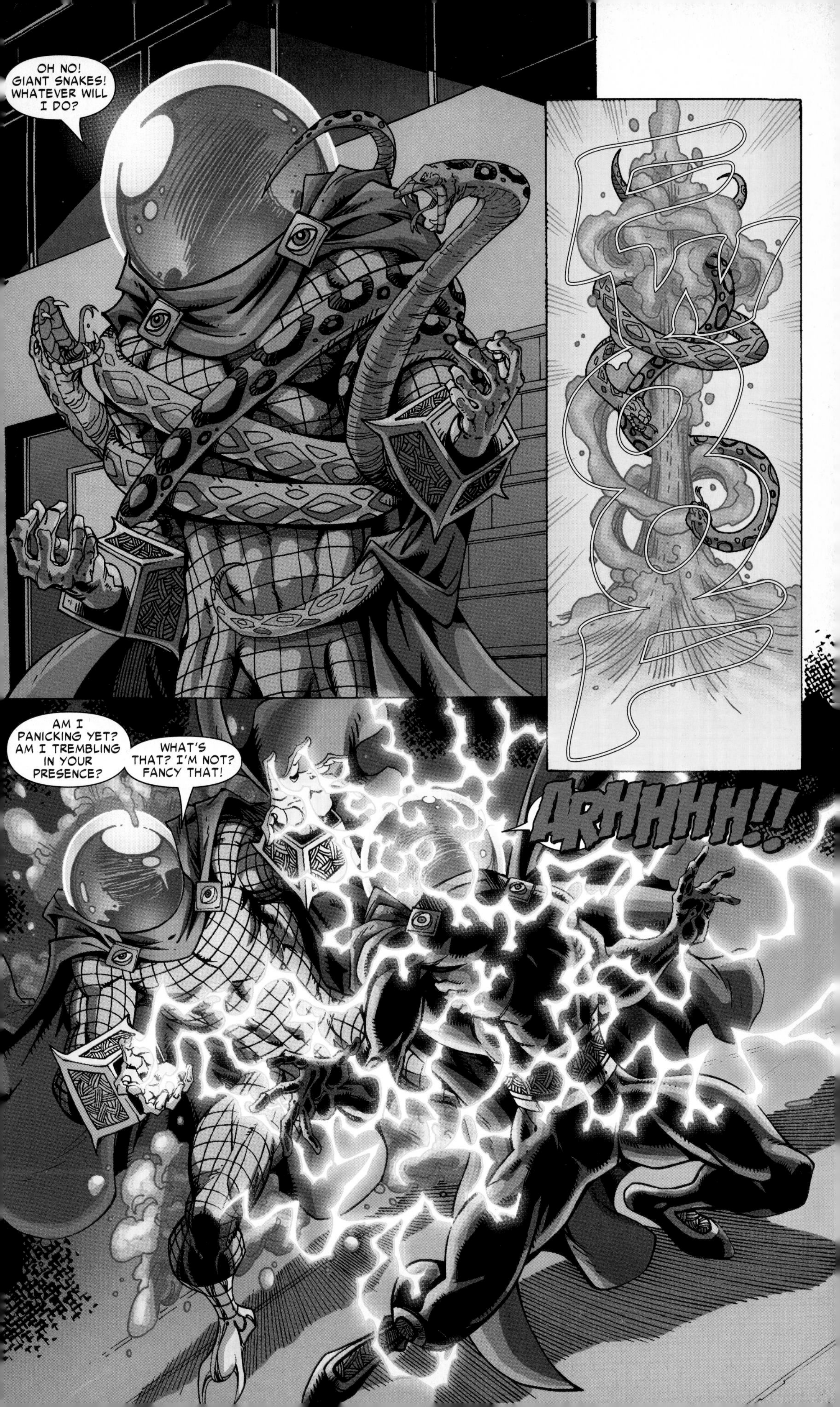
OH NO! GIANT SNAKES! WHATEVER WILL I DO?
AM I PANICKING YET? AM I TREMBLING IN YOUR PRESENCE?
WHAT'S THAT? I'M NOT? FANCY THAT!
ARHHHH!!

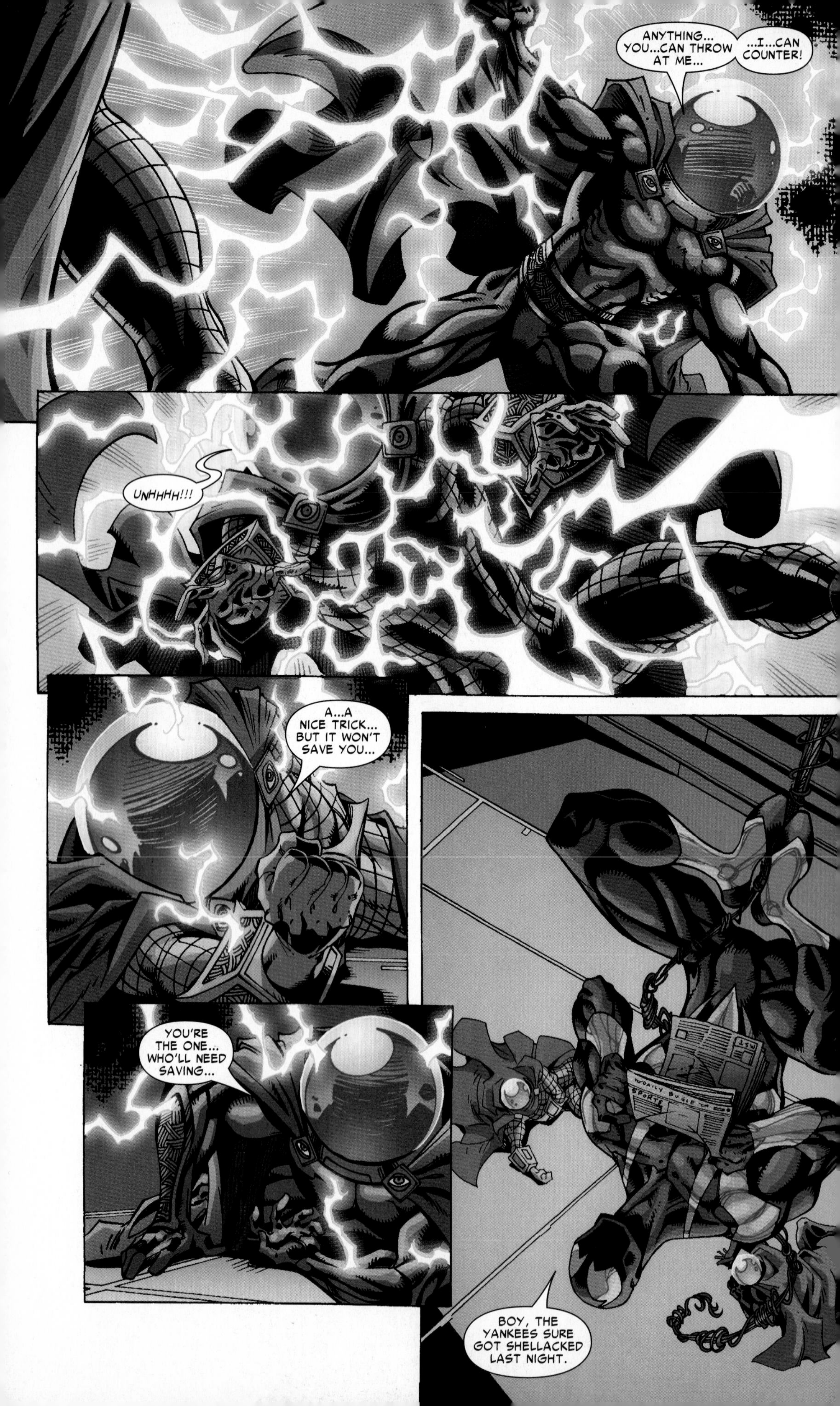
ANYTHING... YOU...CAN THROW AT ME...
...I...CAN COUNTER!
UNHHHH!!!
A...A NICE TRICK... BUT IT WON'T SAVE YOU...
YOU'RE THE ONE... WHO'LL NEED SAVING...
BOY, THE YANKEES SURE GOT SHELLACKED LAST NIGHT.

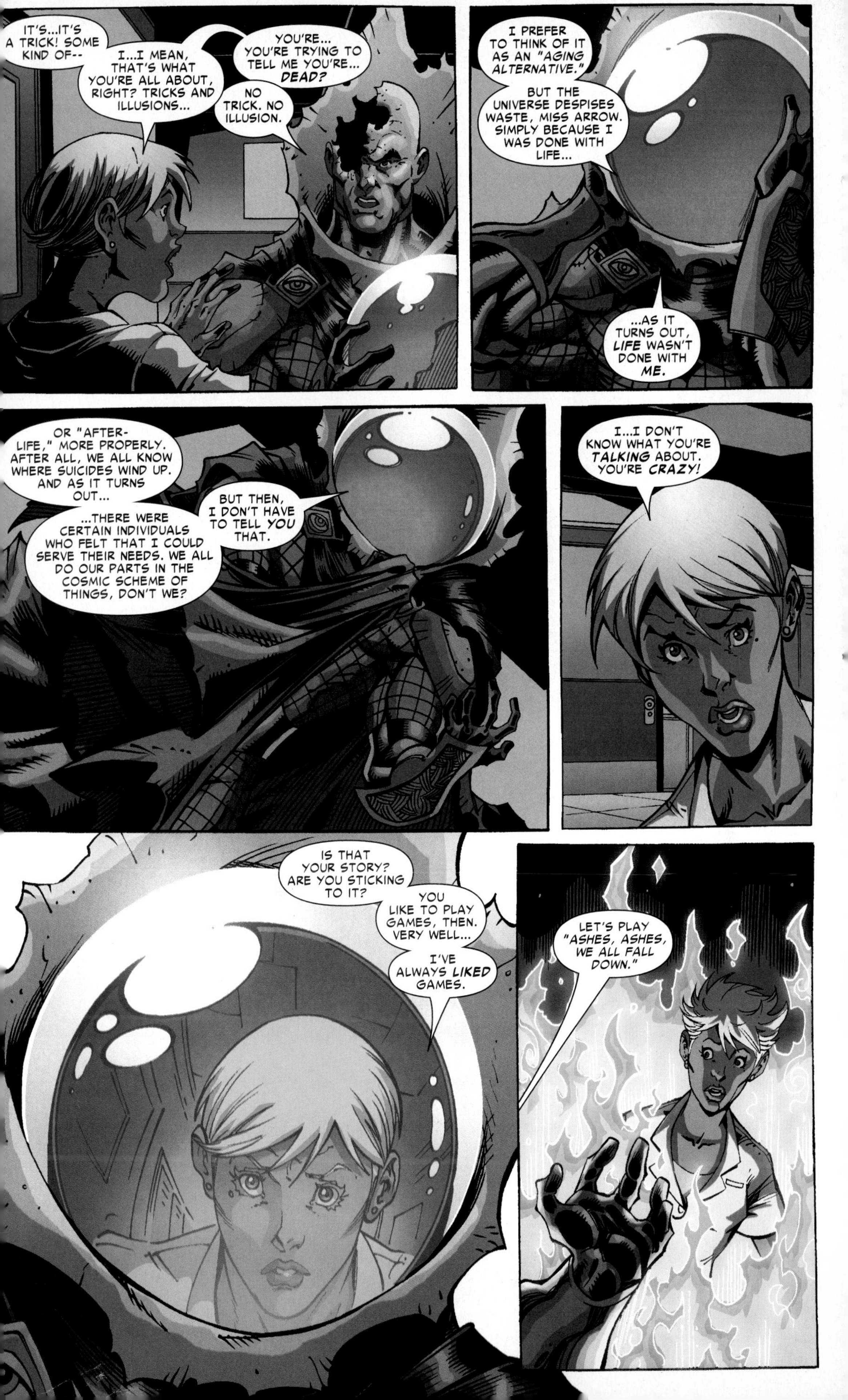
IT'S...IT'S A TRICK! SOME KIND OF--
I...I MEAN, THAT'S WHAT YOU'RE ALL ABOUT, RIGHT? TRICKS AND ILLUSIONS...
YOU'RE... YOU'RE TRYING TO TELL ME YOU'RE... DEAD?
NO TRICK. NO ILLUSION.
I PREFER TO THINK OF IT AS AN "AGING ALTERNATIVE."
BUT THE UNIVERSE DESPISES WASTE, MISS ARROW. SIMPLY BECAUSE I WAS DONE WITH LIFE...
...AS IT TURNS OUT, LIFE WASN'T DONE WITH ME.
OR "AFTER-LIFE," MORE PROPERLY. AFTER ALL, WE ALL KNOW WHERE SUICIDES WIND UP. AND AS IT TURNS OUT...
...THERE WERE CERTAIN INDIVIDUALS WHO FELT THAT I COULD SERVE THEIR NEEDS. WE ALL DO OUR PARTS IN THE COSMIC SCHEME OF THINGS, DON'T WE?
BUT THEN, I DON'T HAVE TO TELL YOU THAT.
I...I DON'T KNOW WHAT YOU'RE TALKING ABOUT. YOU'RE CRAZY!
IS THAT YOUR STORY? ARE YOU STICKING TO IT?
YOU LIKE TO PLAY GAMES, THEN. VERY WELL...
I'VE ALWAYS LIKED GAMES.
LET'S PLAY "ASHES, ASHES, WE ALL FALL DOWN."

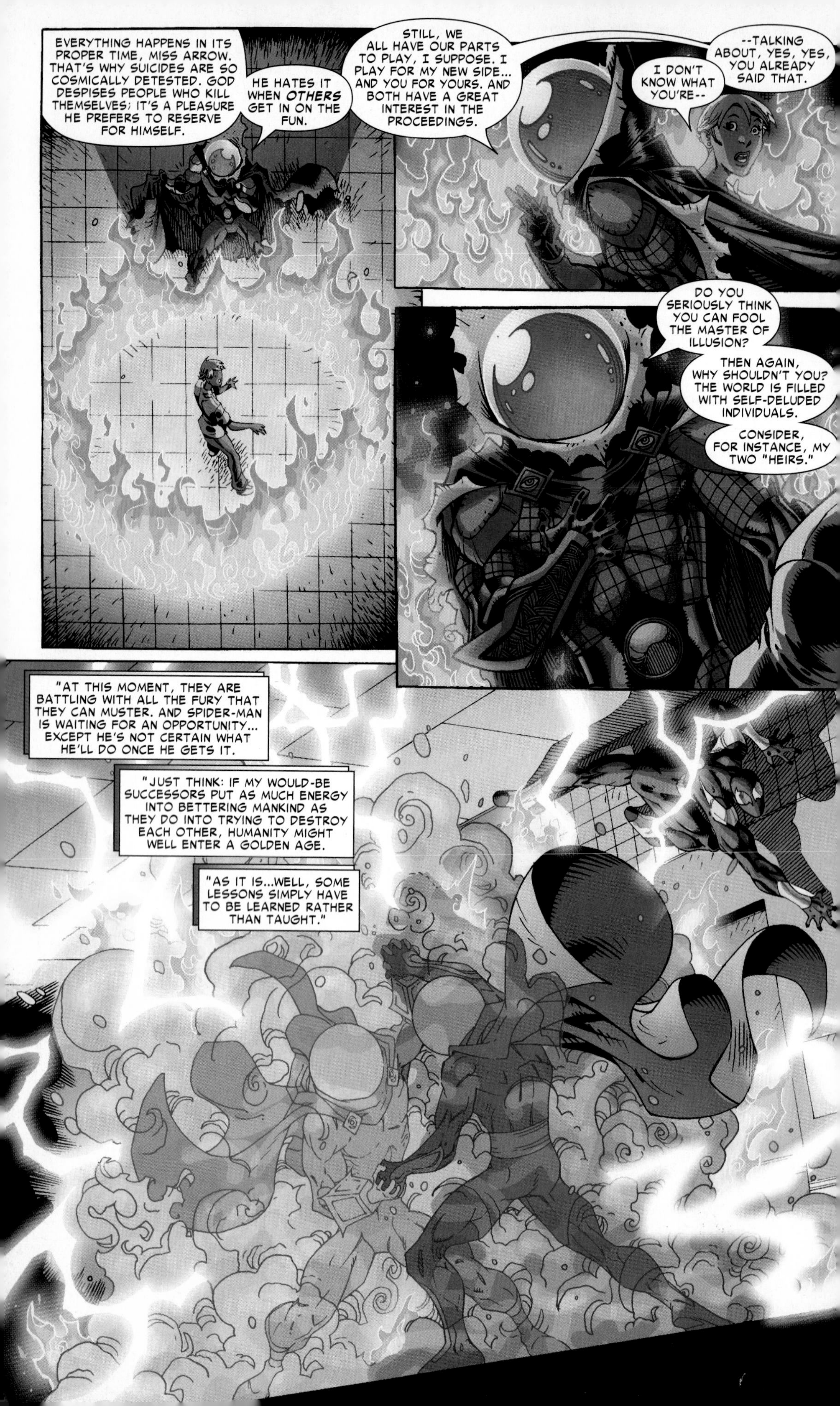
EVERYTHING HAPPENS IN ITS PROPER TIME, MISS ARROW. THAT'S WHY SUICIDES ARE SO COSMICALLY DETESTED. GOD DESPISES PEOPLE WHO KILL THEMSELVES; IT'S A PLEASURE HE PREFERS TO RESERVE FOR HIMSELF.
HE HATES IT WHEN *OTHERS* GET IN ON THE FUN.
STILL, WE ALL HAVE OUR PARTS TO PLAY, I SUPPOSE. I PLAY FOR MY NEW SIDE... AND YOU FOR YOURS. AND BOTH HAVE A GREAT INTEREST IN THE PROCEEDINGS.
I DON'T KNOW WHAT YOU'RE--
--TALKING ABOUT, YES, YES, YOU ALREADY SAID THAT.
DO YOU SERIOUSLY THINK YOU CAN FOOL THE MASTER OF ILLUSION?
THEN AGAIN, WHY SHOULDN'T YOU? THE WORLD IS FILLED WITH SELF-DELUDED INDIVIDUALS.
CONSIDER, FOR INSTANCE, MY TWO "HEIRS."
"AT THIS MOMENT, THEY ARE BATTLING WITH ALL THE FURY THAT THEY CAN MUSTER. AND SPIDER-MAN IS WAITING FOR AN OPPORTUNITY... EXCEPT HE'S NOT CERTAIN WHAT HE'LL DO ONCE HE GETS IT.
"JUST THINK: IF MY WOULD-BE SUCCESSORS PUT AS MUCH ENERGY INTO BETTERING MANKIND AS THEY DO INTO TRYING TO DESTROY EACH OTHER, HUMANITY MIGHT WELL ENTER A GOLDEN AGE.
"AS IT IS...WELL, SOME LESSONS SIMPLY HAVE TO BE LEARNED RATHER THAN TAUGHT."

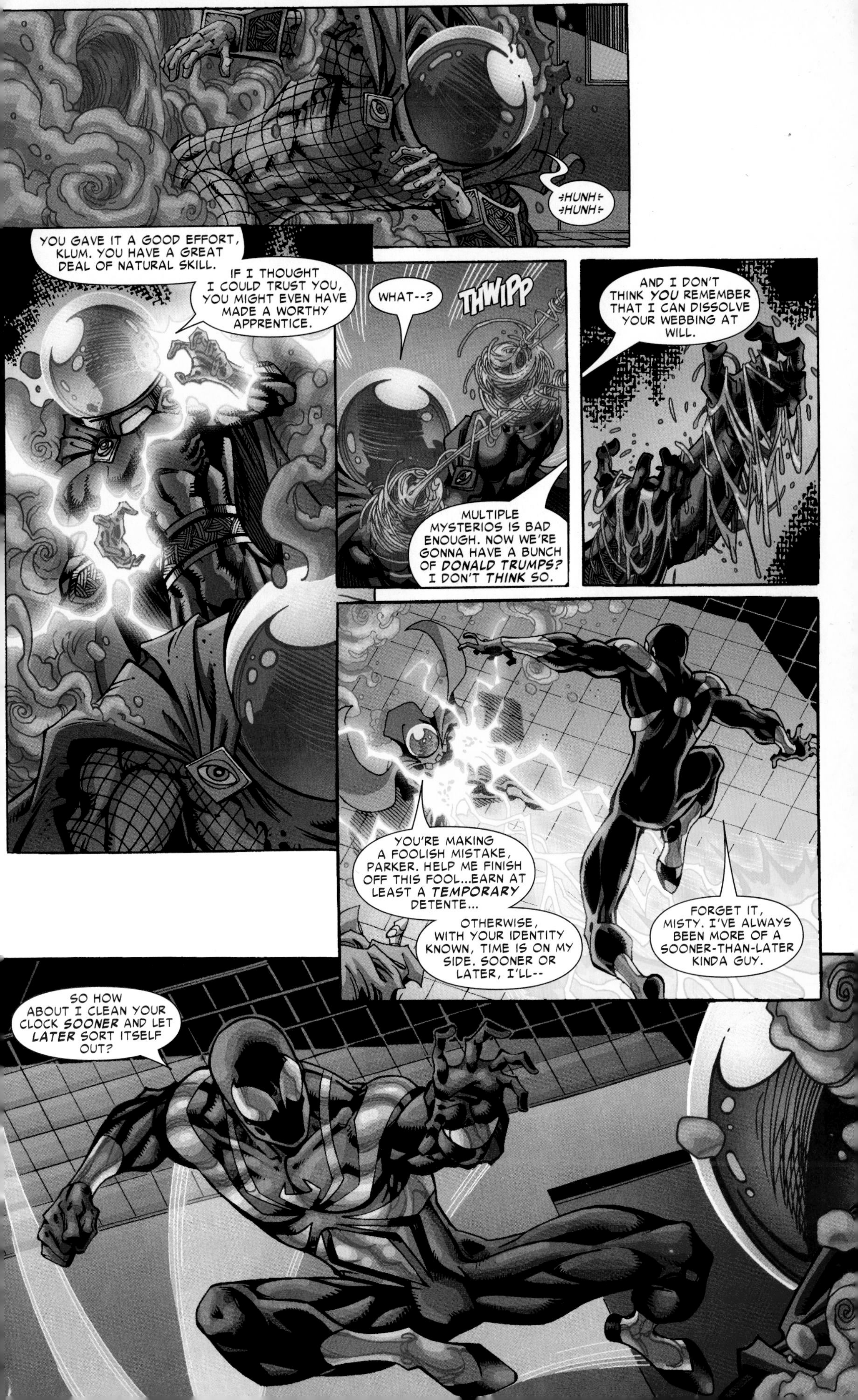
HUNH
HUNH
YOU GAVE IT A GOOD EFFORT, KLUM. YOU HAVE A GREAT DEAL OF NATURAL SKILL.
IF I THOUGHT I COULD TRUST YOU, YOU MIGHT EVEN HAVE MADE A WORTHY APPRENTICE.
WHAT--?
THWIPP
MULTIPLE MYSTERIOS IS BAD ENOUGH. NOW WE'RE GONNA HAVE A BUNCH OF DONALD TRUMPS? I DON'T THINK SO.
AND I DON'T THINK YOU REMEMBER THAT I CAN DISSOLVE YOUR WEBBING AT WILL.
YOU'RE MAKING A FOOLISH MISTAKE, PARKER. HELP ME FINISH OFF THIS FOOL...EARN AT LEAST A TEMPORARY DETENTE...
OTHERWISE, WITH YOUR IDENTITY KNOWN, TIME IS ON MY SIDE. SOONER OR LATER, I'LL--
FORGET IT, MISTY. I'VE ALWAYS BEEN MORE OF A SOONER-THAN-LATER KINDA GUY.
SO HOW ABOUT I CLEAN YOUR CLOCK SOONER AND LET LATER SORT ITSELF OUT?

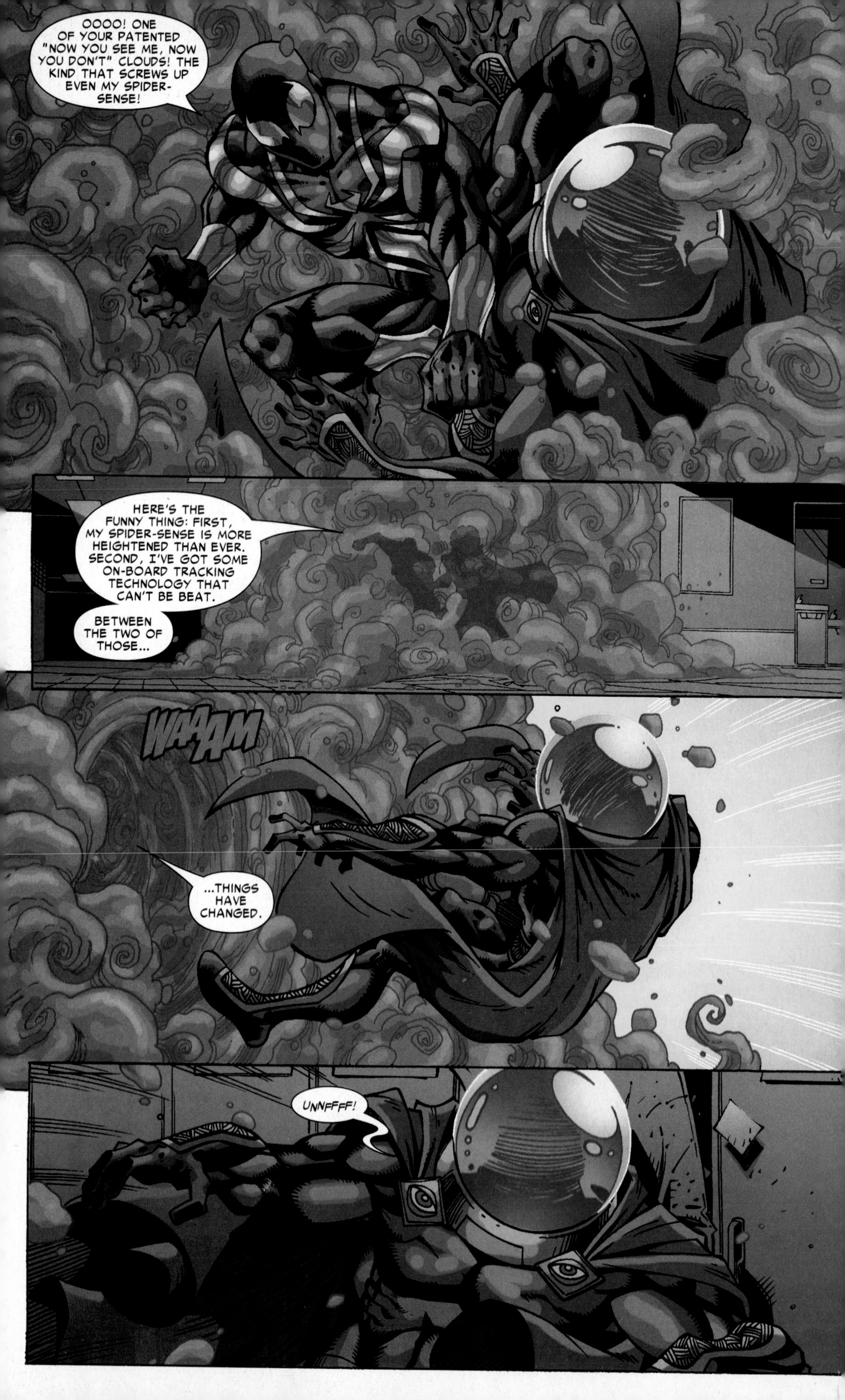
OOOO! ONE OF YOUR PATENTED "NOW YOU SEE ME, NOW YOU DON'T" CLOUDS! THE KIND THAT SCREWS UP EVEN MY SPIDER-SENSE!
HERE'S THE FUNNY THING: FIRST, MY SPIDER-SENSE IS MORE HEIGHTENED THAN EVER. SECOND, I'VE GOT SOME ON-BOARD TRACKING TECHNOLOGY THAT CAN'T BE BEAT.
BETWEEN THE TWO OF THOSE...
WAAAM
...THINGS HAVE CHANGED.
UNNFFFF!

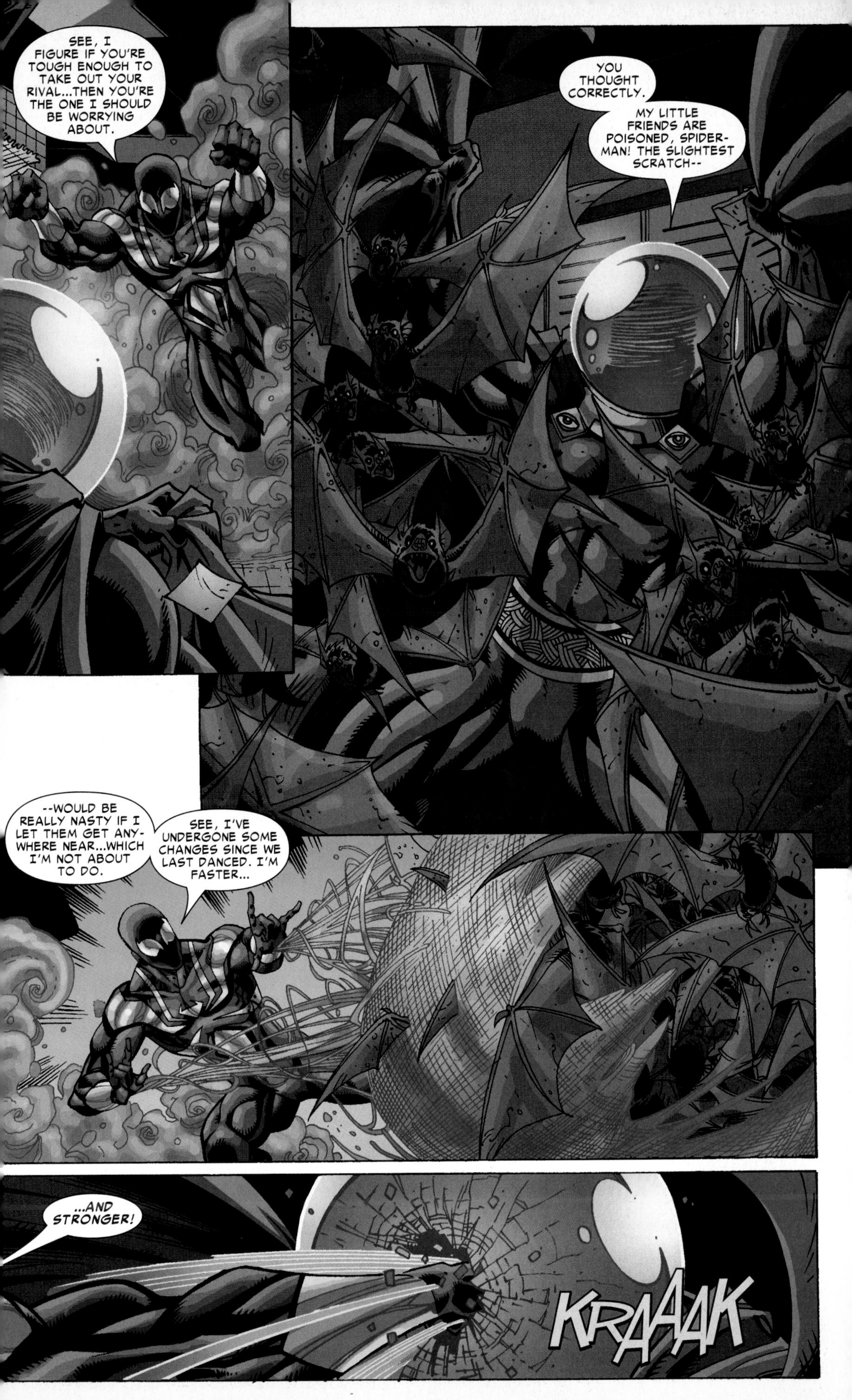
SEE, I FIGURE IF YOU'RE TOUGH ENOUGH TO TAKE OUT YOUR RIVAL...THEN YOU'RE THE ONE I SHOULD BE WORRYING ABOUT.
YOU THOUGHT CORRECTLY.
MY LITTLE FRIENDS ARE POISONED, SPIDER-MAN! THE SLIGHTEST SCRATCH--
--WOULD BE REALLY NASTY IF I LET THEM GET ANY-WHERE NEAR...WHICH I'M NOT ABOUT TO DO.
SEE, I'VE UNDERGONE SOME CHANGES SINCE WE LAST DANCED. I'M FASTER...
...AND STRONGER!
KRAAAK

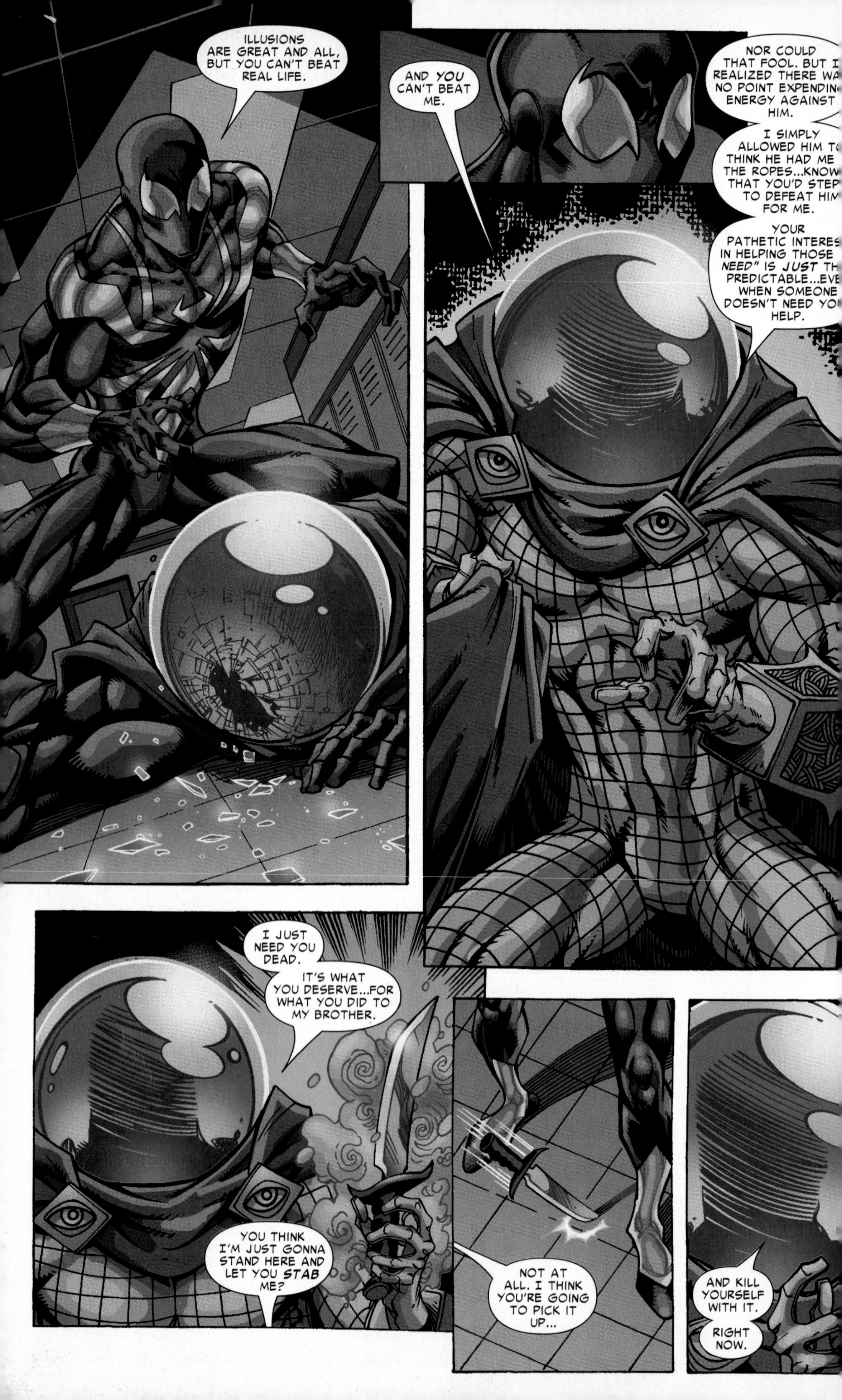

ILLUSIONS ARE GREAT AND ALL, BUT YOU CAN'T BEAT REAL LIFE.
AND YOU CAN'T BEAT ME.
NOR COULD THAT FOOL. BUT I REALIZED THERE WA NO POINT EXPENDIN ENERGY AGAINST HIM.
I SIMPLY ALLOWED HIM T THINK HE HAD ME THE ROPES...KNOW THAT YOU'D STEP TO DEFEAT HIM FOR ME.
YOUR PATHETIC INTERES IN HELPING THOSE NEED" IS JUST TH PREDICTABLE...EVE WHEN SOMEONE DOESN'T NEED YO HELP.
I JUST NEED YOU DEAD.
IT'S WHAT YOU DESERVE...FOR WHAT YOU DID TO MY BROTHER.
YOU THINK I'M JUST GONNA STAND HERE AND LET YOU STAB ME?
NOT AT ALL. I THINK YOU'RE GOING TO PICK IT UP...
AND KILL YOURSELF WITH IT.
RIGHT NOW.

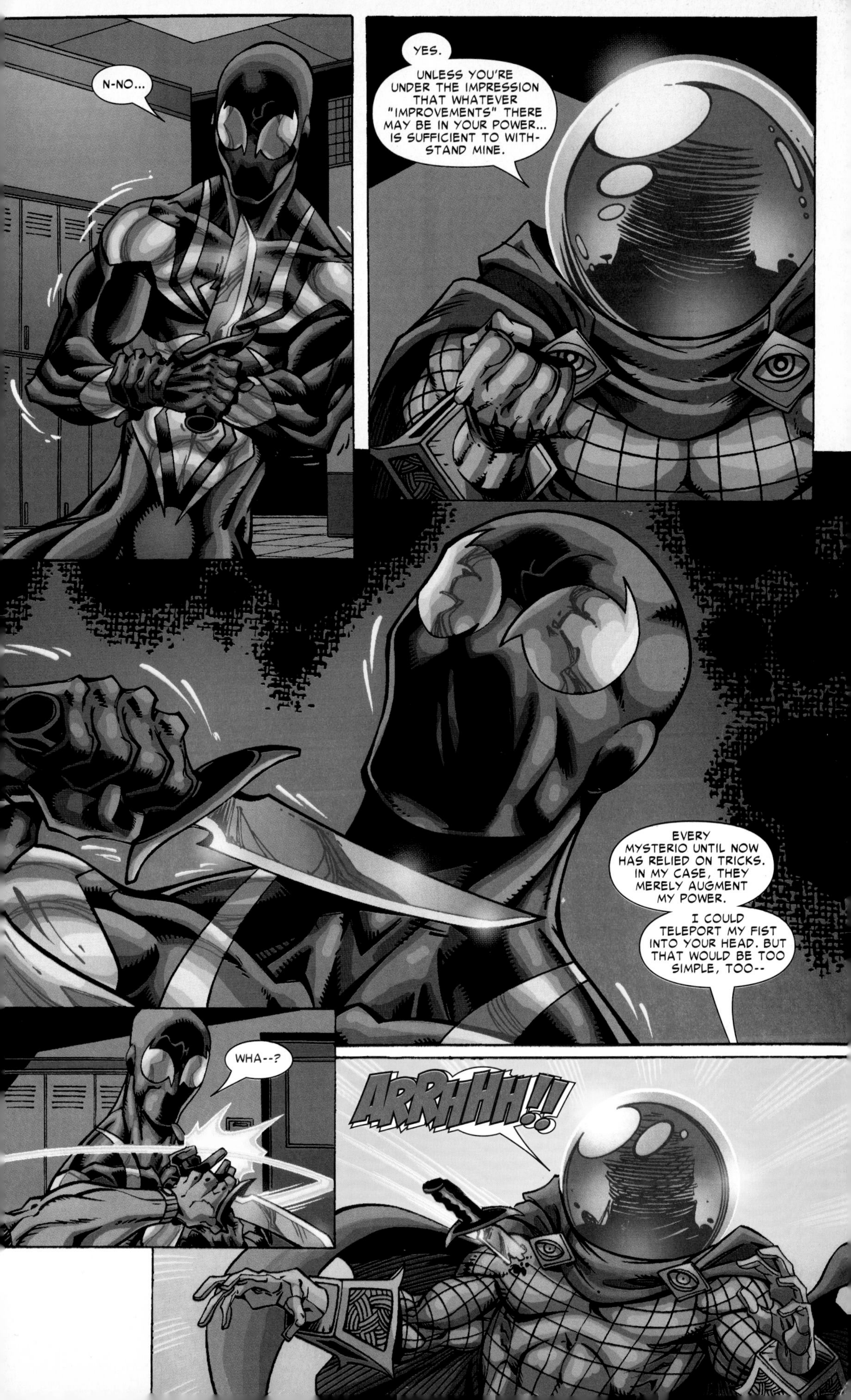
N-NO...
YES.
UNLESS YOU'RE UNDER THE IMPRESSION THAT WHATEVER "IMPROVEMENTS" THERE MAY BE IN YOUR POWER... IS SUFFICIENT TO WITH-STAND MINE.
EVERY MYSTERIO UNTIL NOW HAS RELIED ON TRICKS. IN MY CASE, THEY MERELY AUGMENT MY POWER.
I COULD TELEPORT MY FIST INTO YOUR HEAD. BUT THAT WOULD BE TOO SIMPLE, TOO--
WHA--?
ARRHHH!!

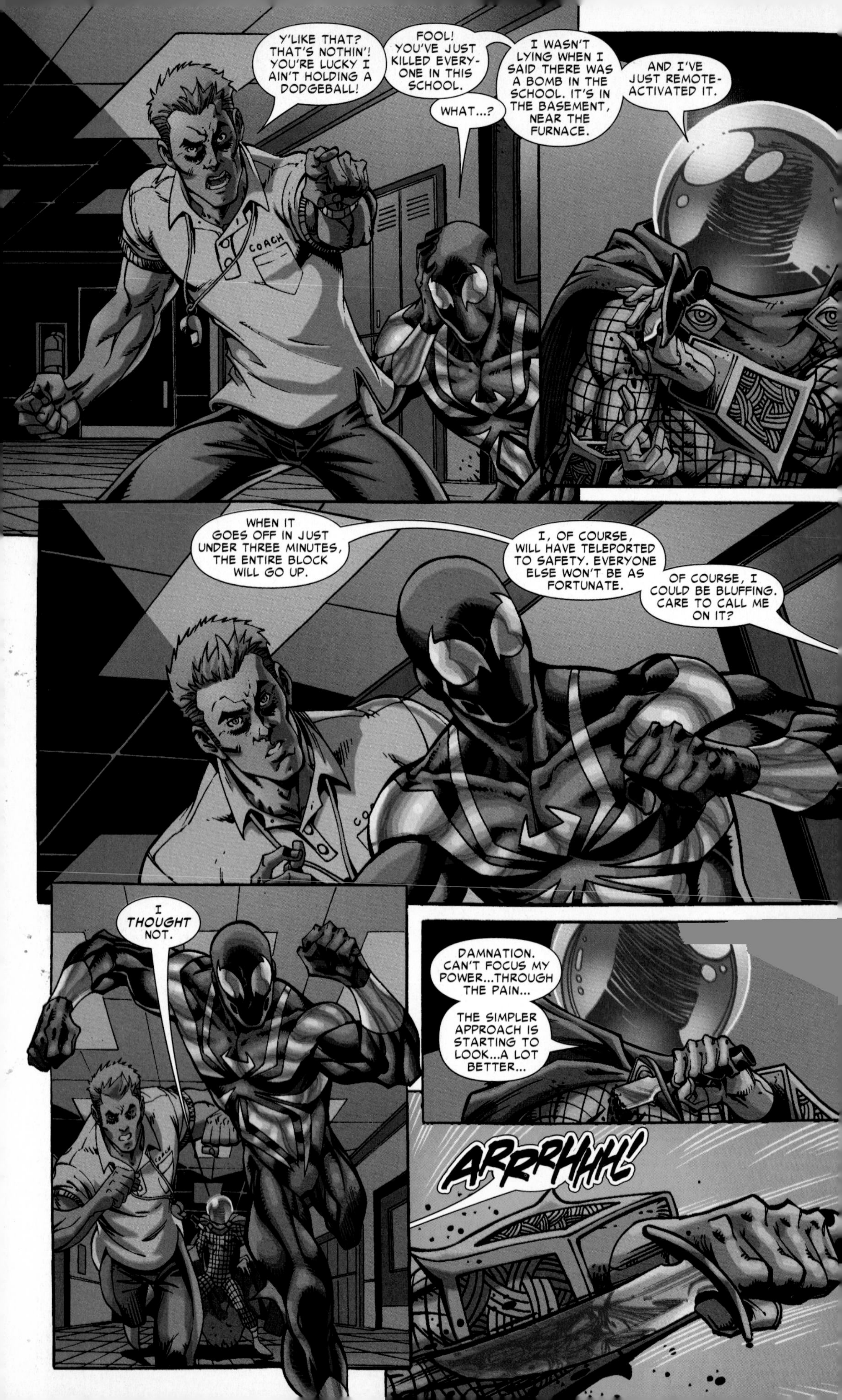
Y'LIKE THAT? THAT'S NOTHIN'! YOU'RE LUCKY I AIN'T HOLDING A DODGEBALL!
FOOL! YOU'VE JUST KILLED EVERY-ONE IN THIS SCHOOL.
WHAT...?
I WASN'T LYING WHEN I SAID THERE WAS A BOMB IN THE SCHOOL. IT'S IN THE BASEMENT, NEAR THE FURNACE.
AND I'VE JUST REMOTE-ACTIVATED IT.
COACH
WHEN IT GOES OFF IN JUST UNDER THREE MINUTES, THE ENTIRE BLOCK WILL GO UP.
I, OF COURSE, WILL HAVE TELEPORTED TO SAFETY. EVERYONE ELSE WON'T BE AS FORTUNATE.
OF COURSE, I COULD BE BLUFFING. CARE TO CALL ME ON IT?
I *THOUGHT* NOT.
DAMNATION. CAN'T FOCUS MY POWER...THROUGH THE PAIN...
THE SIMPLER APPROACH IS STARTING TO LOOK...A LOT BETTER...
ARRRHHH!

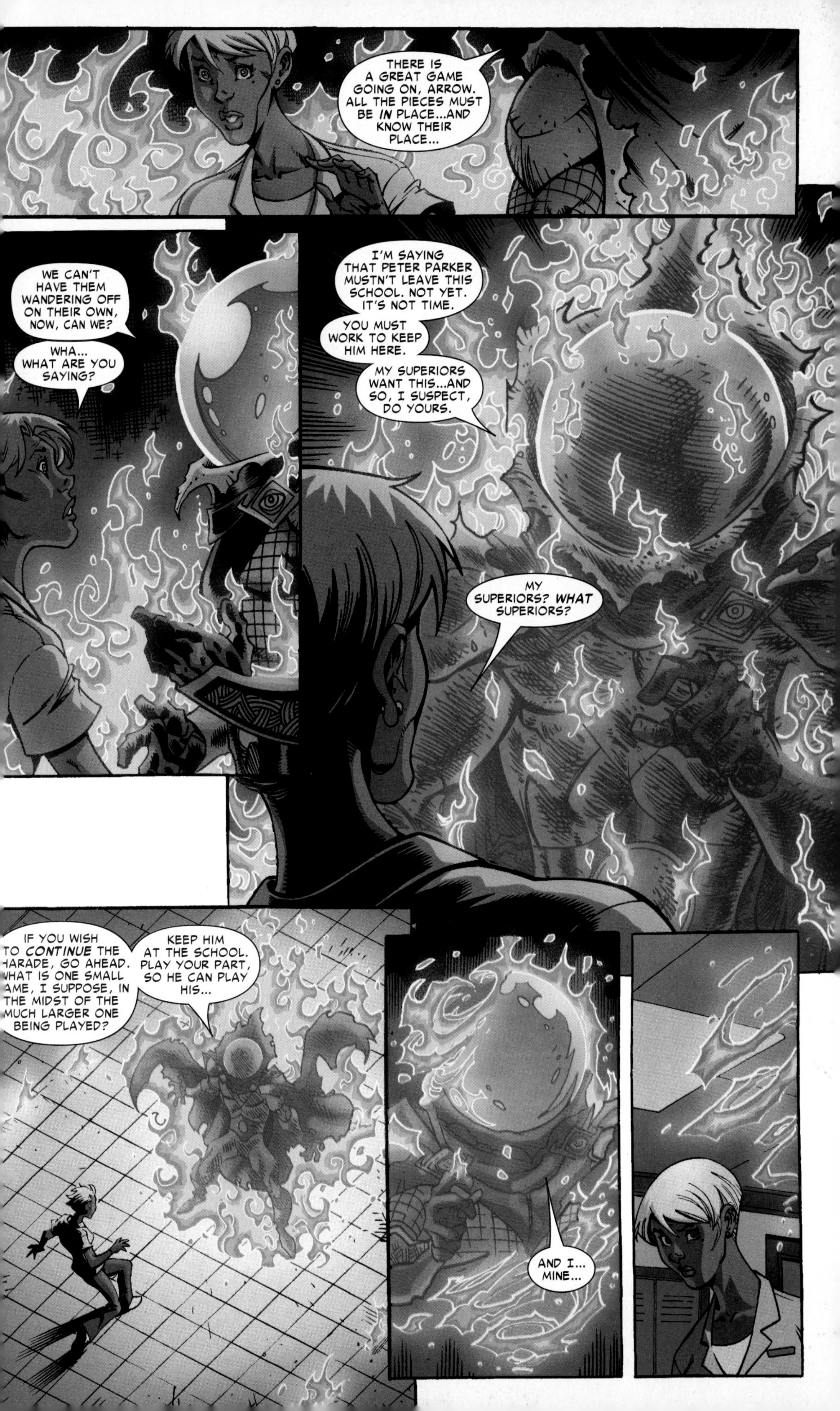

THERE IS A GREAT GAME GOING ON, ARROW. ALL THE PIECES MUST BE *IN* PLACE...AND KNOW THEIR PLACE...
WE CAN'T HAVE THEM WANDERING OFF ON THEIR OWN, NOW, CAN WE?
WHA... WHAT ARE YOU SAYING?
I'M SAYING THAT PETER PARKER MUSTN'T LEAVE THIS SCHOOL. NOT YET. IT'S NOT TIME.
YOU MUST WORK TO KEEP HIM HERE.
MY SUPERIORS WANT THIS...AND SO, I SUSPECT, DO YOURS.
MY SUPERIORS? *WHAT* SUPERIORS?
IF YOU WISH TO *CONTINUE* THE HARADE, GO AHEAD. WHAT IS ONE SMALL AME, I SUPPOSE, IN THE MIDST OF THE MUCH LARGER ONE BEING PLAYED?
KEEP HIM AT THE SCHOOL. PLAY YOUR PART, SO HE CAN PLAY HIS...
AND I... MINE...

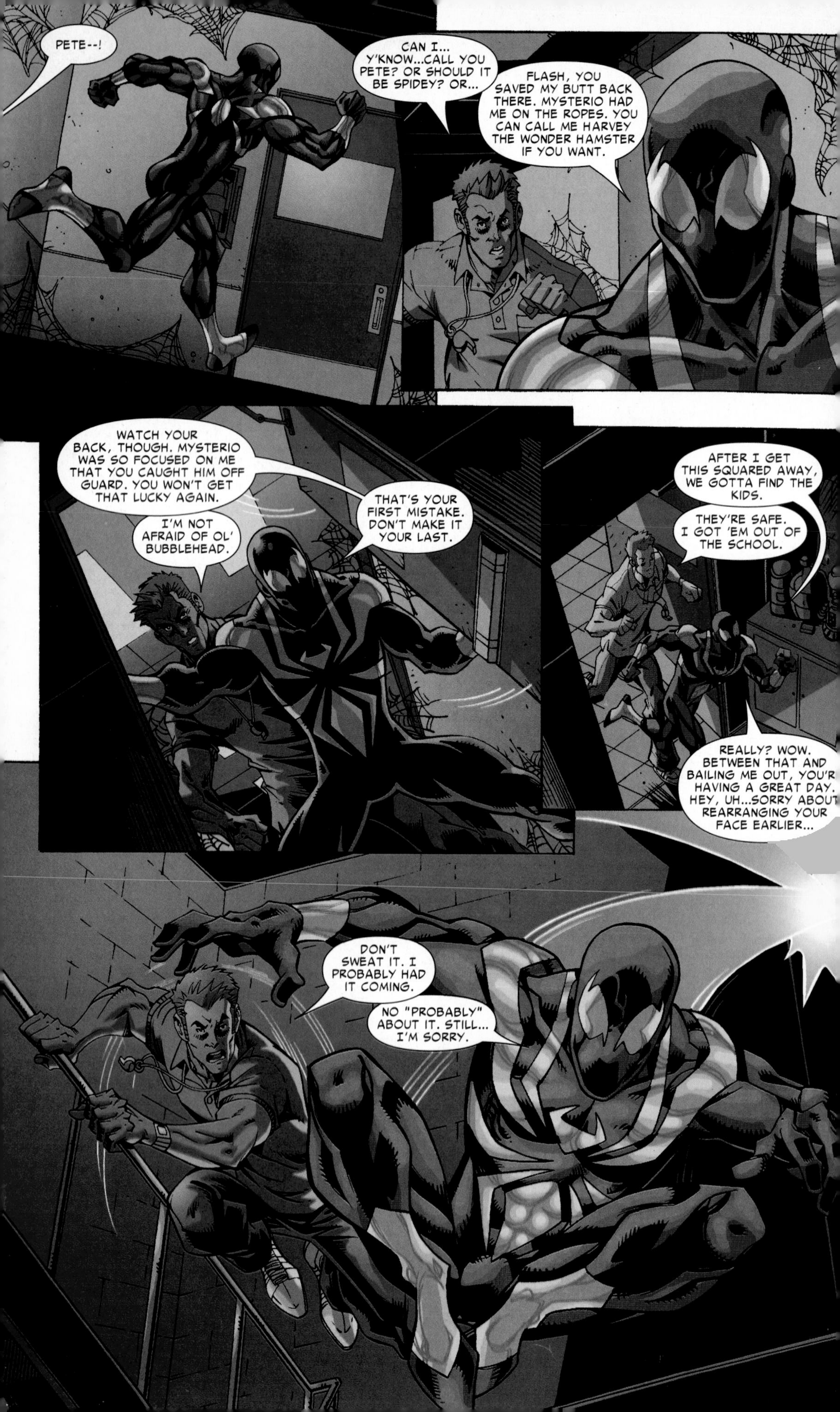
PETE--!
CAN I... Y'KNOW...CALL YOU PETE? OR SHOULD IT BE SPIDEY? OR...
FLASH, YOU SAVED MY BUTT BACK THERE. MYSTERIO HAD ME ON THE ROPES. YOU CAN CALL ME HARVEY THE WONDER HAMSTER IF YOU WANT.
WATCH YOUR BACK, THOUGH. MYSTERIO WAS SO FOCUSED ON ME THAT YOU CAUGHT HIM OFF GUARD. YOU WON'T GET THAT LUCKY AGAIN.
I'M NOT AFRAID OF OL' BUBBLEHEAD.
THAT'S YOUR FIRST MISTAKE. DON'T MAKE IT YOUR LAST.
AFTER I GET THIS SQUARED AWAY, WE GOTTA FIND THE KIDS.
THEY'RE SAFE. I GOT 'EM OUT OF THE SCHOOL.
REALLY? WOW. BETWEEN THAT AND BAILING ME OUT, YOU'R HAVING A GREAT DAY. HEY, UH...SORRY ABOUT REARRANGING YOUR FACE EARLIER...
DON'T SWEAT IT. I PROBABLY HAD IT COMING.
NO "PROBABLY" ABOUT IT. STILL... I'M SORRY.

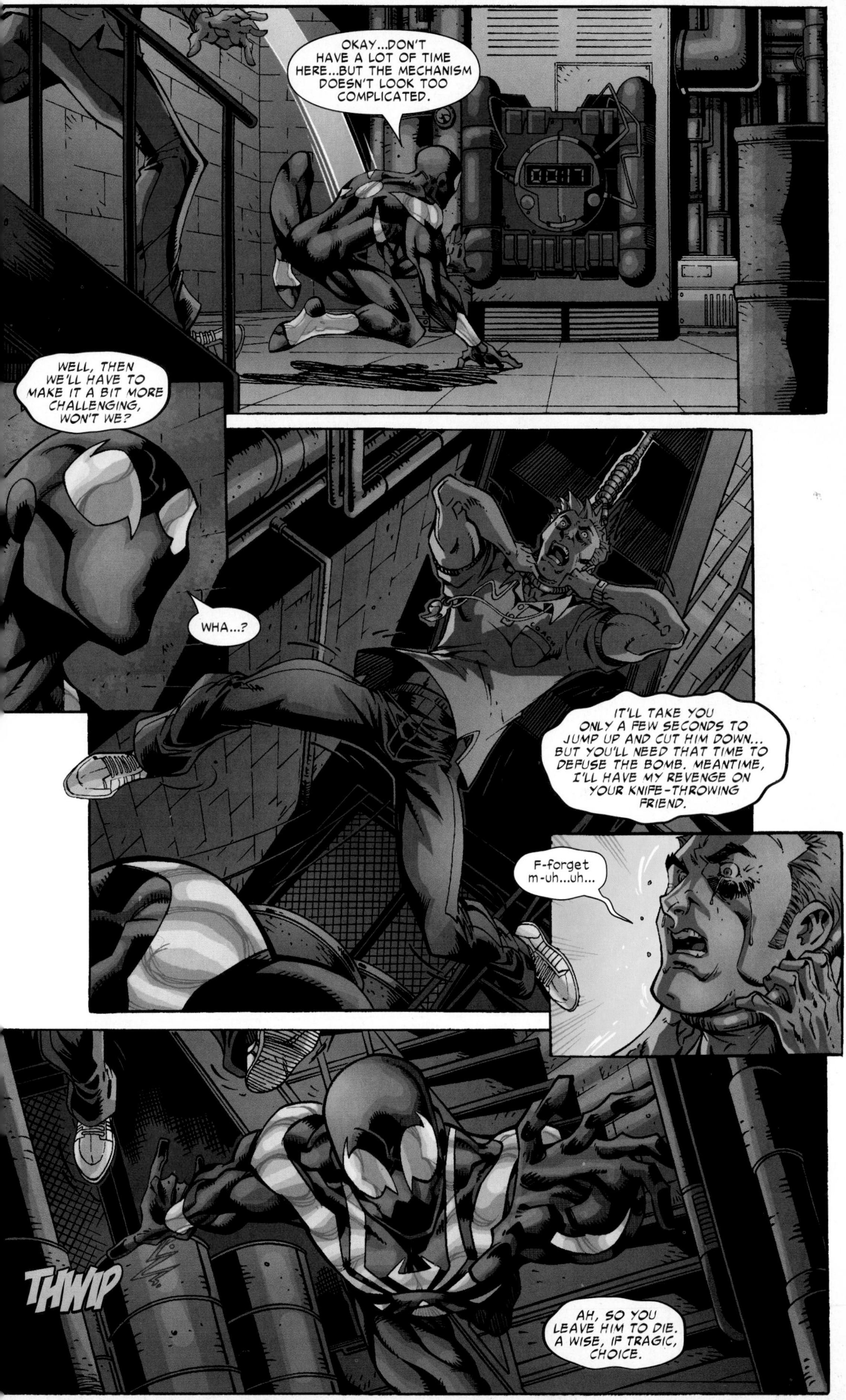
OKAY...DON'T HAVE A LOT OF TIME HERE...BUT THE MECHANISM DOESN'T LOOK TOO COMPLICATED.
WELL, THEN WE'LL HAVE TO MAKE IT A BIT MORE CHALLENGING, WON'T WE?
WHA...?
IT'LL TAKE YOU ONLY A FEW SECONDS TO JUMP UP AND CUT HIM DOWN... BUT YOU'LL NEED THAT TIME TO DEFUSE THE BOMB. MEANTIME, I'LL HAVE MY REVENGE ON YOUR KNIFE-THROWING FRIEND.
F-forget m-uh...uh...
THWIP
AH, SO YOU LEAVE HIM TO DIE. A WISE, IF TRAGIC, CHOICE.

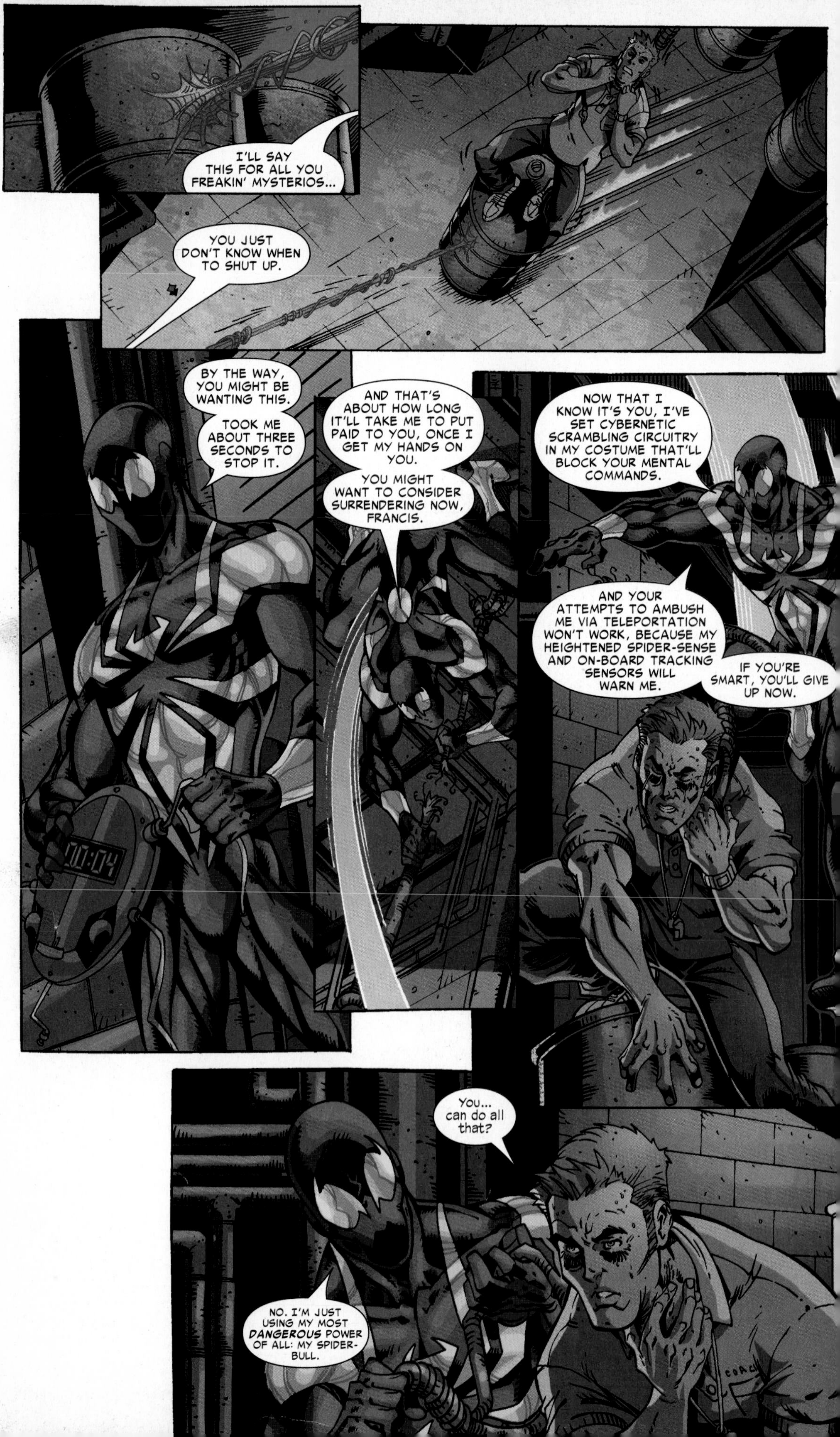
I'LL SAY THIS FOR ALL YOU FREAKIN' MYSTERIOS...
YOU JUST DON'T KNOW WHEN TO SHUT UP.
BY THE WAY, YOU MIGHT BE WANTING THIS.
TOOK ME ABOUT THREE SECONDS TO STOP IT.
00:04
AND THAT'S ABOUT HOW LONG IT'LL TAKE ME TO PUT PAID TO YOU, ONCE I GET MY HANDS ON YOU.
YOU MIGHT WANT TO CONSIDER SURRENDERING NOW, FRANCIS.
NOW THAT I KNOW IT'S YOU, I'VE SET CYBERNETIC SCRAMBLING CIRCUITRY IN MY COSTUME THAT'LL BLOCK YOUR MENTAL COMMANDS.
AND YOUR ATTEMPTS TO AMBUSH ME VIA TELEPORTATION WON'T WORK, BECAUSE MY HEIGHTENED SPIDER-SENSE AND ON-BOARD TRACKING SENSORS WILL WARN ME.
IF YOU'RE SMART, YOU'LL GIVE UP NOW.
You... can do all that?
NO. I'M JUST USING MY MOST *DANGEROUS* POWER OF ALL: MY SPIDER-BULL.

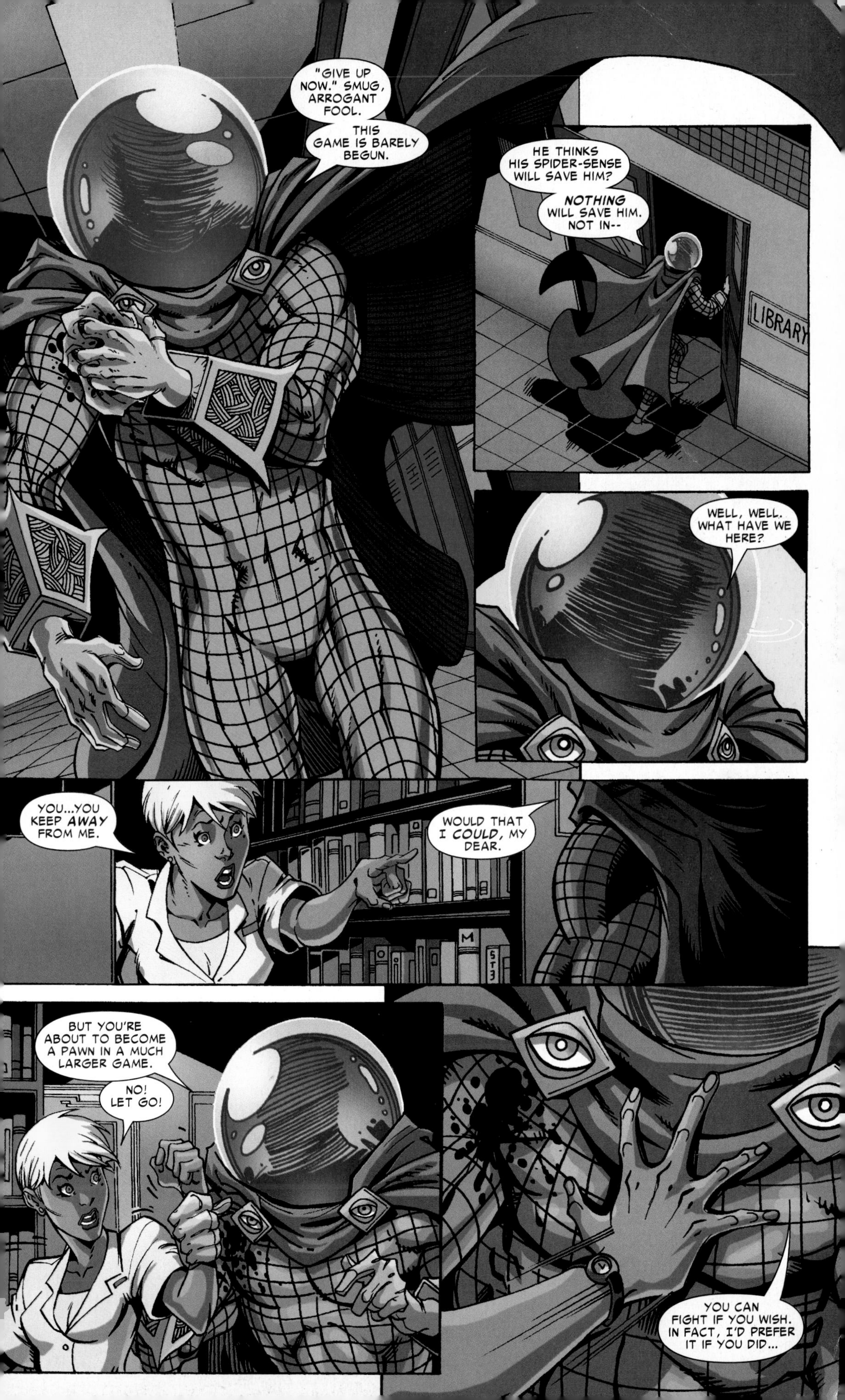
"GIVE UP NOW." SMUG, ARROGANT FOOL.
THIS GAME IS BARELY BEGUN.
HE THINKS HIS SPIDER-SENSE WILL SAVE HIM?
NOTHING WILL SAVE HIM. NOT IN--
LIBRARY
WELL, WELL. WHAT HAVE WE HERE?
YOU...YOU KEEP AWAY FROM ME.
WOULD THAT I COULD, MY DEAR.
BUT YOU'RE ABOUT TO BECOME A PAWN IN A MUCH LARGER GAME.
NO! LET GO!
YOU CAN FIGHT IF YOU WISH. IN FACT, I'D PREFER IT IF YOU DID...

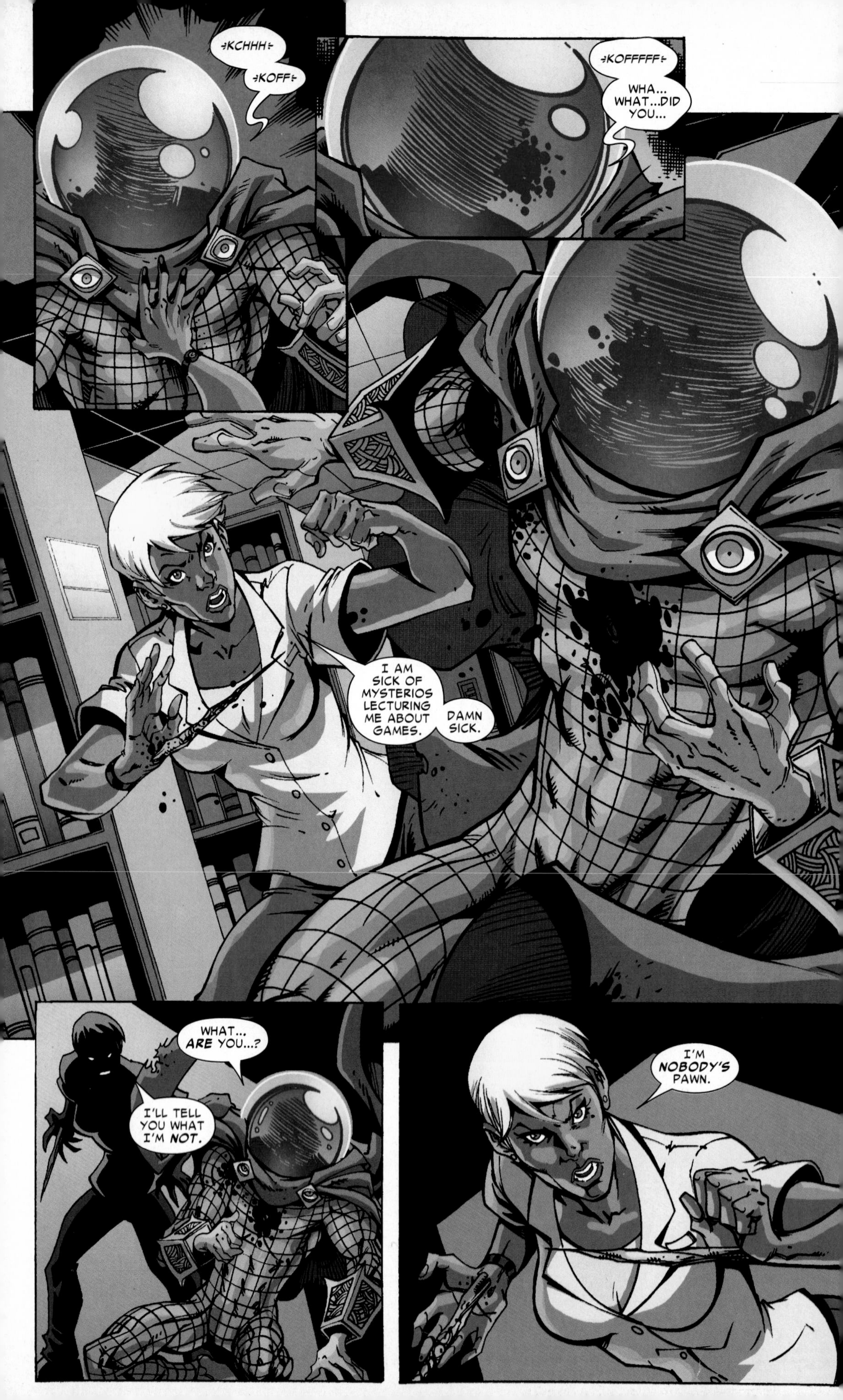

KCHHH
KOFF
KOFFFFF
WHA... WHAT...DID YOU...
I AM SICK OF MYSTERIOS LECTURING ME ABOUT GAMES.
DAMN SICK.
WHAT... ARE YOU...?
I'LL TELL YOU WHAT I'M NOT.
I'M NOBODY'S PAWN.

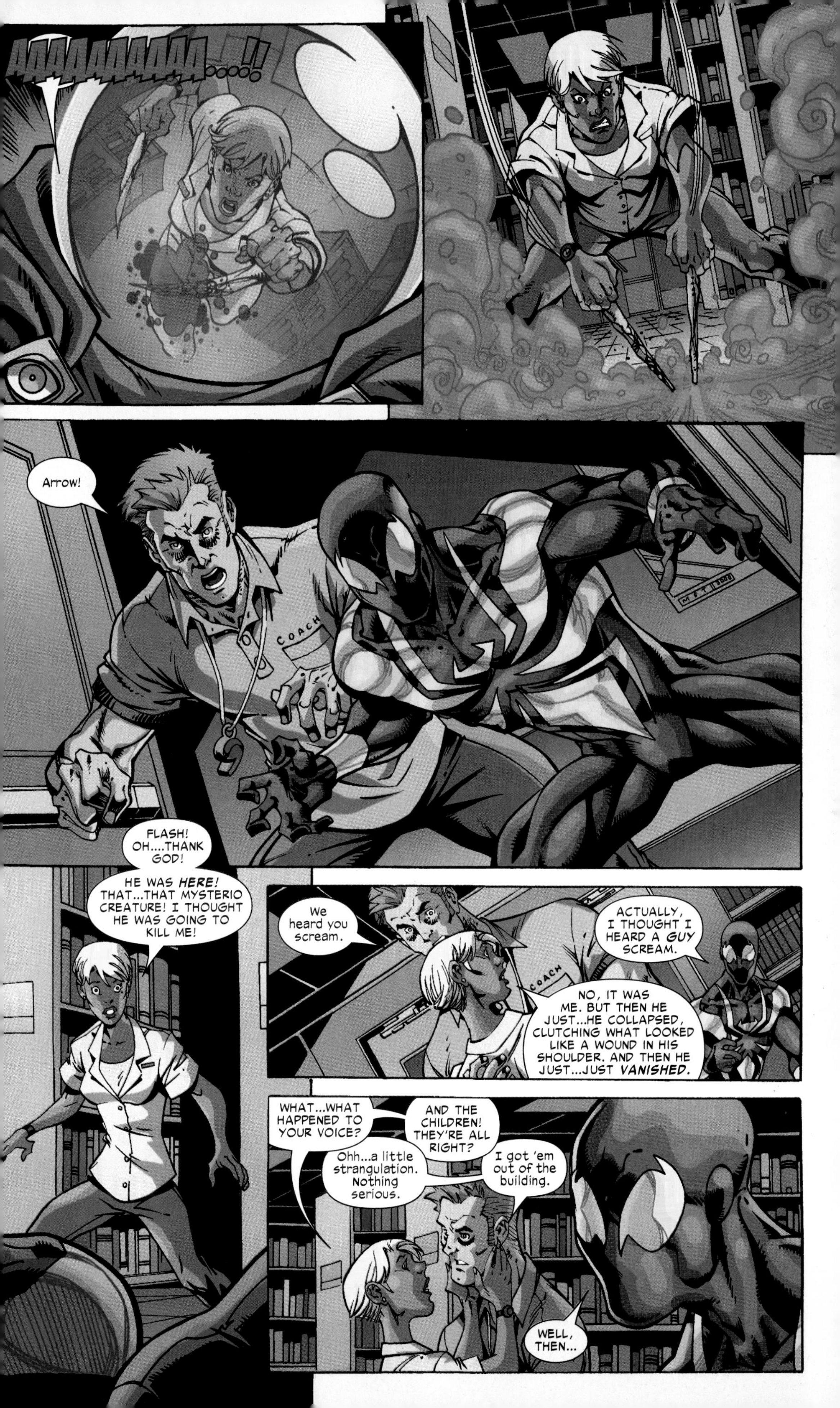
AAAAAAAAAA...oooo!!
Arrow!
FLASH! OH....THANK GOD!
HE WAS HERE! THAT...THAT MYSTERIO CREATURE! I THOUGHT HE WAS GOING TO KILL ME!
We heard you scream.
ACTUALLY, I THOUGHT I HEARD A GUY SCREAM.
NO, IT WAS ME. BUT THEN HE JUST...HE COLLAPSED, CLUTCHING WHAT LOOKED LIKE A WOUND IN HIS SHOULDER. AND THEN HE JUST...JUST VANISHED.
WHAT...WHAT HAPPENED TO YOUR VOICE?
AND THE CHILDREN! THEY'RE ALL RIGHT?
Ohh...a little strangulation. Nothing serious.
I got 'em out of the building.
WELL, THEN...

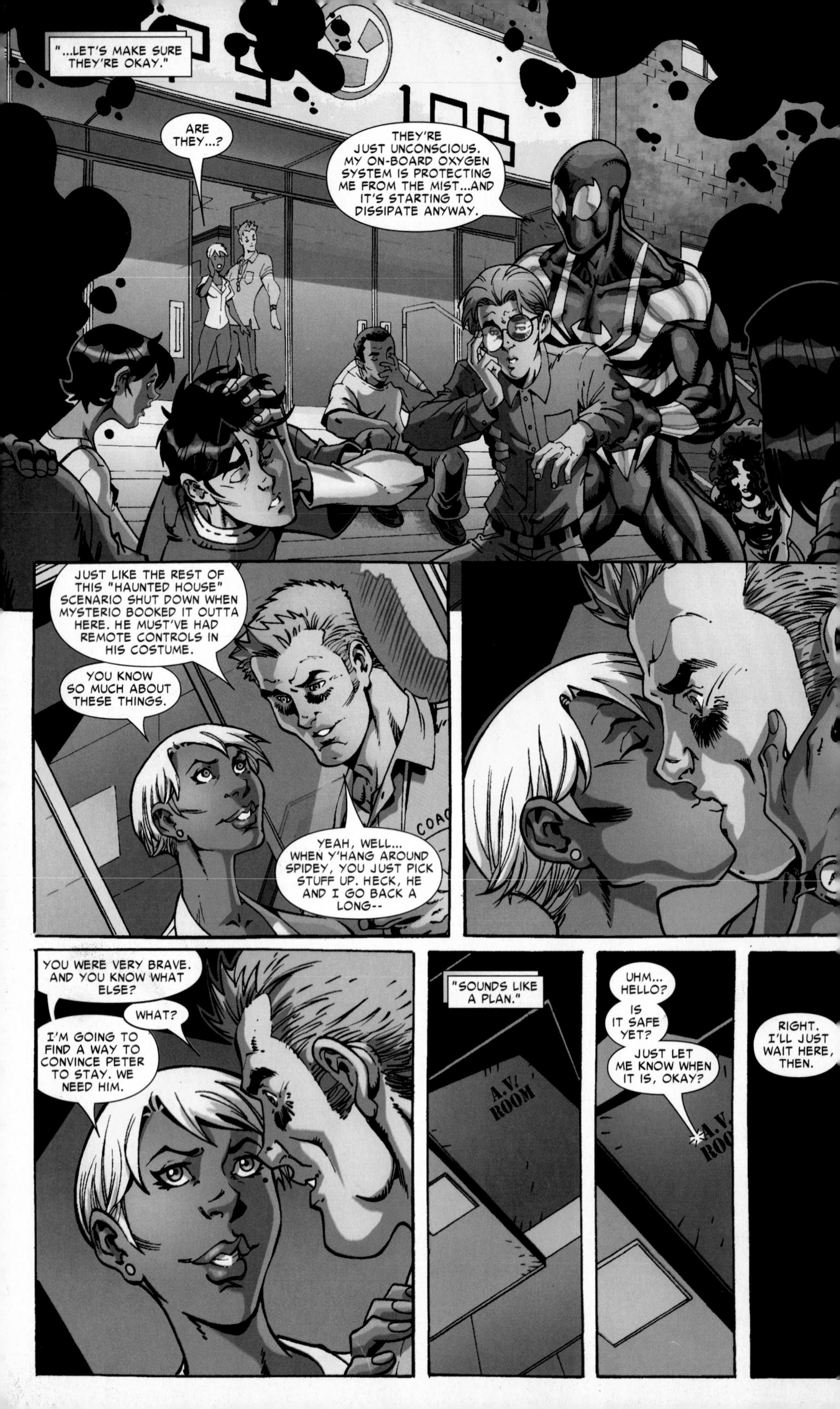
"...LET'S MAKE SURE THEY'RE OKAY."
108
ARE THEY...?
THEY'RE JUST UNCONSCIOUS. MY ON-BOARD OXYGEN SYSTEM IS PROTECTING ME FROM THE MIST...AND IT'S STARTING TO DISSIPATE ANYWAY.
JUST LIKE THE REST OF THIS "HAUNTED HOUSE" SCENARIO SHUT DOWN WHEN MYSTERIO BOOKED IT OUTTA HERE. HE MUST'VE HAD REMOTE CONTROLS IN HIS COSTUME.
YOU KNOW SO MUCH ABOUT THESE THINGS.
YEAH, WELL... WHEN Y'HANG AROUND SPIDEY, YOU JUST PICK STUFF UP. HECK, HE AND I GO BACK A LONG--
YOU WERE VERY BRAVE. AND YOU KNOW WHAT ELSE?
WHAT?
I'M GOING TO FIND A WAY TO CONVINCE PETER TO STAY. WE NEED HIM.
"SOUNDS LIKE A PLAN."
A.V. ROOM
UHM... HELLO?
IS IT SAFE YET?
JUST LET ME KNOW WHEN IT IS, OKAY?
RIGHT. I'LL JUST WAIT HERE, THEN.

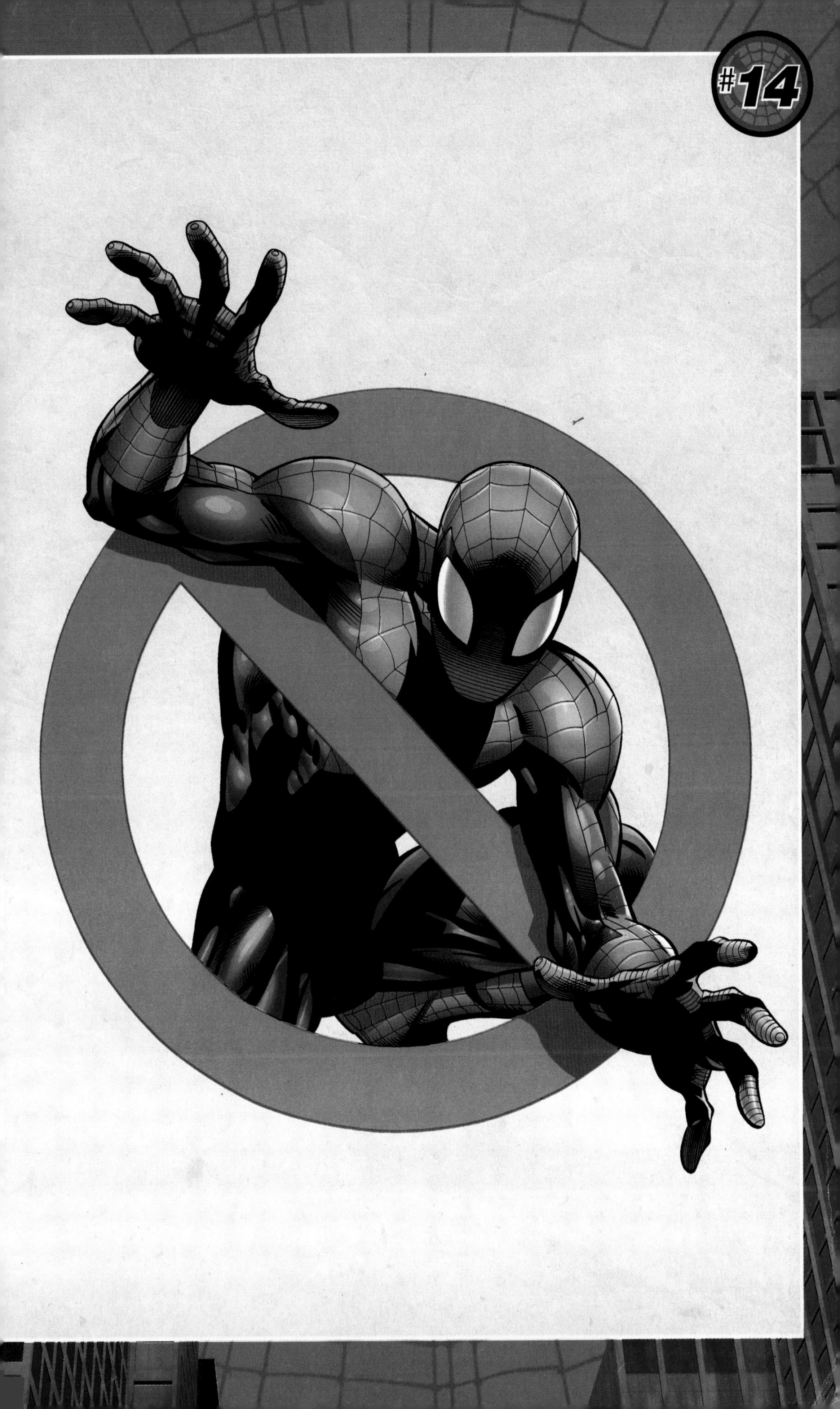
#14

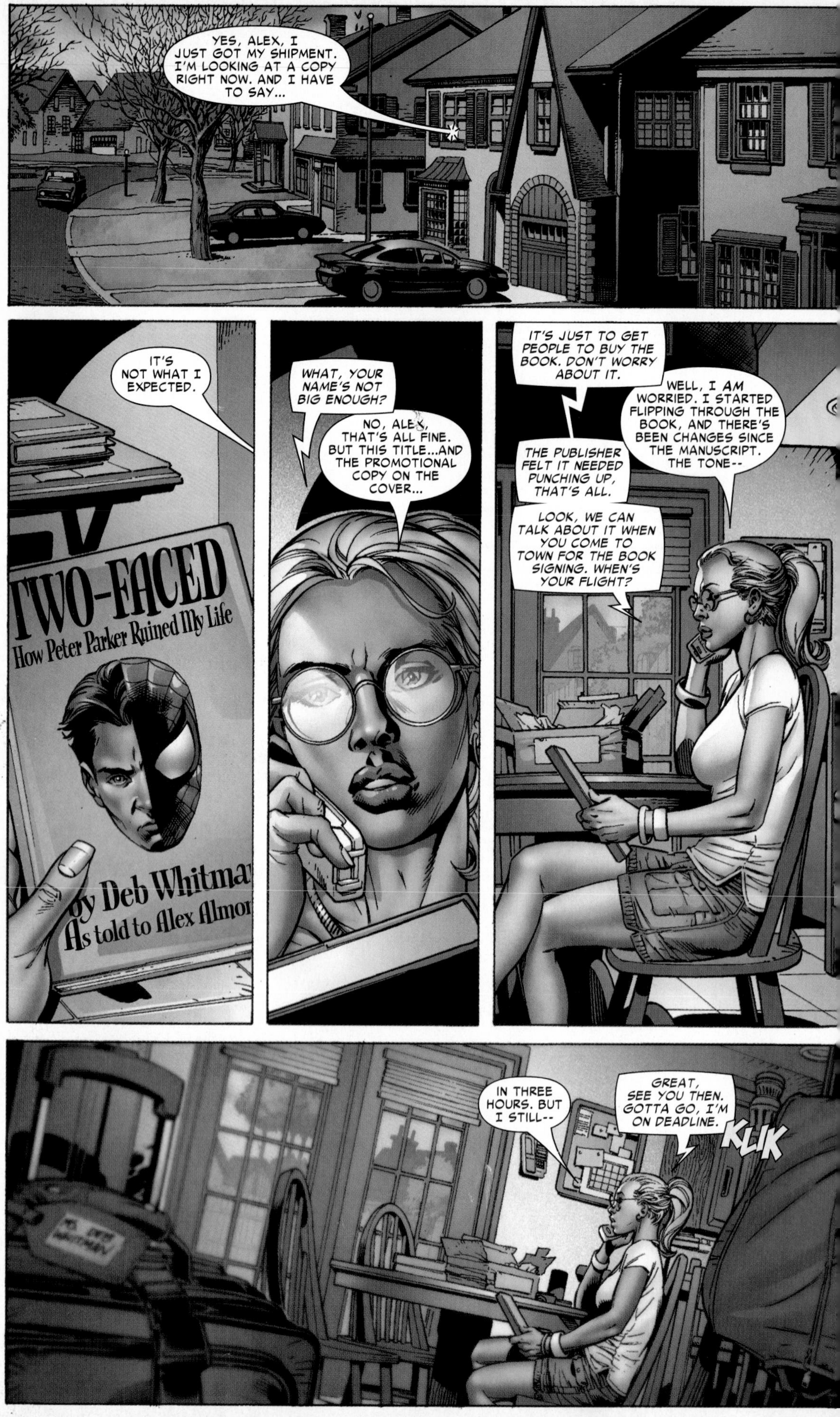
YES, ALEX, I JUST GOT MY SHIPMENT. I'M LOOKING AT A COPY RIGHT NOW. AND I HAVE TO SAY...
IT'S NOT WHAT I EXPECTED.
TWO-FACED
How Peter Parker Ruined My Life
by Deb Whitman
As told to Alex Almon
WHAT, YOUR NAME'S NOT BIG ENOUGH?
NO, ALEX, THAT'S ALL FINE. BUT THIS TITLE...AND THE PROMOTIONAL COPY ON THE COVER...
IT'S JUST TO GET PEOPLE TO BUY THE BOOK. DON'T WORRY ABOUT IT.
WELL, I AM WORRIED. I STARTED FLIPPING THROUGH THE BOOK, AND THERE'S BEEN CHANGES SINCE THE MANUSCRIPT. THE TONE--
THE PUBLISHER FELT IT NEEDED PUNCHING UP, THAT'S ALL.
LOOK, WE CAN TALK ABOUT IT WHEN YOU COME TO TOWN FOR THE BOOK SIGNING. WHEN'S YOUR FLIGHT?
IN THREE HOURS. BUT I STILL--
GREAT, SEE YOU THEN. GOTTA GO, I'M ON DEADLINE.
KLIK

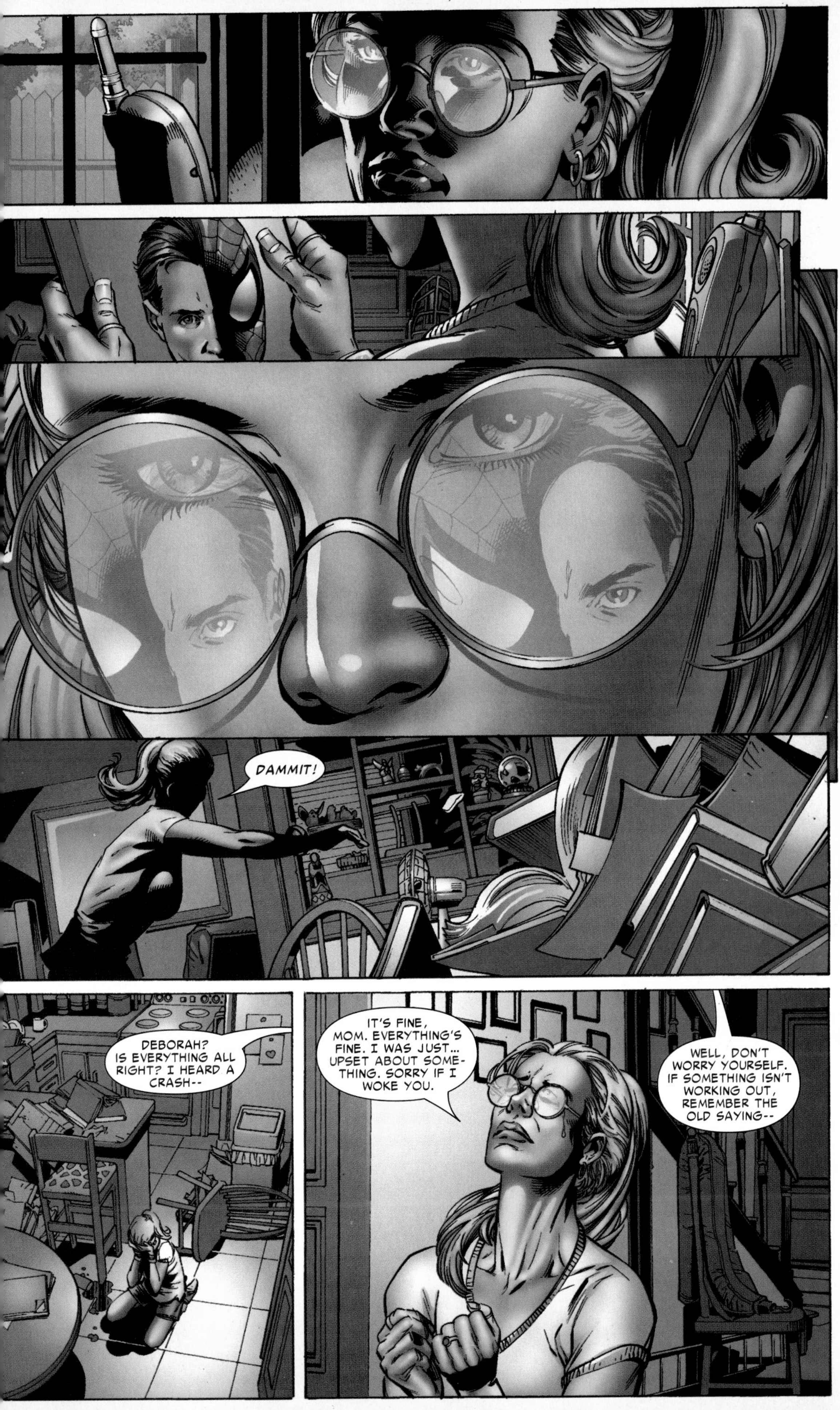
DAMMIT!
DEBORAH? IS EVERYTHING ALL RIGHT? I HEARD A CRASH--
IT'S FINE, MOM. EVERYTHING'S FINE. I WAS JUST... UPSET ABOUT SOMETHING. SORRY IF I WOKE YOU.
WELL, DON'T WORRY YOURSELF. IF SOMETHING ISN'T WORKING OUT, REMEMBER THE OLD SAYING--

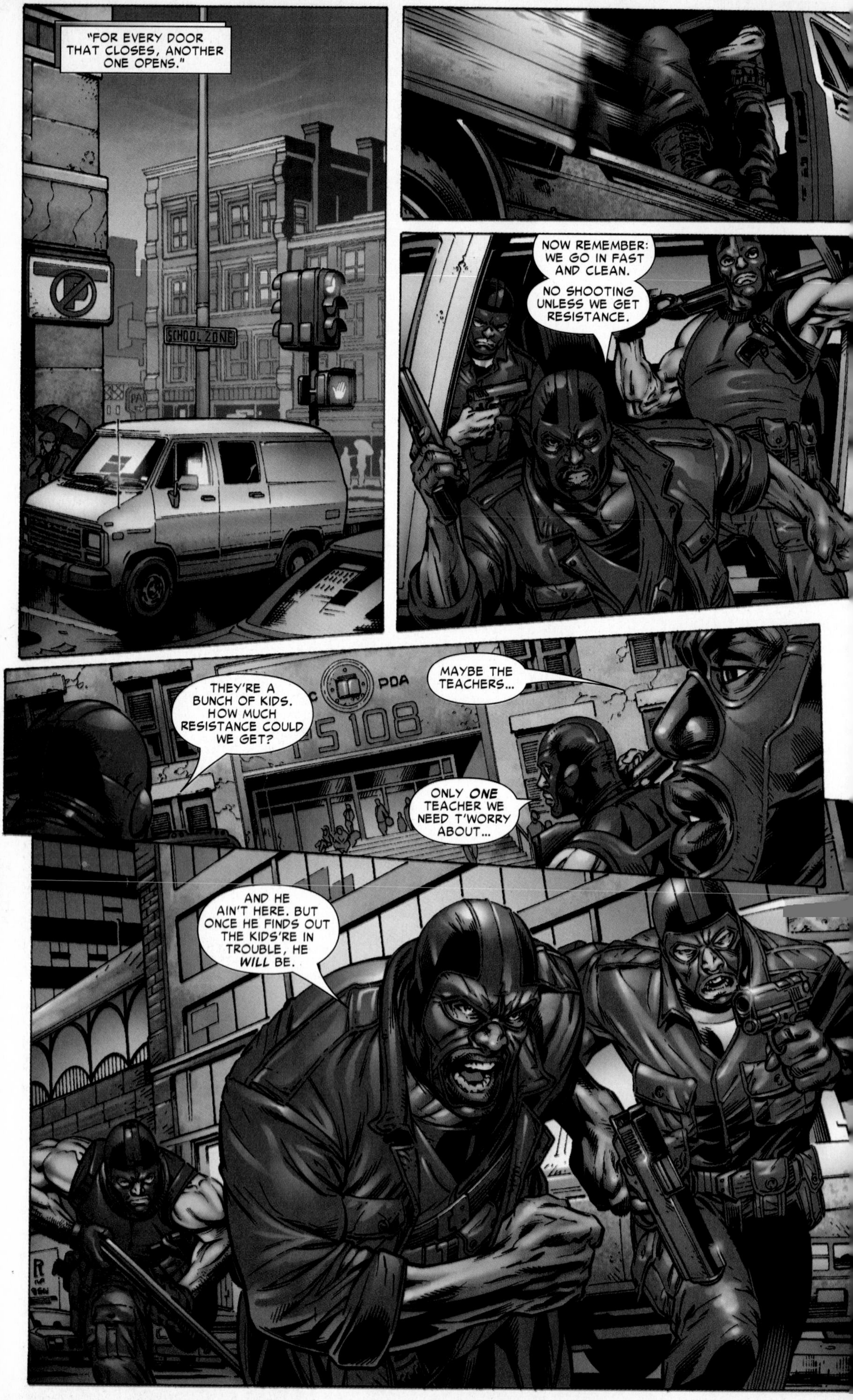
"FOR EVERY DOOR THAT CLOSES, ANOTHER ONE OPENS."
SCHOOL ZONE
NOW REMEMBER: WE GO IN FAST AND CLEAN.
NO SHOOTING UNLESS WE GET RESISTANCE.
THEY'RE A BUNCH OF KIDS. HOW MUCH RESISTANCE COULD WE GET?
PDA
PS 108
MAYBE THE TEACHERS...
ONLY ONE TEACHER WE NEED T'WORRY ABOUT...
AND HE AIN'T HERE. BUT ONCE HE FINDS OUT THE KIDS'RE IN TROUBLE, HE WILL BE.

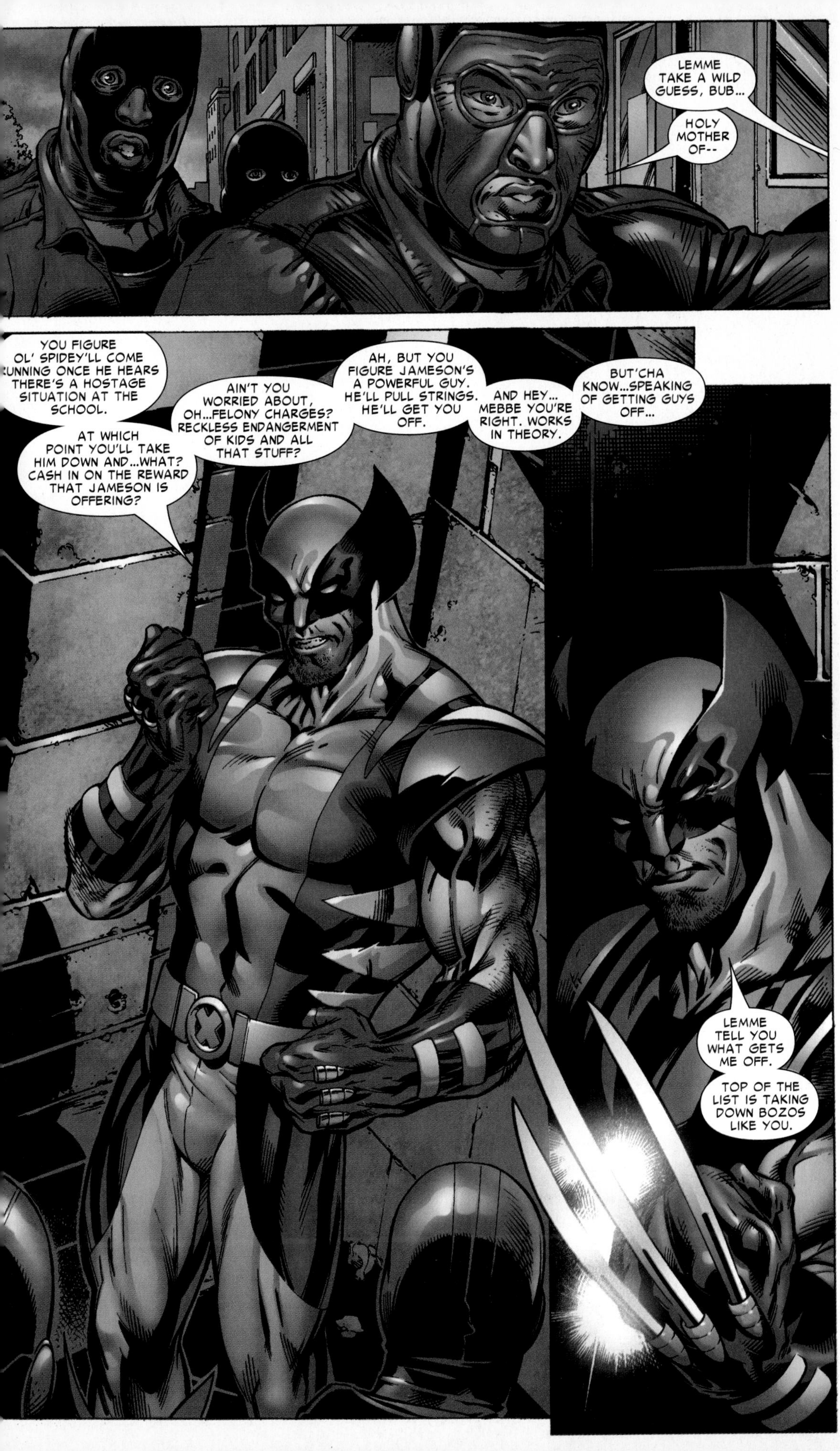
LEMME TAKE A WILD GUESS, BUB...
HOLY MOTHER OF--
YOU FIGURE OL' SPIDEY'LL COME RUNNING ONCE HE HEARS THERE'S A HOSTAGE SITUATION AT THE SCHOOL.
AT WHICH POINT YOU'LL TAKE HIM DOWN AND...WHAT? CASH IN ON THE REWARD THAT JAMESON IS OFFERING?
AIN'T YOU WORRIED ABOUT, OH...FELONY CHARGES? RECKLESS ENDANGERMENT OF KIDS AND ALL THAT STUFF?
AH, BUT YOU FIGURE JAMESON'S A POWERFUL GUY. HE'LL PULL STRINGS. HE'LL GET YOU OFF.
AND HEY... MEBBE YOU'RE RIGHT. WORKS IN THEORY.
BUT'CHA KNOW...SPEAKING OF GETTING GUYS OFF...
LEMME TELL YOU WHAT GETS ME OFF.
TOP OF THE LIST IS TAKING DOWN BOZOS LIKE YOU.

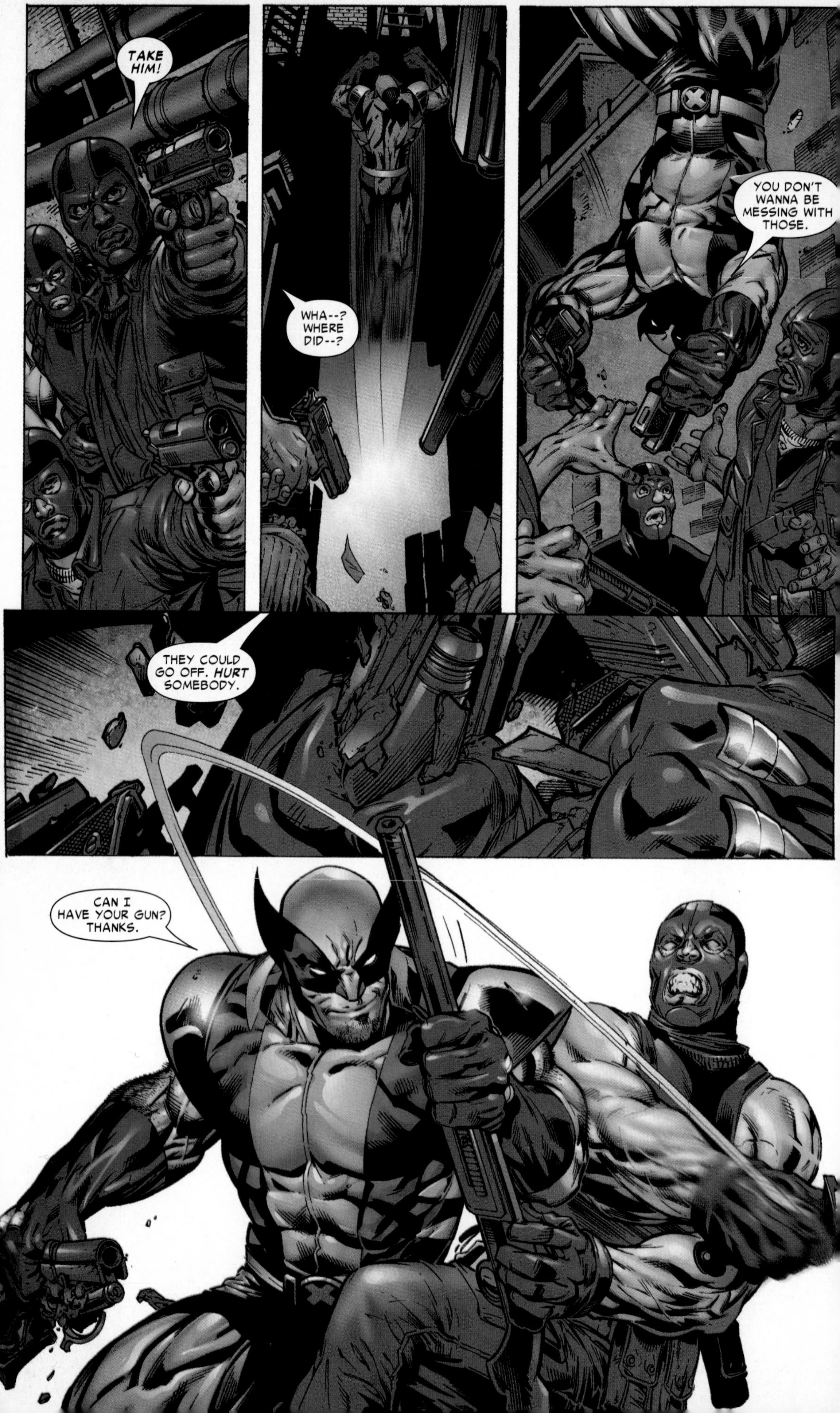
TAKE HIM!
WHA--? WHERE DID--?
YOU DON'T WANNA BE MESSING WITH THOSE.
THEY COULD GO OFF. *HURT* SOMEBODY.
CAN I HAVE YOUR GUN? THANKS.

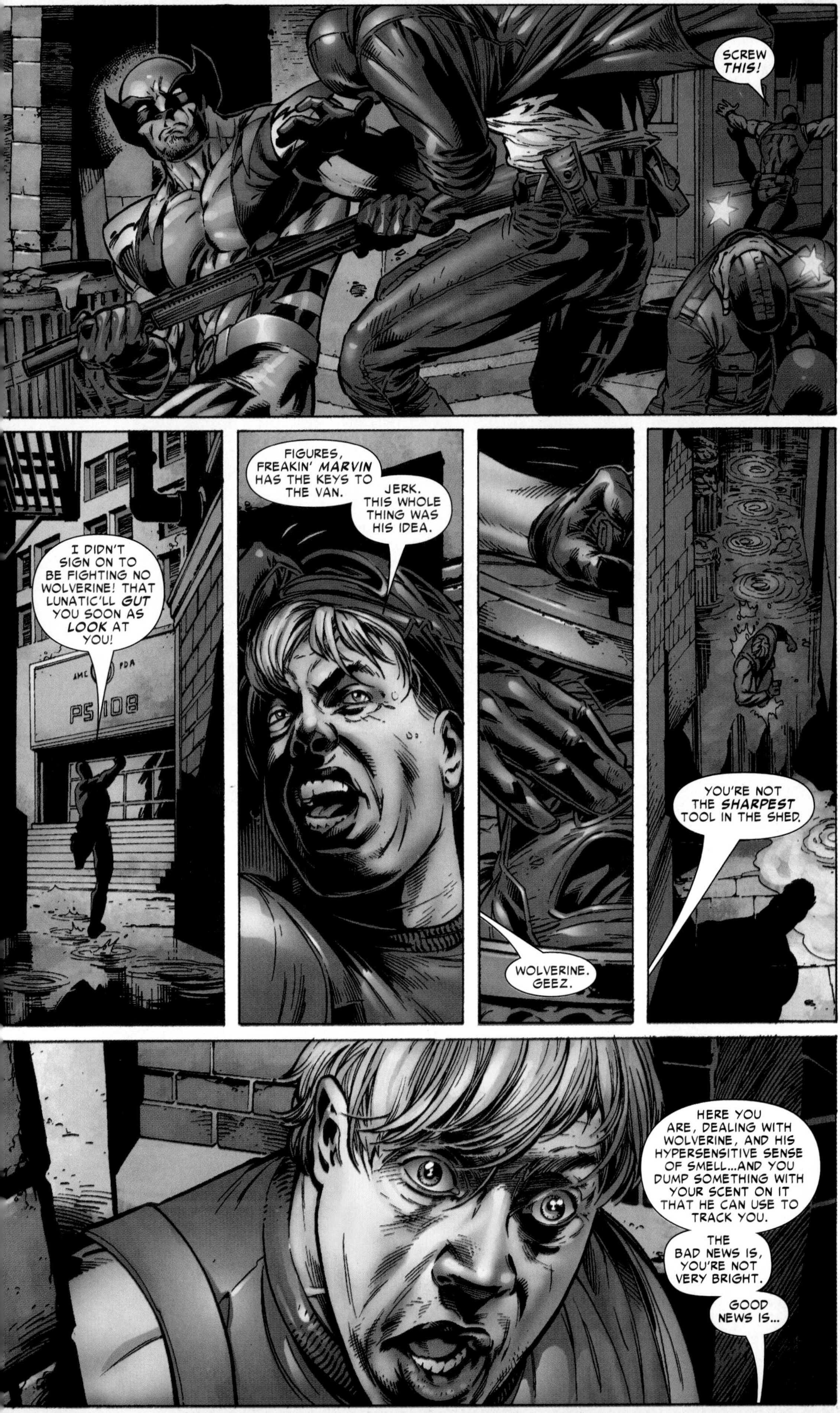
SCREW THIS!
I DIDN'T SIGN ON TO BE FIGHTING NO WOLVERINE! THAT LUNATIC'LL GUT YOU SOON AS LOOK AT YOU!
PS 108
FIGURES, FREAKIN' MARVIN HAS THE KEYS TO THE VAN.
JERK. THIS WHOLE THING WAS HIS IDEA.
WOLVERINE. GEEZ.
YOU'RE NOT THE SHARPEST TOOL IN THE SHED.
HERE YOU ARE, DEALING WITH WOLVERINE, AND HIS HYPERSENSITIVE SENSE OF SMELL...AND YOU DUMP SOMETHING WITH YOUR SCENT ON IT THAT HE CAN USE TO TRACK YOU.
THE BAD NEWS IS, YOU'RE NOT VERY BRIGHT.
GOOD NEWS IS...

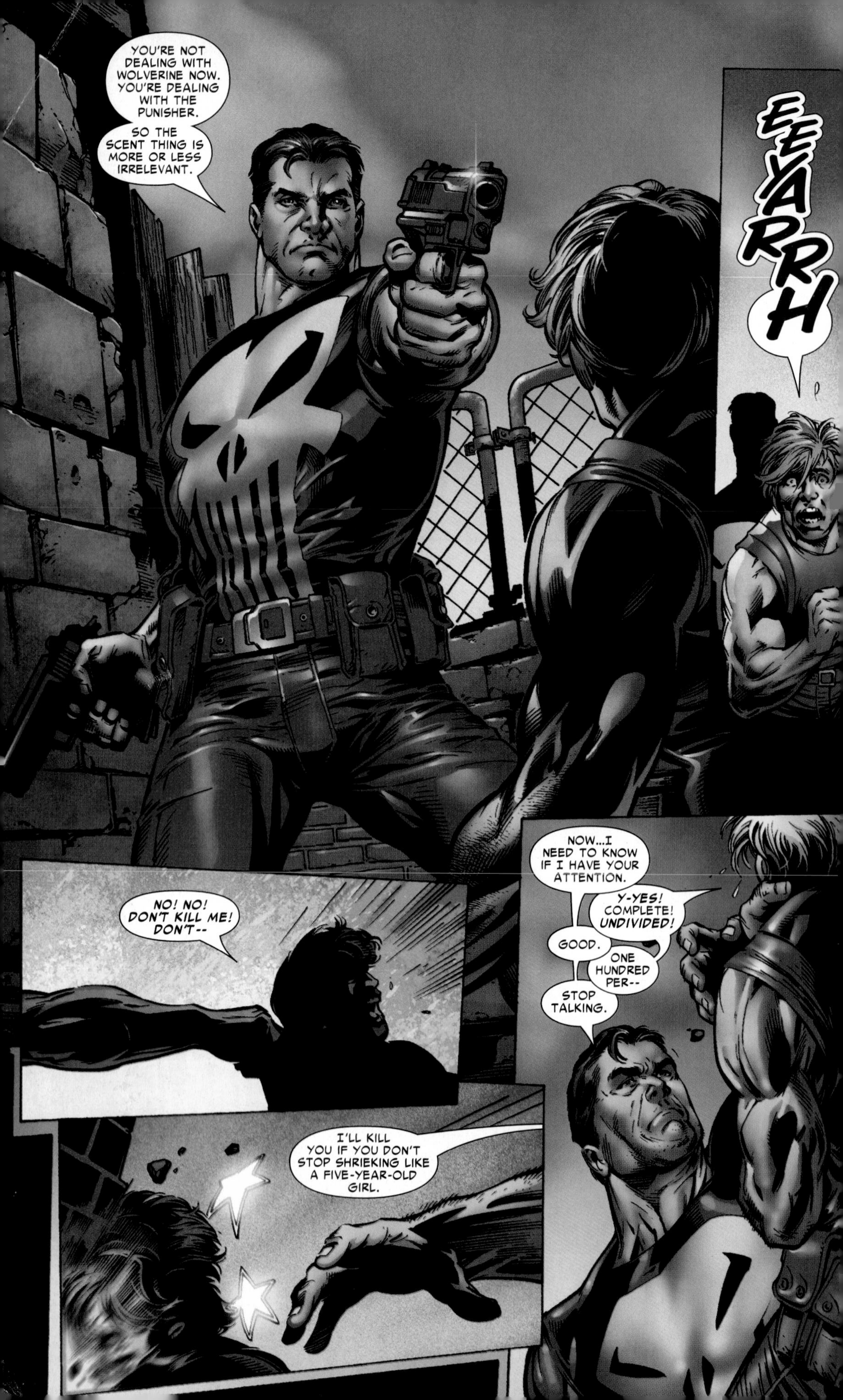
YOU'RE NOT DEALING WITH WOLVERINE NOW. YOU'RE DEALING WITH THE PUNISHER.
SO THE SCENT THING IS MORE OR LESS IRRELEVANT.
EEYARRH
NO! NO! DON'T KILL ME! DON'T--
I'LL KILL YOU IF YOU DON'T STOP SHRIEKING LIKE A FIVE-YEAR-OLD GIRL.
NOW...I NEED TO KNOW IF I HAVE YOUR ATTENTION.
Y-YES! COMPLETE! UNDIVIDED!
GOOD.
ONE HUNDRED PER--
STOP TALKING.

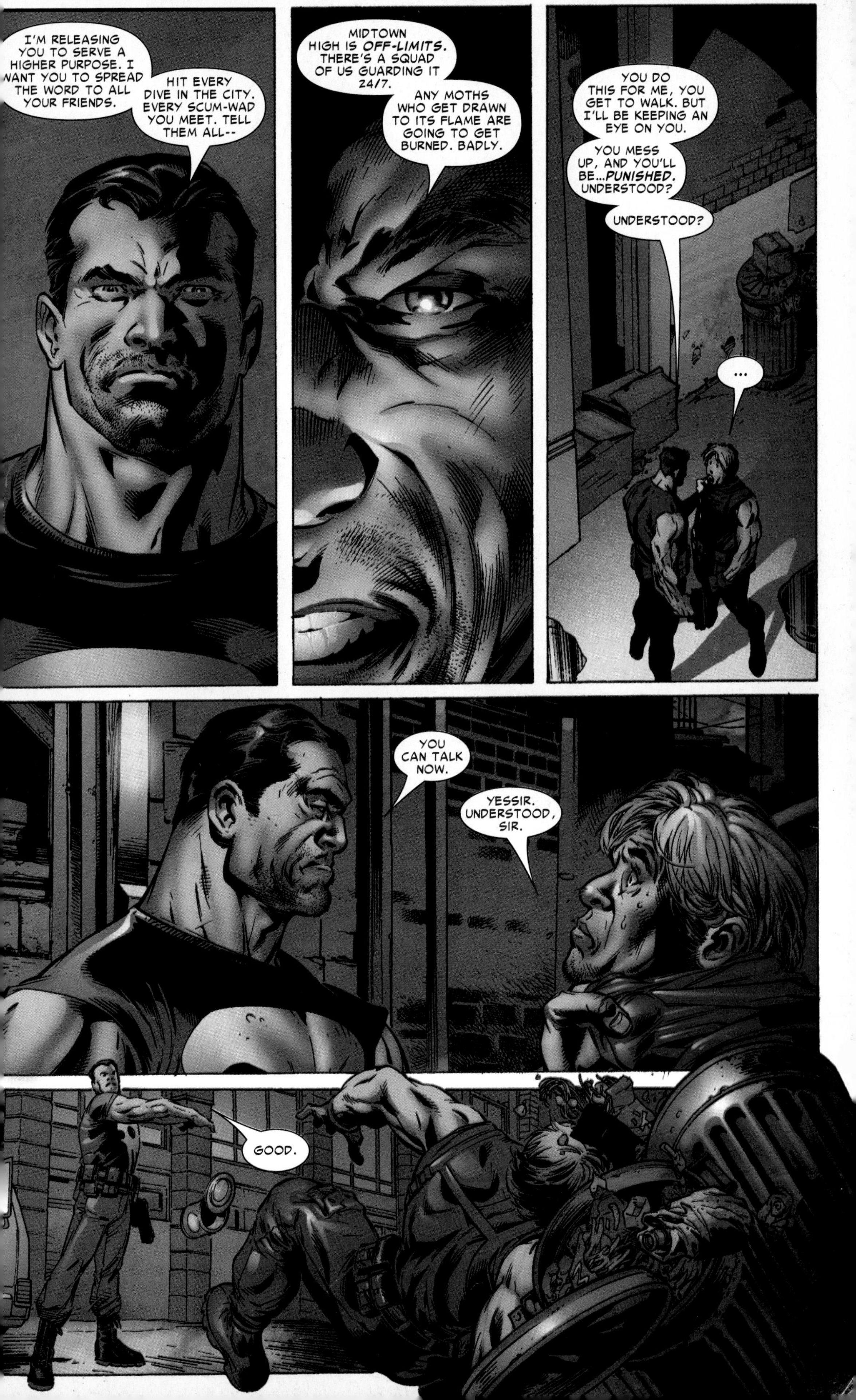
I'M RELEASING YOU TO SERVE A HIGHER PURPOSE. I WANT YOU TO SPREAD THE WORD TO ALL YOUR FRIENDS.
HIT EVERY DIVE IN THE CITY. EVERY SCUM-WAD YOU MEET. TELL THEM ALL--
MIDTOWN HIGH IS *OFF-LIMITS.* THERE'S A SQUAD OF US GUARDING IT 24/7.
ANY MOTHS WHO GET DRAWN TO ITS FLAME ARE GOING TO GET BURNED. BADLY.
YOU DO THIS FOR ME, YOU GET TO WALK. BUT I'LL BE KEEPING AN EYE ON YOU.
YOU MESS UP, AND YOU'LL BE...*PUNISHED.* UNDERSTOOD?
UNDERSTOOD?
...
YOU CAN TALK NOW.
YESSIR. UNDERSTOOD, SIR.
GOOD.

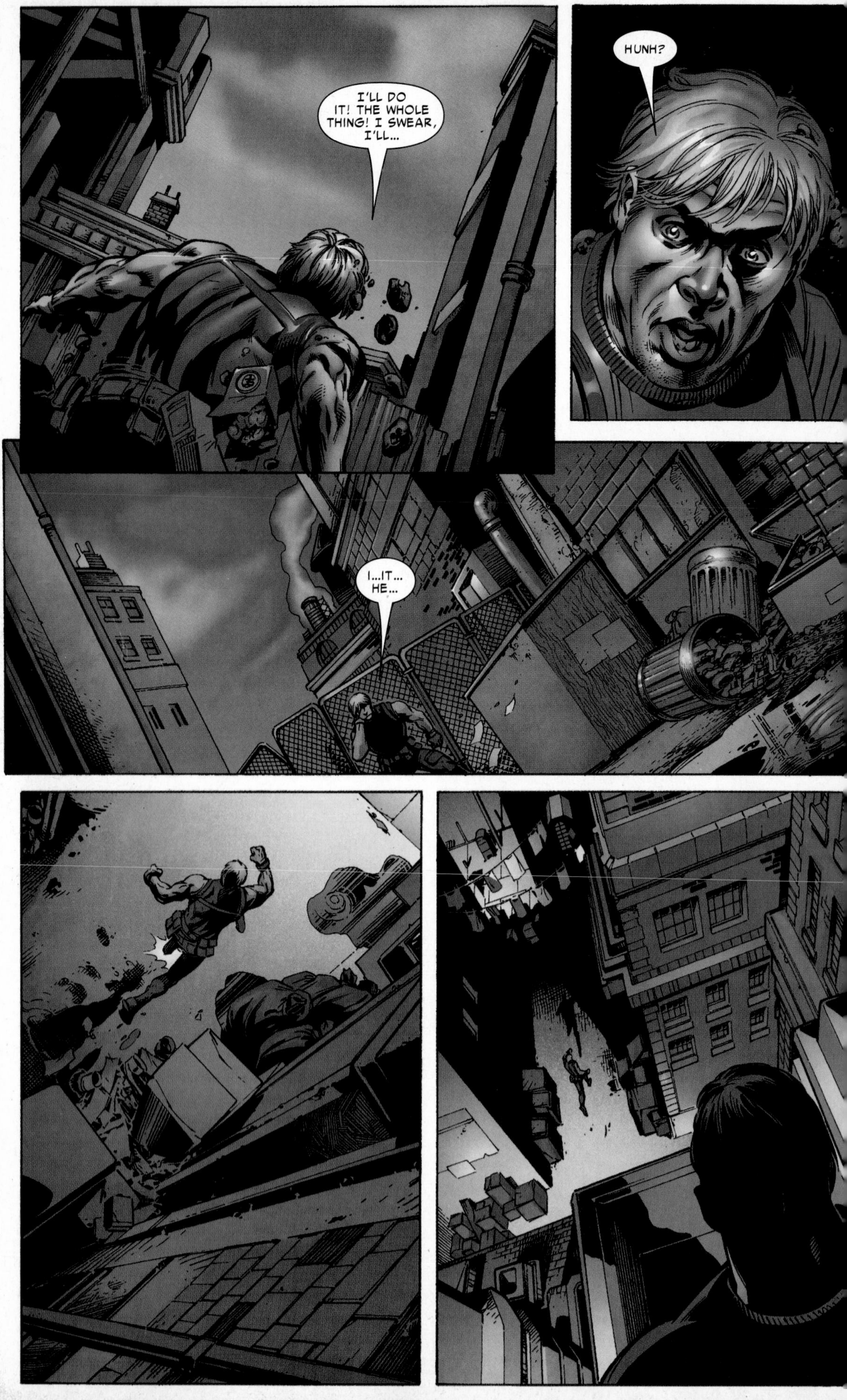
I'LL DO IT! THE WHOLE THING! I SWEAR, I'LL...
HUNH?
I...IT... HE...

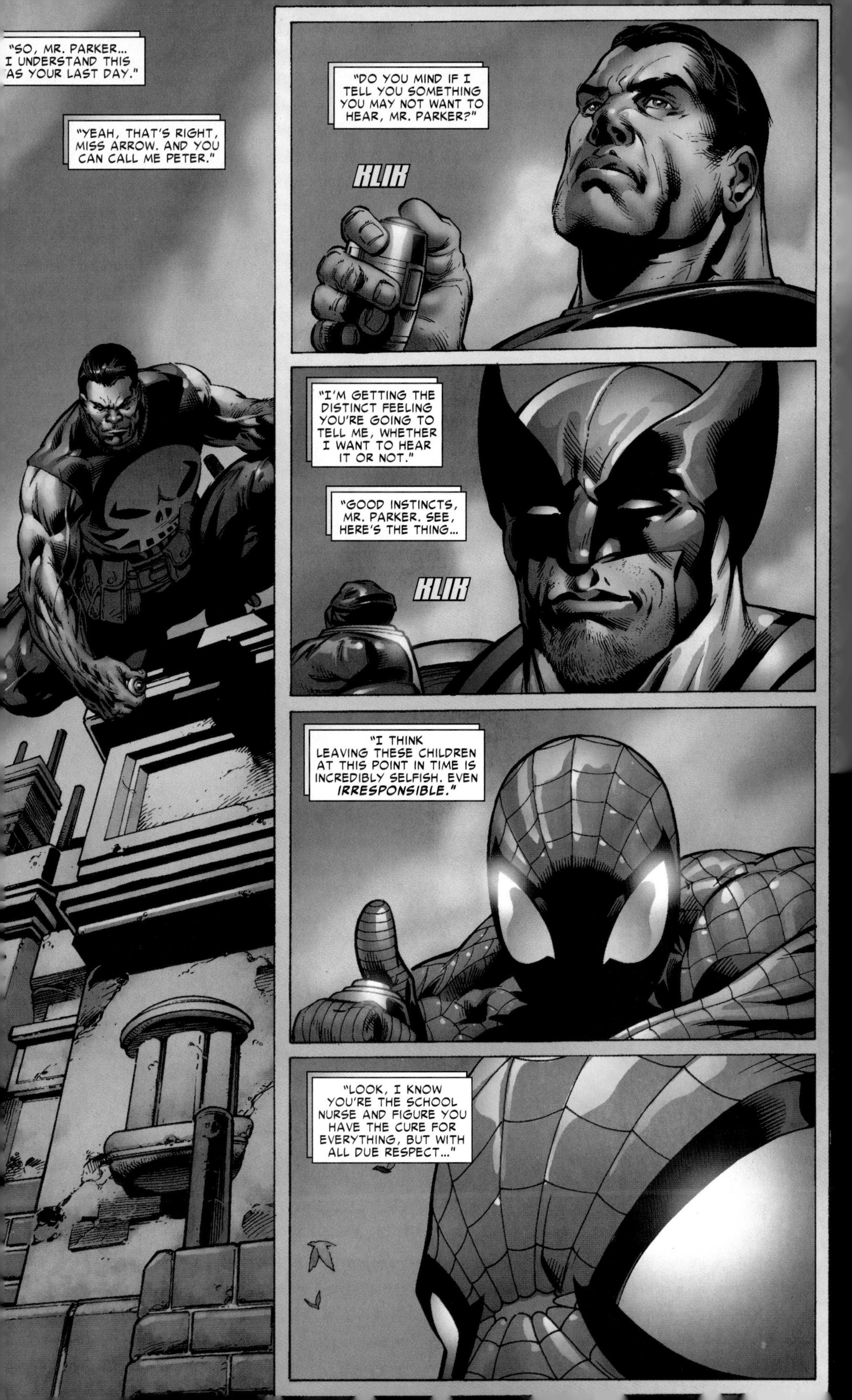
"SO, MR. PARKER... I UNDERSTAND THIS WAS YOUR LAST DAY."
"YEAH, THAT'S RIGHT, MISS ARROW. AND YOU CAN CALL ME PETER."
"DO YOU MIND IF I TELL YOU SOMETHING YOU MAY NOT WANT TO HEAR, MR. PARKER?"
KLIK
"I'M GETTING THE DISTINCT FEELING YOU'RE GOING TO TELL ME, WHETHER I WANT TO HEAR IT OR NOT."
"GOOD INSTINCTS, MR. PARKER. SEE, HERE'S THE THING...
KLIK
"I THINK LEAVING THESE CHILDREN AT THIS POINT IN TIME IS INCREDIBLY SELFISH. EVEN *IRRESPONSIBLE.*"
"LOOK, I KNOW YOU'RE THE SCHOOL NURSE AND FIGURE YOU HAVE THE CURE FOR EVERYTHING, BUT WITH ALL DUE RESPECT..."

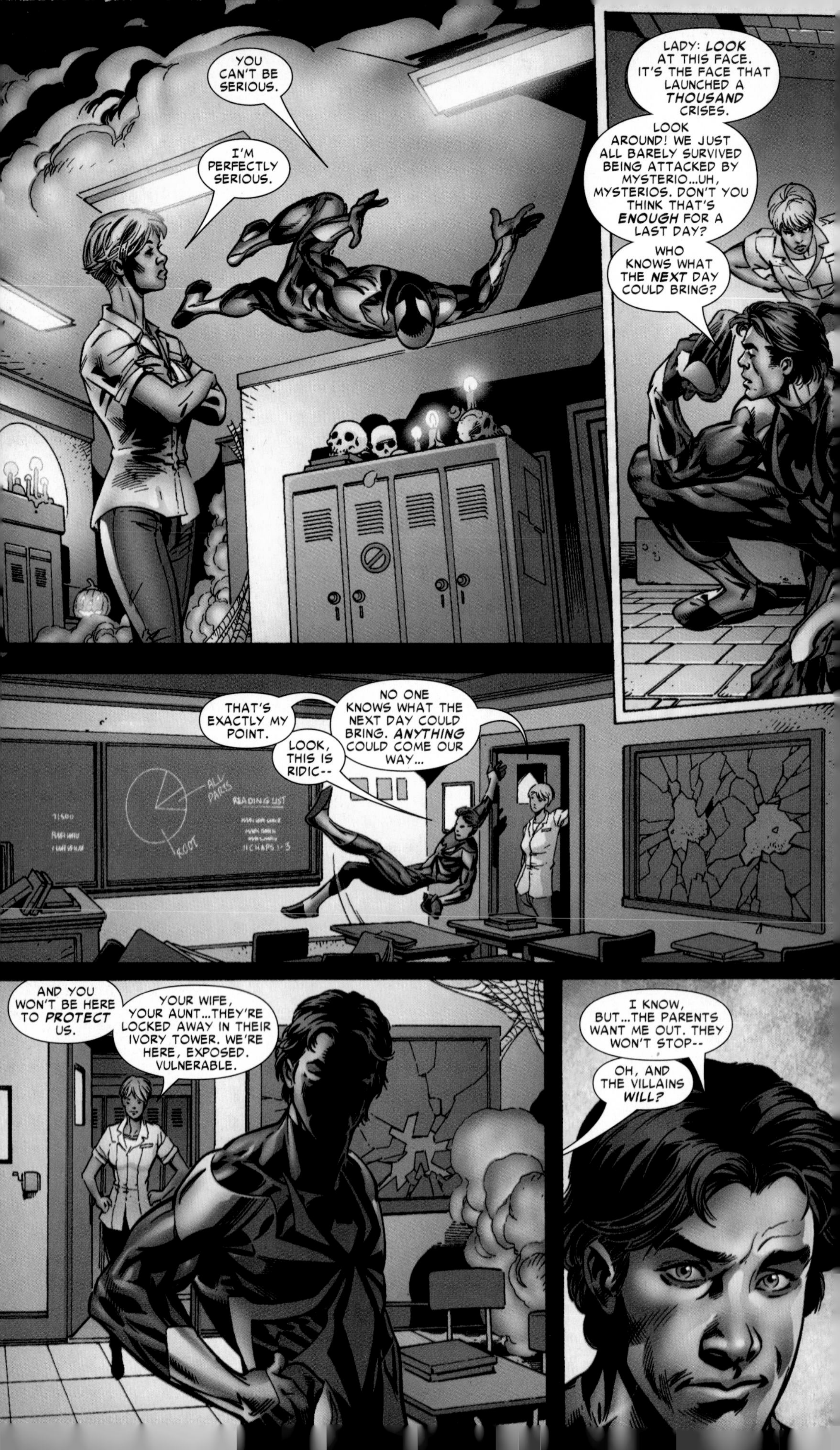
YOU CAN'T BE SERIOUS.
I'M PERFECTLY SERIOUS.
LADY: LOOK AT THIS FACE. IT'S THE FACE THAT LAUNCHED A THOUSAND CRISES.
LOOK AROUND! WE JUST ALL BARELY SURVIVED BEING ATTACKED BY MYSTERIO...UH, MYSTERIOS. DON'T YOU THINK THAT'S ENOUGH FOR A LAST DAY?
WHO KNOWS WHAT THE NEXT DAY COULD BRING?
THAT'S EXACTLY MY POINT.
NO ONE KNOWS WHAT THE NEXT DAY COULD BRING. ANYTHING COULD COME OUR WAY...
LOOK, THIS IS RIDIC--
READING LIST
AND YOU WON'T BE HERE TO PROTECT US.
YOUR WIFE, YOUR AUNT...THEY'RE LOCKED AWAY IN THEIR IVORY TOWER. WE'RE HERE, EXPOSED. VULNERABLE.
I KNOW, BUT...THE PARENTS WANT ME OUT. THEY WON'T STOP--
OH, AND THE VILLAINS WILL?

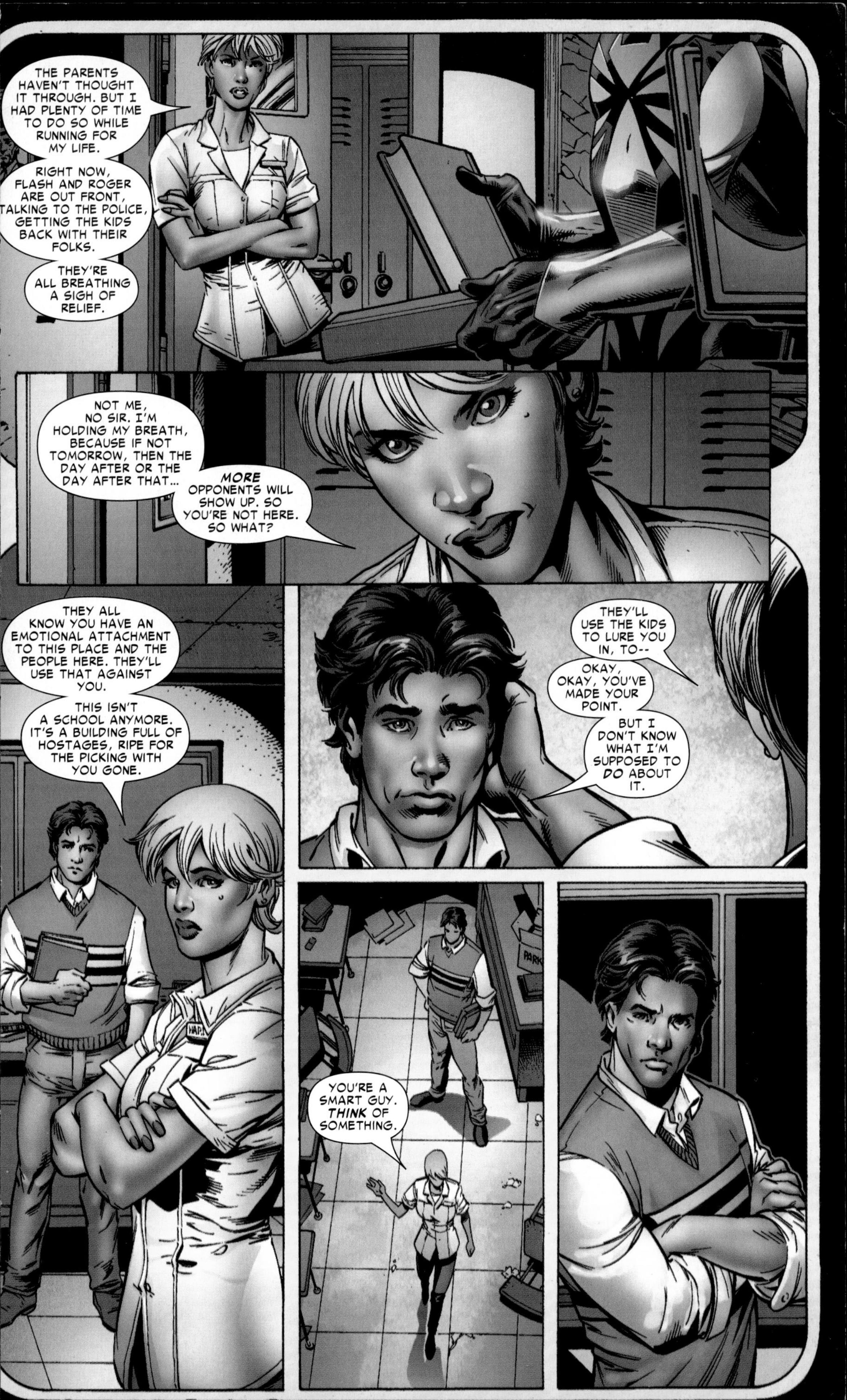

THE PARENTS HAVEN'T THOUGHT IT THROUGH. BUT I HAD PLENTY OF TIME TO DO SO WHILE RUNNING FOR MY LIFE.
RIGHT NOW, FLASH AND ROGER ARE OUT FRONT, TALKING TO THE POLICE, GETTING THE KIDS BACK WITH THEIR FOLKS.
THEY'RE ALL BREATHING A SIGH OF RELIEF.
NOT ME, NO SIR. I'M HOLDING MY BREATH, BECAUSE IF NOT TOMORROW, THEN THE DAY AFTER OR THE DAY AFTER THAT...
MORE OPPONENTS WILL SHOW UP. SO YOU'RE NOT HERE. SO WHAT?
THEY ALL KNOW YOU HAVE AN EMOTIONAL ATTACHMENT TO THIS PLACE AND THE PEOPLE HERE. THEY'LL USE THAT AGAINST YOU.
THIS ISN'T A SCHOOL ANYMORE. IT'S A BUILDING FULL OF HOSTAGES, RIPE FOR THE PICKING WITH YOU GONE.
THEY'LL USE THE KIDS TO LURE YOU IN, TO--
OKAY, OKAY, YOU'VE MADE YOUR POINT.
BUT I DON'T KNOW WHAT I'M SUPPOSED TO DO ABOUT IT.
YOU'RE A SMART GUY. THINK OF SOMETHING.

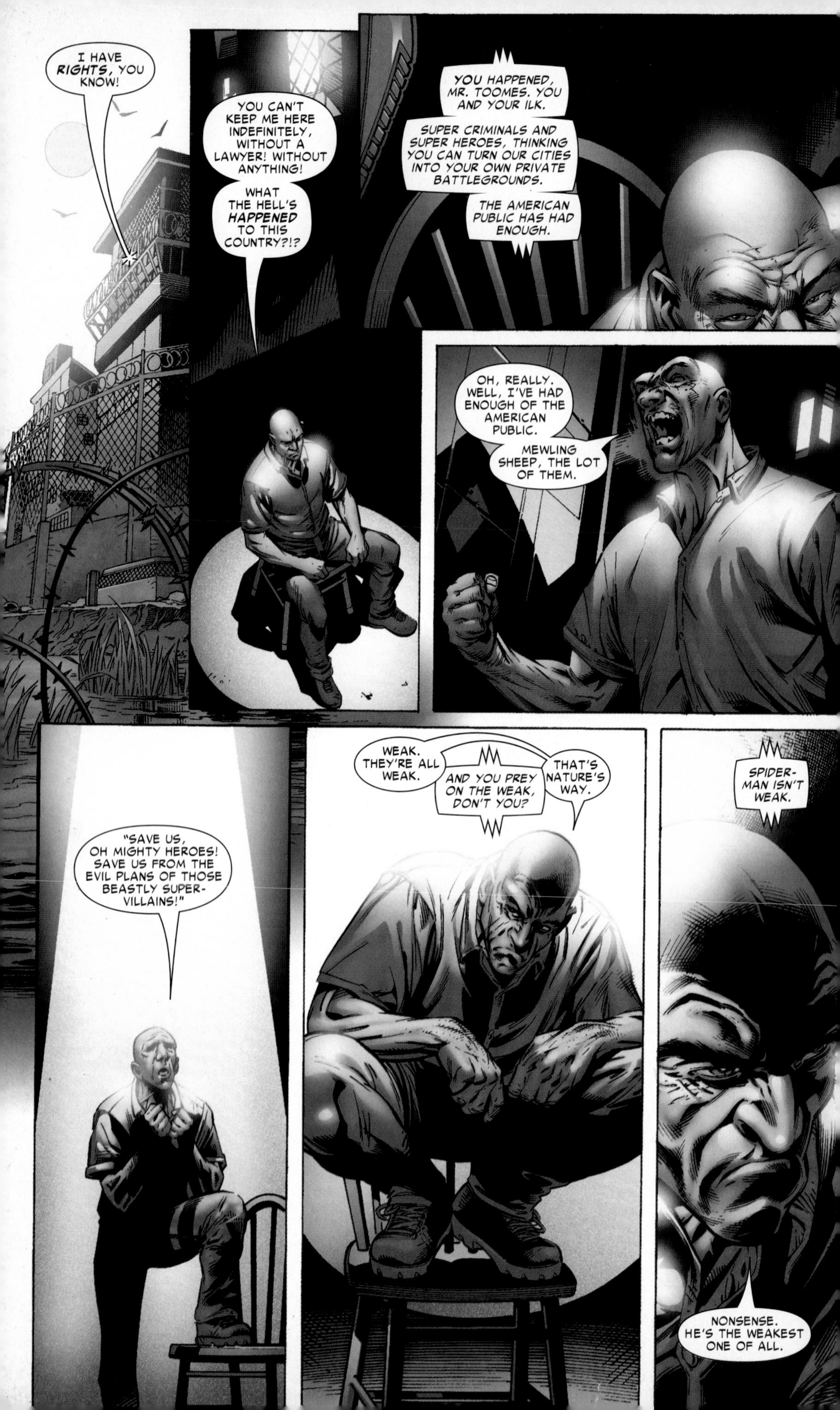
I HAVE RIGHTS, YOU KNOW!
YOU CAN'T KEEP ME HERE INDEFINITELY, WITHOUT A LAWYER! WITHOUT ANYTHING!
WHAT THE HELL'S HAPPENED TO THIS COUNTRY?!?
YOU HAPPENED, MR. TOOMES. YOU AND YOUR ILK.
SUPER CRIMINALS AND SUPER HEROES, THINKING YOU CAN TURN OUR CITIES INTO YOUR OWN PRIVATE BATTLEGROUNDS.
THE AMERICAN PUBLIC HAS HAD ENOUGH.
OH, REALLY. WELL, I'VE HAD ENOUGH OF THE AMERICAN PUBLIC.
MEWLING SHEEP, THE LOT OF THEM.
"SAVE US, OH MIGHTY HEROES! SAVE US FROM THE EVIL PLANS OF THOSE BEASTLY SUPER-VILLAINS!"
WEAK. THEY'RE ALL WEAK.
AND YOU PREY ON THE WEAK, DON'T YOU?
THAT'S NATURE'S WAY.
SPIDER-MAN ISN'T WEAK.
NONSENSE. HE'S THE WEAKEST ONE OF ALL.

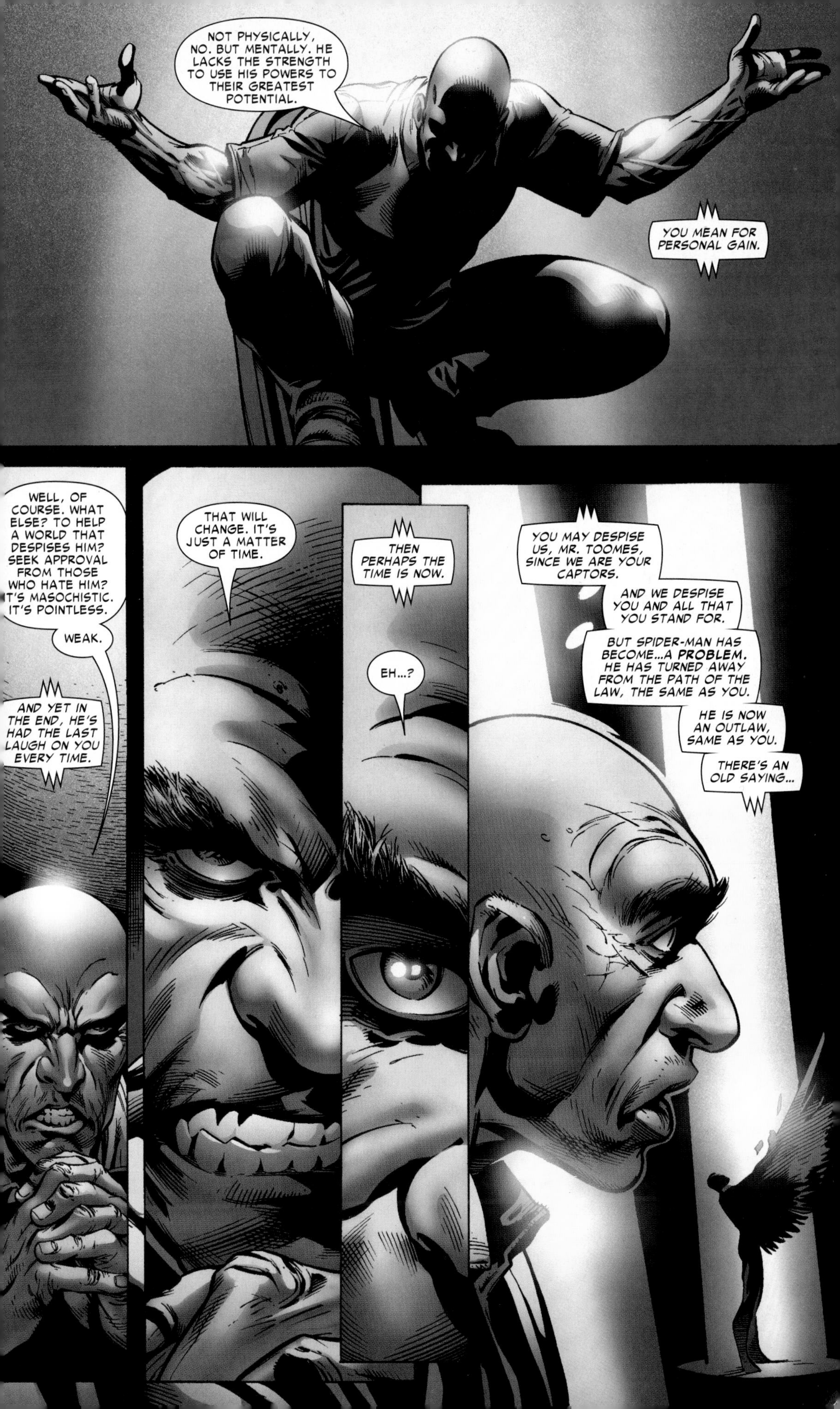

NOT PHYSICALLY, NO. BUT MENTALLY. HE LACKS THE STRENGTH TO USE HIS POWERS TO THEIR GREATEST POTENTIAL.
YOU MEAN FOR PERSONAL GAIN.
WELL, OF COURSE. WHAT ELSE? TO HELP A WORLD THAT DESPISES HIM? SEEK APPROVAL FROM THOSE WHO HATE HIM? IT'S MASOCHISTIC. IT'S POINTLESS.
WEAK.
AND YET IN THE END, HE'S HAD THE LAST LAUGH ON YOU EVERY TIME.
THAT WILL CHANGE. IT'S JUST A MATTER OF TIME.
THEN PERHAPS THE TIME IS NOW.
EH...?
YOU MAY DESPISE US, MR. TOOMES, SINCE WE ARE YOUR CAPTORS.
AND WE DESPISE YOU AND ALL THAT YOU STAND FOR.
BUT SPIDER-MAN HAS BECOME...A **PROBLEM**. HE HAS TURNED AWAY FROM THE PATH OF THE LAW, THE SAME AS YOU.
HE IS NOW AN OUTLAW, SAME AS YOU.
THERE'S AN OLD SAYING...

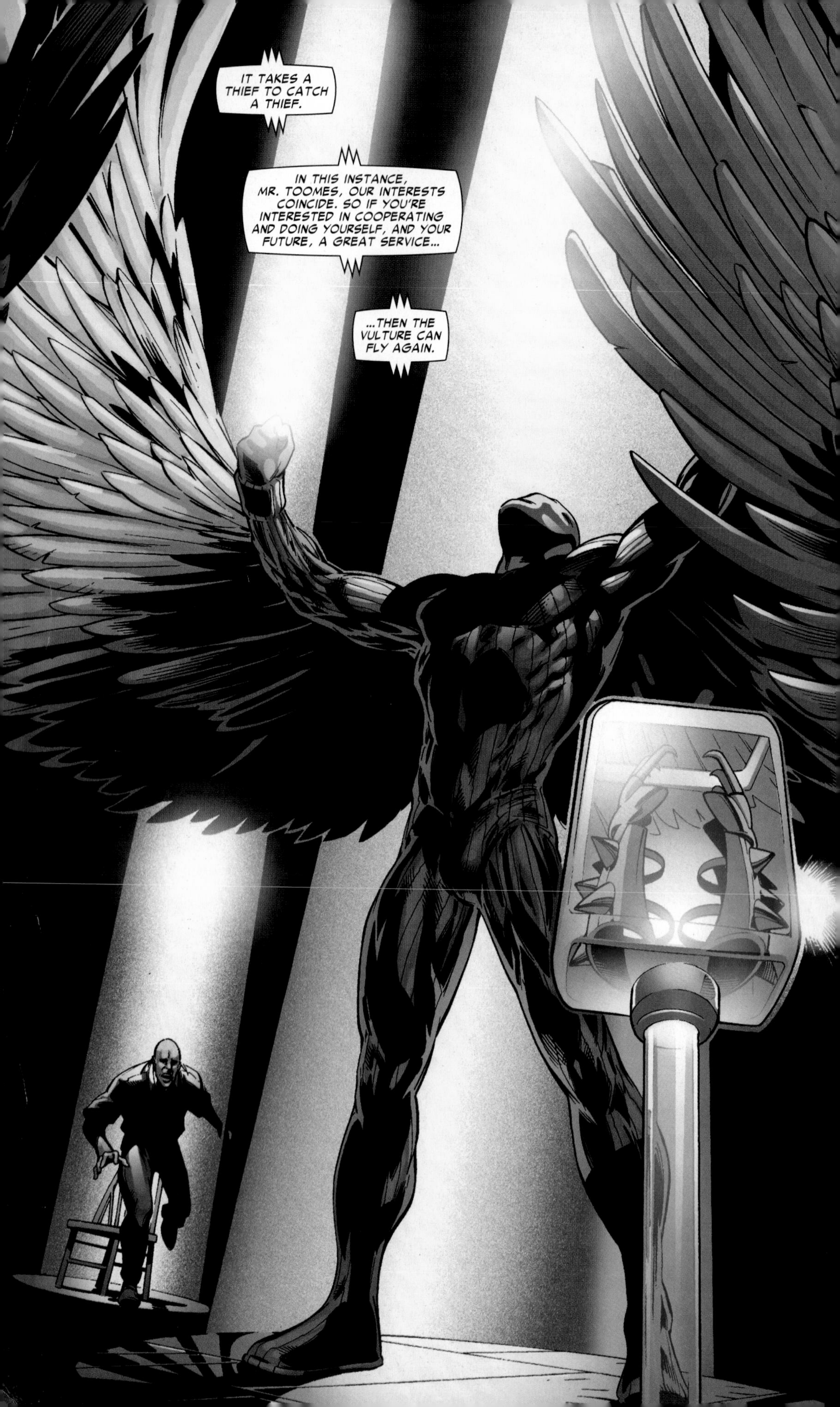
IT TAKES A THIEF TO CATCH A THIEF.
IN THIS INSTANCE, MR. TOOMES, OUR INTERESTS COINCIDE. SO IF YOU'RE INTERESTED IN COOPERATING AND DOING YOURSELF, AND YOUR FUTURE, A GREAT SERVICE...
...THEN THE VULTURE CAN FLY AGAIN.

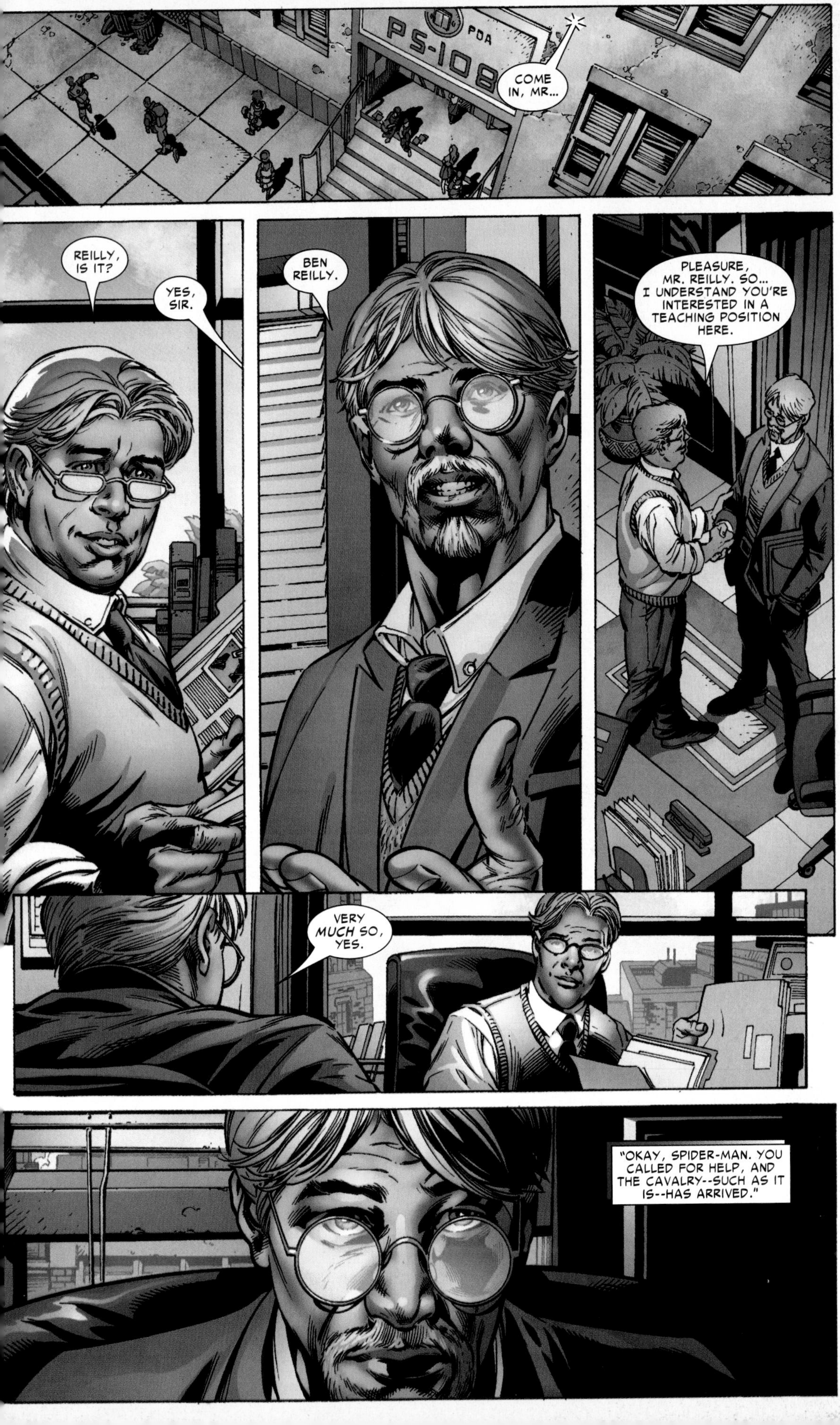
PS-108
PDA
COME IN, MR...
REILLY, IS IT?
YES, SIR.
BEN REILLY.
PLEASURE, MR. REILLY. SO... I UNDERSTAND YOU'RE INTERESTED IN A TEACHING POSITION HERE.
VERY MUCH SO, YES.
"OKAY, SPIDER-MAN. YOU CALLED FOR HELP, AND THE CAVALRY--SUCH AS IT IS--HAS ARRIVED."

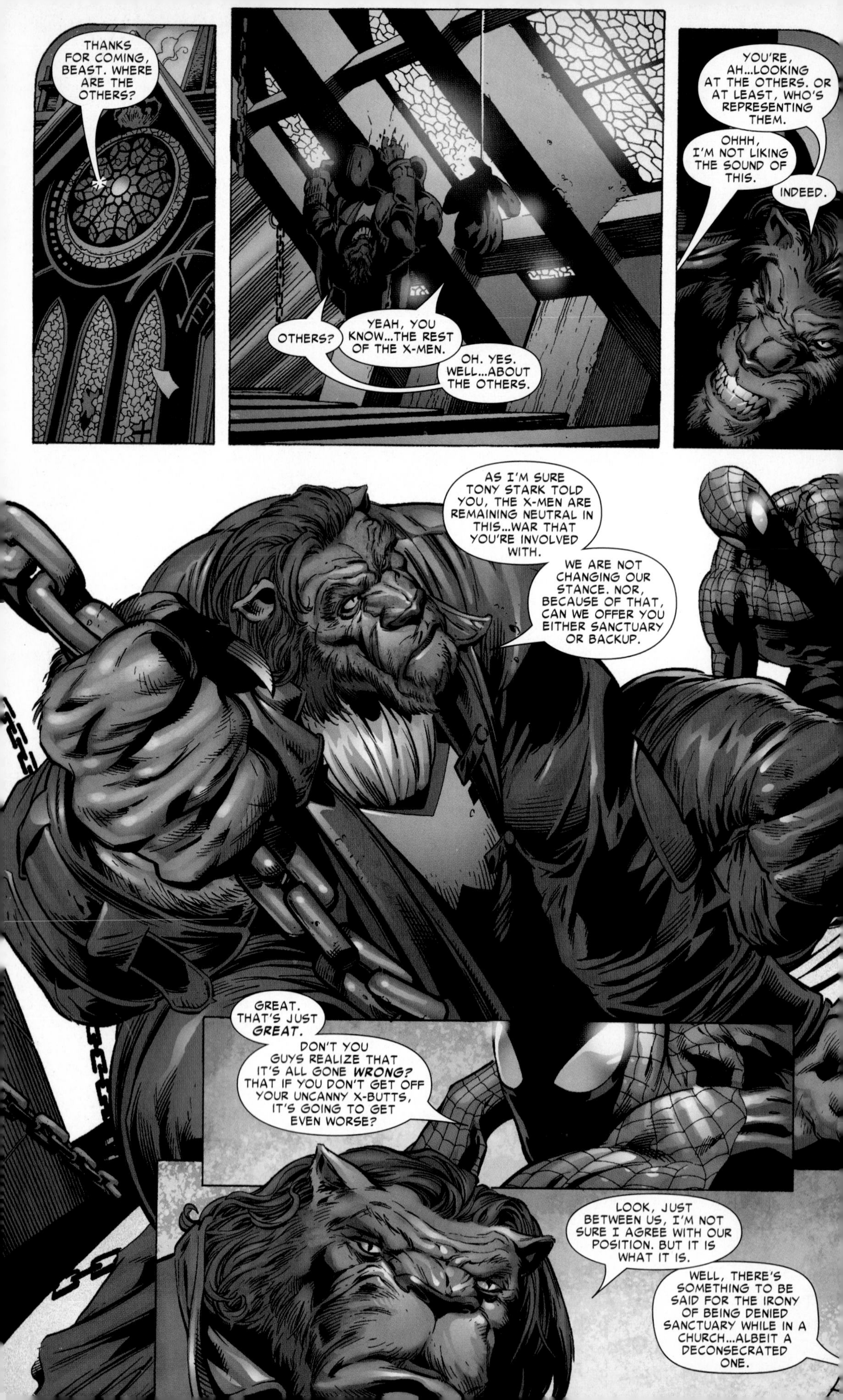
THANKS FOR COMING, BEAST. WHERE ARE THE OTHERS?
OTHERS?
YEAH, YOU KNOW...THE REST OF THE X-MEN.
OH. YES. WELL...ABOUT THE OTHERS.
YOU'RE, AH...LOOKING AT THE OTHERS. OR AT LEAST, WHO'S REPRESENTING THEM.
OHHH, I'M NOT LIKING THE SOUND OF THIS.
INDEED.
AS I'M SURE TONY STARK TOLD YOU, THE X-MEN ARE REMAINING NEUTRAL IN THIS...WAR THAT YOU'RE INVOLVED WITH.
WE ARE NOT CHANGING OUR STANCE. NOR, BECAUSE OF THAT, CAN WE OFFER YOU EITHER SANCTUARY OR BACKUP.
GREAT. THAT'S JUST *GREAT*.
DON'T YOU GUYS REALIZE THAT IT'S ALL GONE *WRONG?* THAT IF YOU DON'T GET OFF YOUR UNCANNY X-BUTTS, IT'S GOING TO GET EVEN WORSE?
LOOK, JUST BETWEEN US, I'M NOT SURE I AGREE WITH OUR POSITION. BUT IT IS WHAT IT IS.
WELL, THERE'S SOMETHING TO BE SAID FOR THE IRONY OF BEING DENIED SANCTUARY WHILE IN A CHURCH...ALBEIT A DECONSECRATED ONE.

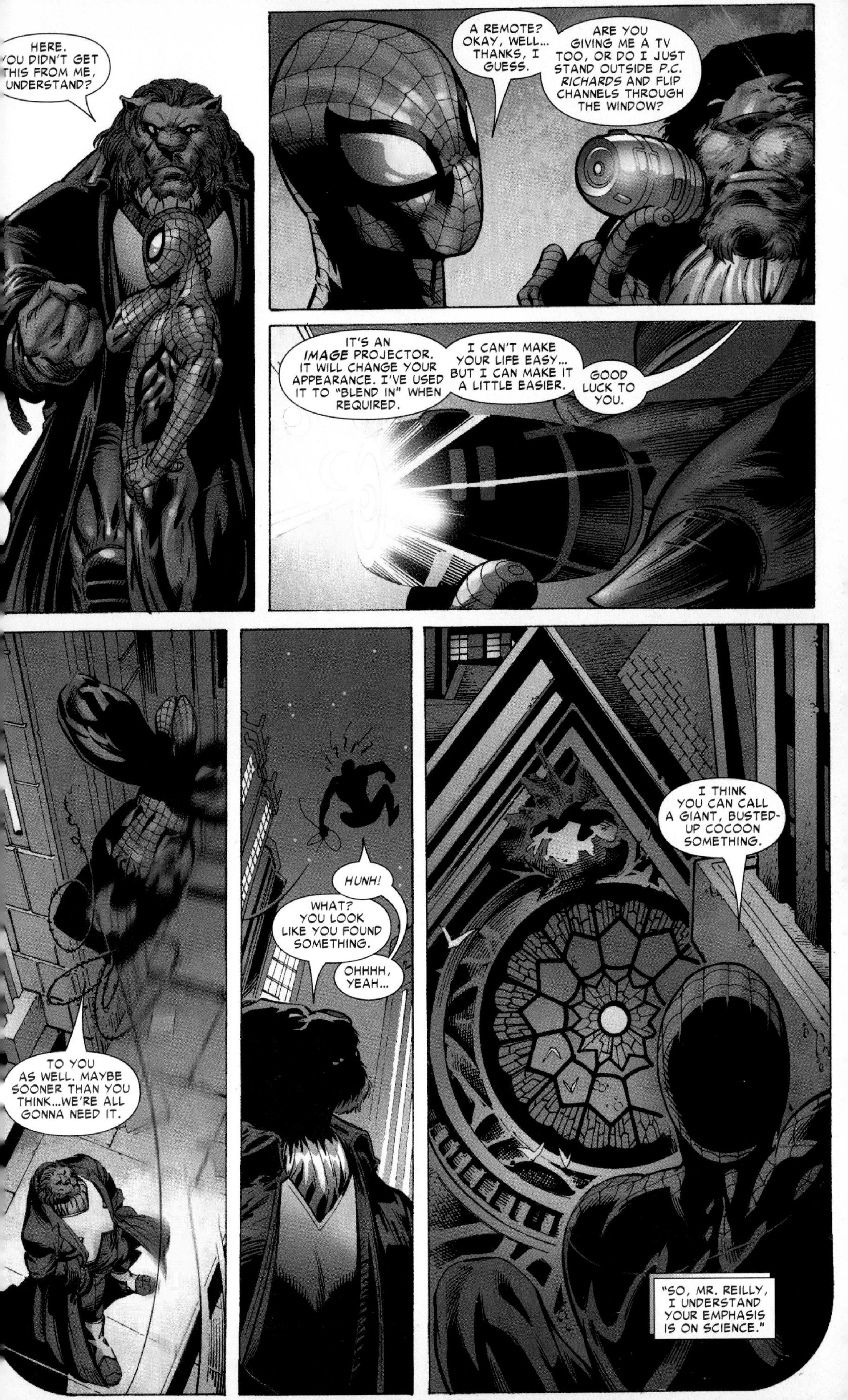
HERE. YOU DIDN'T GET THIS FROM ME, UNDERSTAND?
A REMOTE? OKAY, WELL... THANKS, I GUESS.
ARE YOU GIVING ME A TV TOO, OR DO I JUST STAND OUTSIDE P.C. RICHARDS AND FLIP CHANNELS THROUGH THE WINDOW?
IT'S AN IMAGE PROJECTOR. IT WILL CHANGE YOUR APPEARANCE. I'VE USED IT TO "BLEND IN" WHEN REQUIRED.
I CAN'T MAKE YOUR LIFE EASY... BUT I CAN MAKE IT A LITTLE EASIER.
GOOD LUCK TO YOU.
TO YOU AS WELL. MAYBE SOONER THAN YOU THINK...WE'RE ALL GONNA NEED IT.
HUNH!
WHAT? YOU LOOK LIKE YOU FOUND SOMETHING.
OHHHH, YEAH...
I THINK YOU CAN CALL A GIANT, BUSTED-UP COCOON SOMETHING.
"SO, MR. REILLY, I UNDERSTAND YOUR EMPHASIS IS ON SCIENCE."

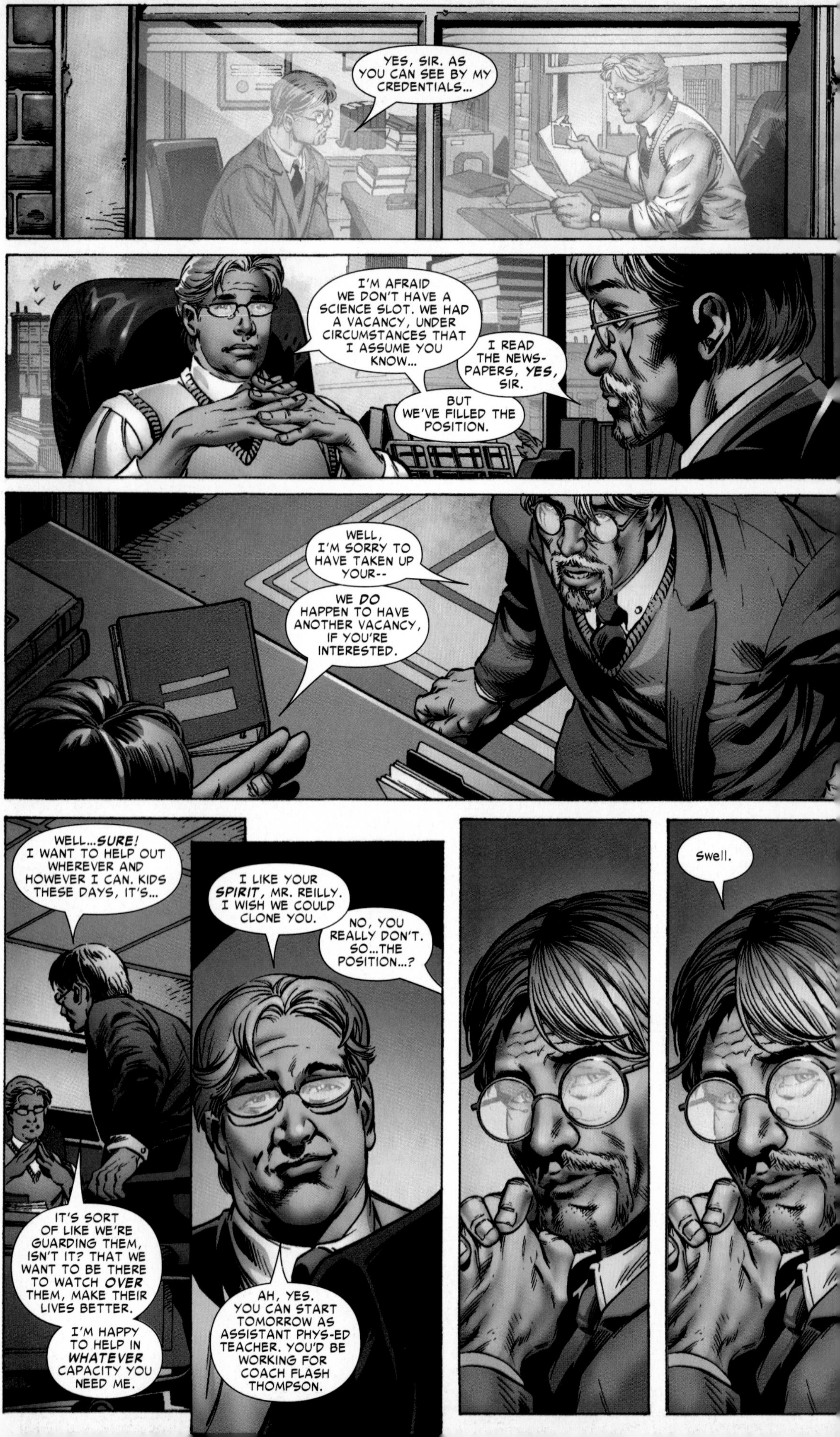

YES, SIR. AS YOU CAN SEE BY MY CREDENTIALS...
I'M AFRAID WE DON'T HAVE A SCIENCE SLOT. WE HAD A VACANCY, UNDER CIRCUMSTANCES THAT I ASSUME YOU KNOW...
I READ THE NEWS-PAPERS, YES, SIR.
BUT WE'VE FILLED THE POSITION.
WELL, I'M SORRY TO HAVE TAKEN UP YOUR--
WE DO HAPPEN TO HAVE ANOTHER VACANCY, IF YOU'RE INTERESTED.
WELL...SURE! I WANT TO HELP OUT WHEREVER AND HOWEVER I CAN. KIDS THESE DAYS, IT'S...
IT'S SORT OF LIKE WE'RE GUARDING THEM, ISN'T IT? THAT WE WANT TO BE THERE TO WATCH OVER THEM, MAKE THEIR LIVES BETTER.
I'M HAPPY TO HELP IN WHATEVER CAPACITY YOU NEED ME.
I LIKE YOUR SPIRIT, MR. REILLY. I WISH WE COULD CLONE YOU.
NO, YOU REALLY DON'T. SO...THE POSITION...?
AH, YES. YOU CAN START TOMORROW AS ASSISTANT PHYS-ED TEACHER. YOU'D BE WORKING FOR COACH FLASH THOMPSON.
Swell.

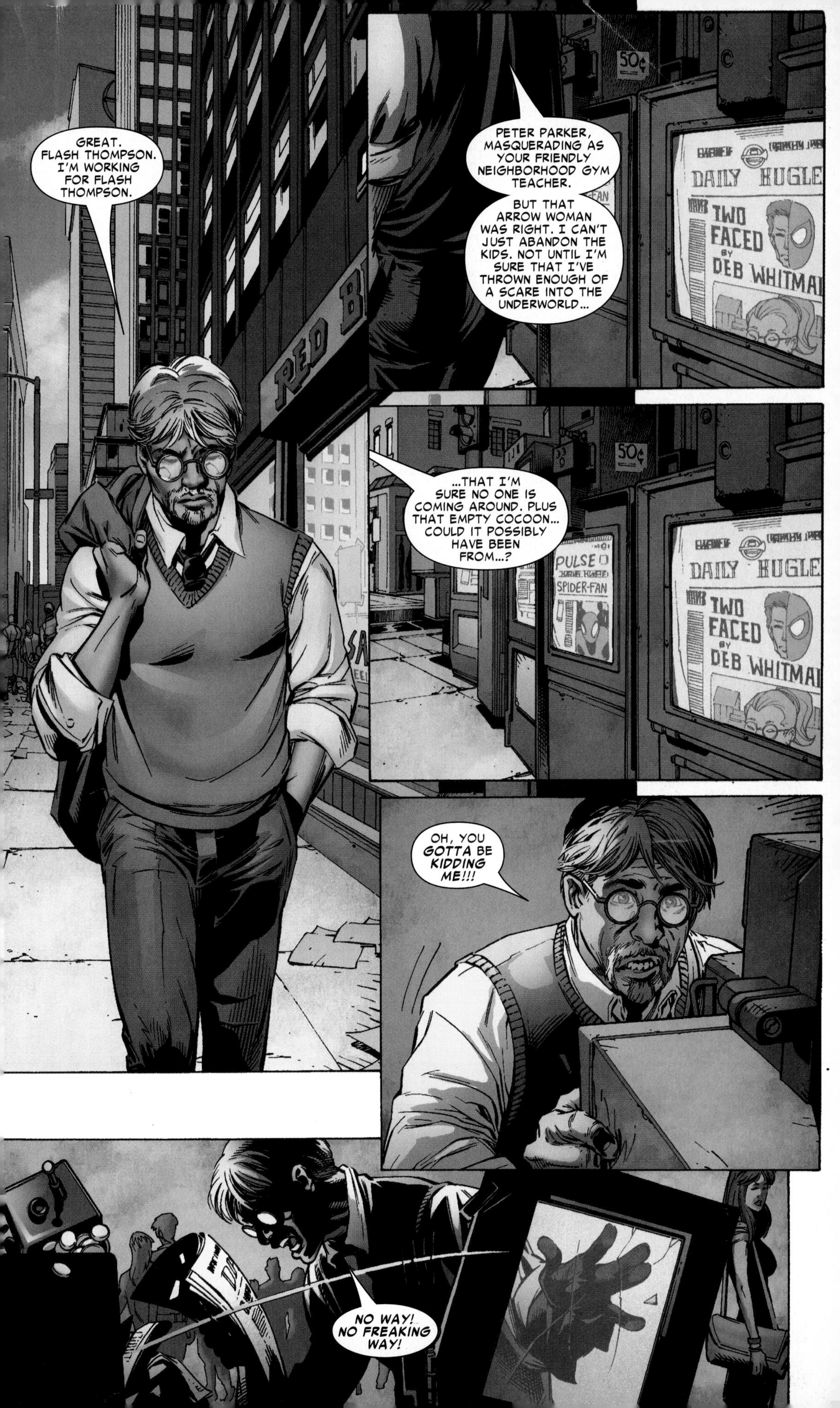

GREAT. FLASH THOMPSON. I'M WORKING FOR FLASH THOMPSON.
PETER PARKER, MASQUERADING AS YOUR FRIENDLY NEIGHBORHOOD GYM TEACHER.
BUT THAT ARROW WOMAN WAS RIGHT. I CAN'T JUST ABANDON THE KIDS. NOT UNTIL I'M SURE THAT I'VE THROWN ENOUGH OF A SCARE INTO THE UNDERWORLD...
50¢
DAILY BUGLE
TWO FACED
BY DEB WHITMAN
...THAT I'M SURE NO ONE IS COMING AROUND. PLUS THAT EMPTY COCOON... COULD IT POSSIBLY HAVE BEEN FROM...?
PULSE
SPIDER-FAN
OH, YOU GOTTA BE KIDDING ME!!!
NO WAY! NO FREAKING WAY!

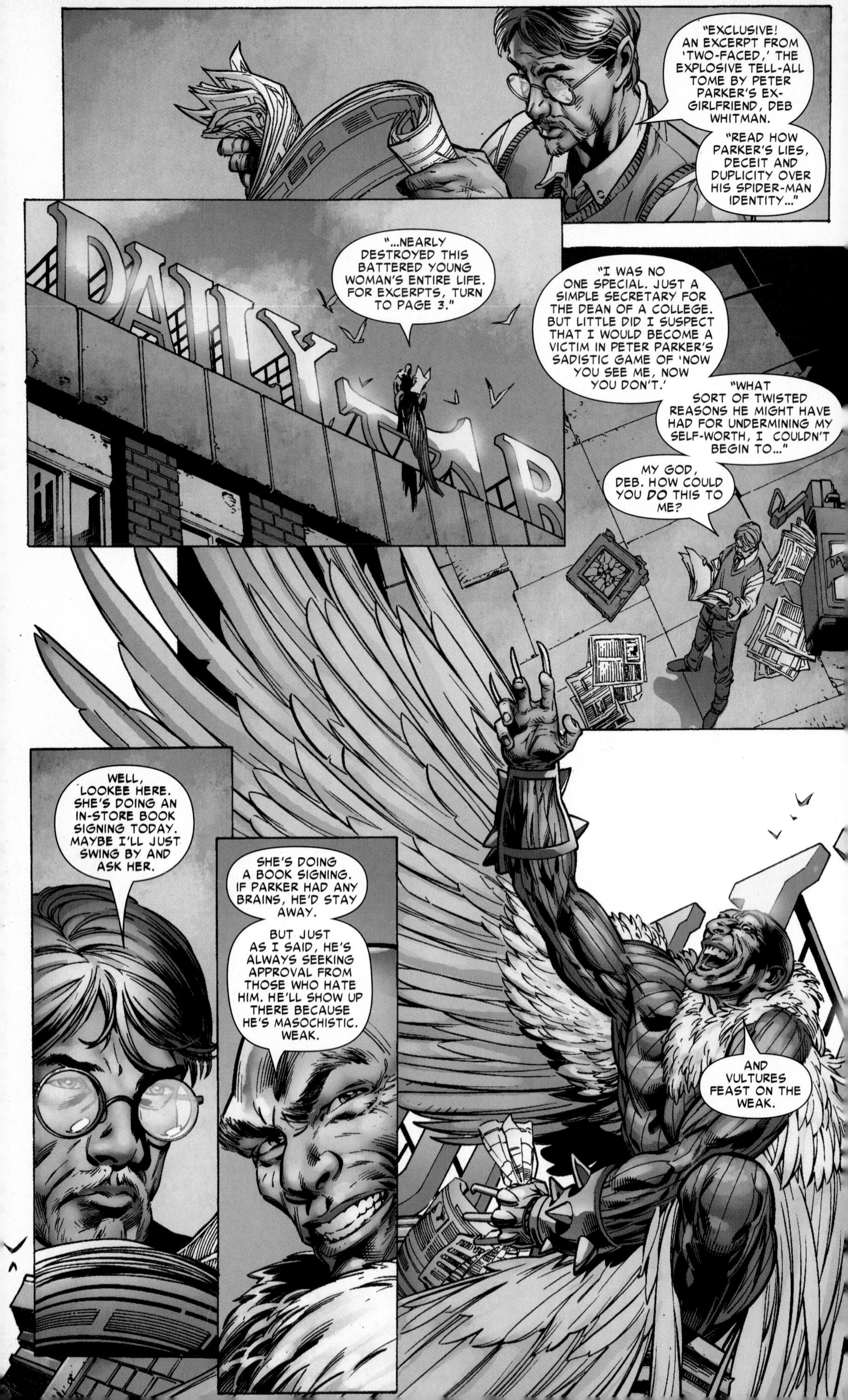
"EXCLUSIVE! AN EXCERPT FROM 'TWO-FACED,' THE EXPLOSIVE TELL-ALL TOME BY PETER PARKER'S EX-GIRLFRIEND, DEB WHITMAN.
"READ HOW PARKER'S LIES, DECEIT AND DUPLICITY OVER HIS SPIDER-MAN IDENTITY..."
"...NEARLY DESTROYED THIS BATTERED YOUNG WOMAN'S ENTIRE LIFE. FOR EXCERPTS, TURN TO PAGE 3."
"I WAS NO ONE SPECIAL. JUST A SIMPLE SECRETARY FOR THE DEAN OF A COLLEGE. BUT LITTLE DID I SUSPECT THAT I WOULD BECOME A VICTIM IN PETER PARKER'S SADISTIC GAME OF 'NOW YOU SEE ME, NOW YOU DON'T.'
"WHAT SORT OF TWISTED REASONS HE MIGHT HAVE HAD FOR UNDERMINING MY SELF-WORTH, I COULDN'T BEGIN TO..."
MY GOD, DEB. HOW COULD YOU DO THIS TO ME?
WELL, LOOKEE HERE. SHE'S DOING AN IN-STORE BOOK SIGNING TODAY. MAYBE I'LL JUST SWING BY AND ASK HER.
SHE'S DOING A BOOK SIGNING. IF PARKER HAD ANY BRAINS, HE'D STAY AWAY.
BUT JUST AS I SAID, HE'S ALWAYS SEEKING APPROVAL FROM THOSE WHO HATE HIM. HE'LL SHOW UP THERE BECAUSE HE'S MASOCHISTIC. WEAK.
AND VULTURES FEAST ON THE WEAK.

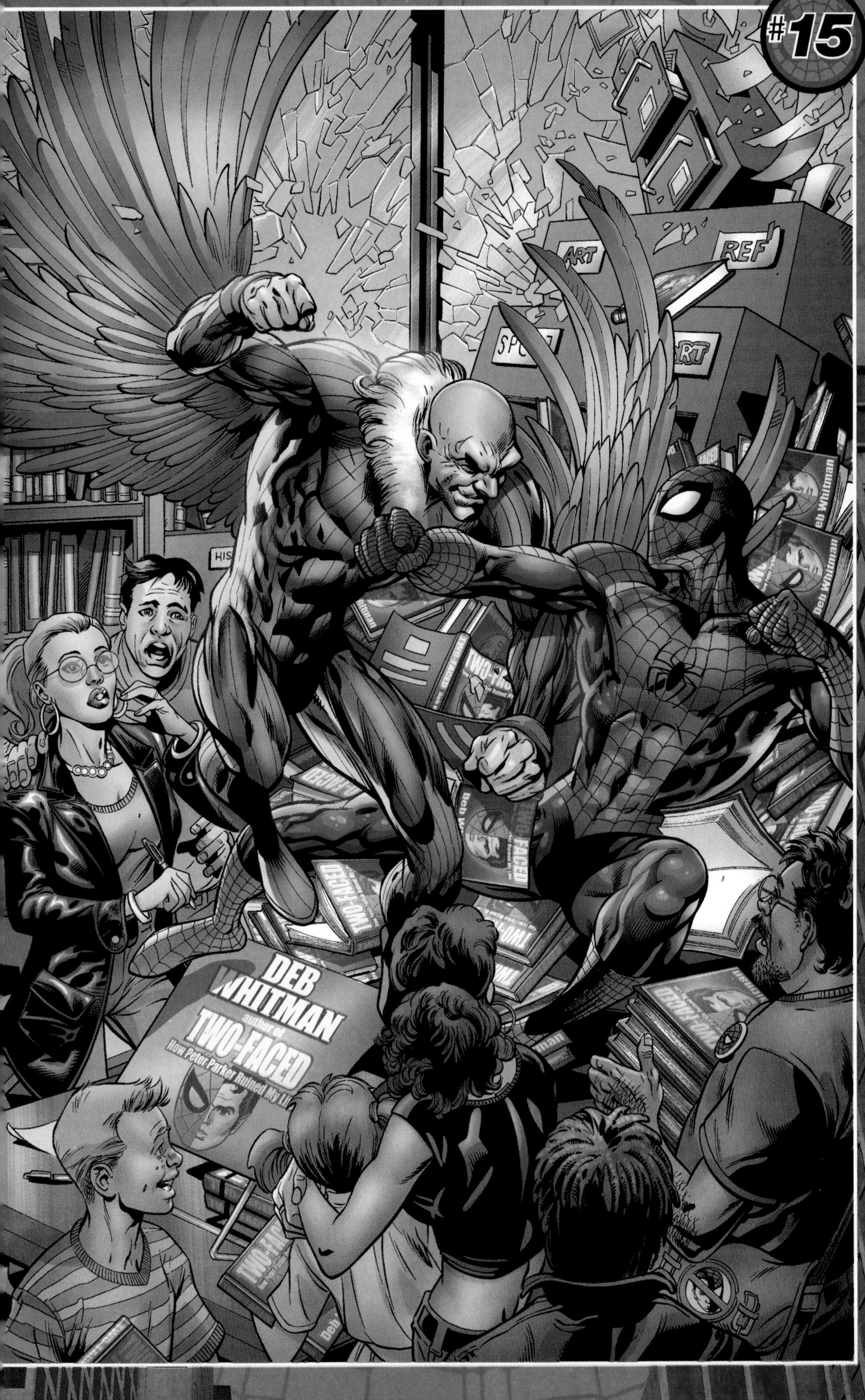

#15
ART
REF
HIS
DEB
WHITMAN
author of
TWO-FACED
How Peter Parker Ruined My Life
Deb Whitman

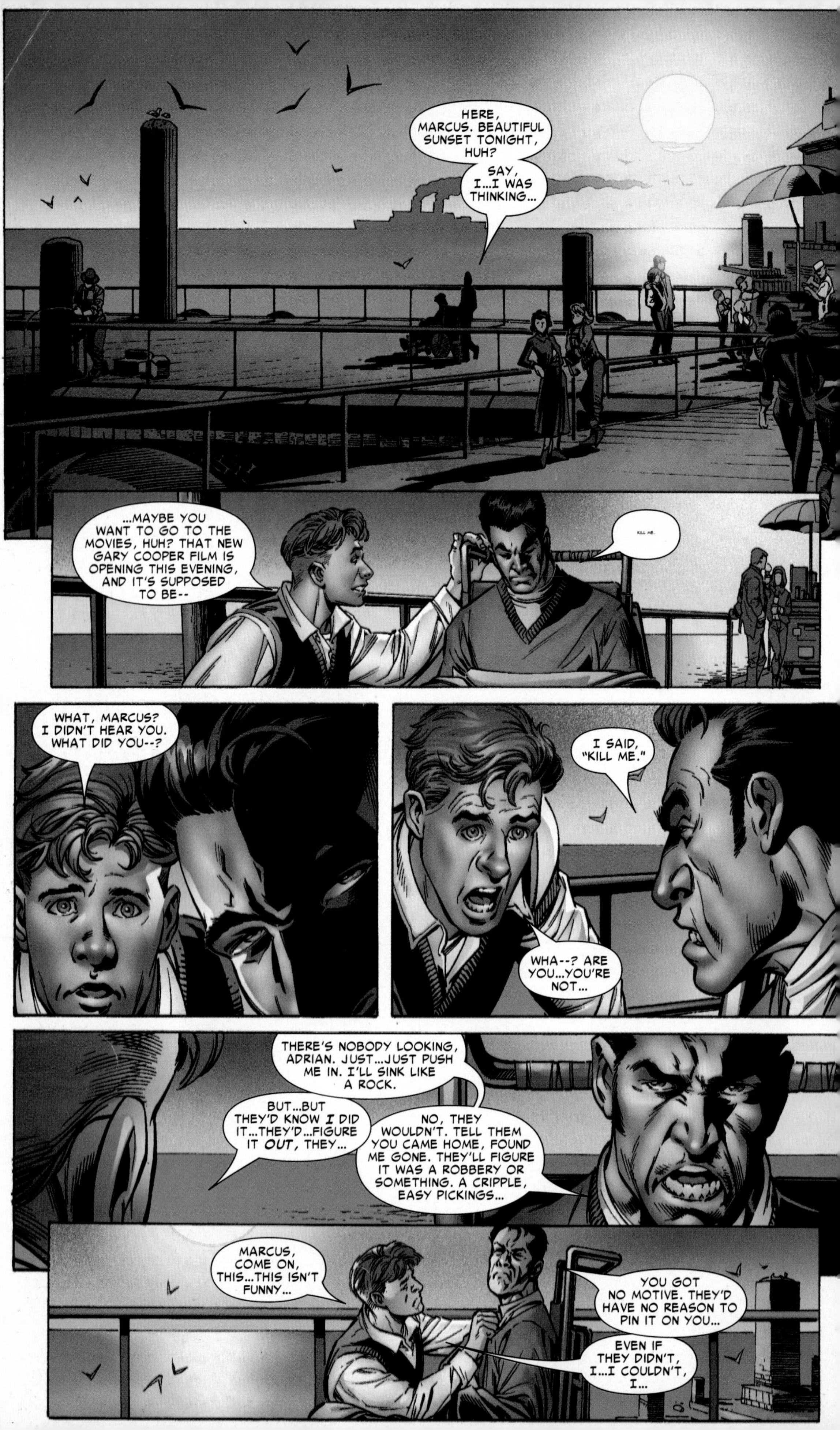
HERE, MARCUS. BEAUTIFUL SUNSET TONIGHT, HUH?
SAY, I...I WAS THINKING...
...MAYBE YOU WANT TO GO TO THE MOVIES, HUH? THAT NEW GARY COOPER FILM IS OPENING THIS EVENING, AND IT'S SUPPOSED TO BE--
KILL ME.
WHAT, MARCUS? I DIDN'T HEAR YOU. WHAT DID YOU--?
I SAID, "KILL ME."
WHA--? ARE YOU...YOU'RE NOT...
THERE'S NOBODY LOOKING, ADRIAN. JUST...JUST PUSH ME IN. I'LL SINK LIKE A ROCK.
BUT...BUT THEY'D KNOW I DID IT...THEY'D...FIGURE IT OUT, THEY...
NO, THEY WOULDN'T. TELL THEM YOU CAME HOME, FOUND ME GONE. THEY'LL FIGURE IT WAS A ROBBERY OR SOMETHING. A CRIPPLE, EASY PICKINGS...
MARCUS, COME ON, THIS...THIS ISN'T FUNNY...
YOU GOT NO MOTIVE. THEY'D HAVE NO REASON TO PIN IT ON YOU...
EVEN IF THEY DIDN'T, I...I COULDN'T, I...

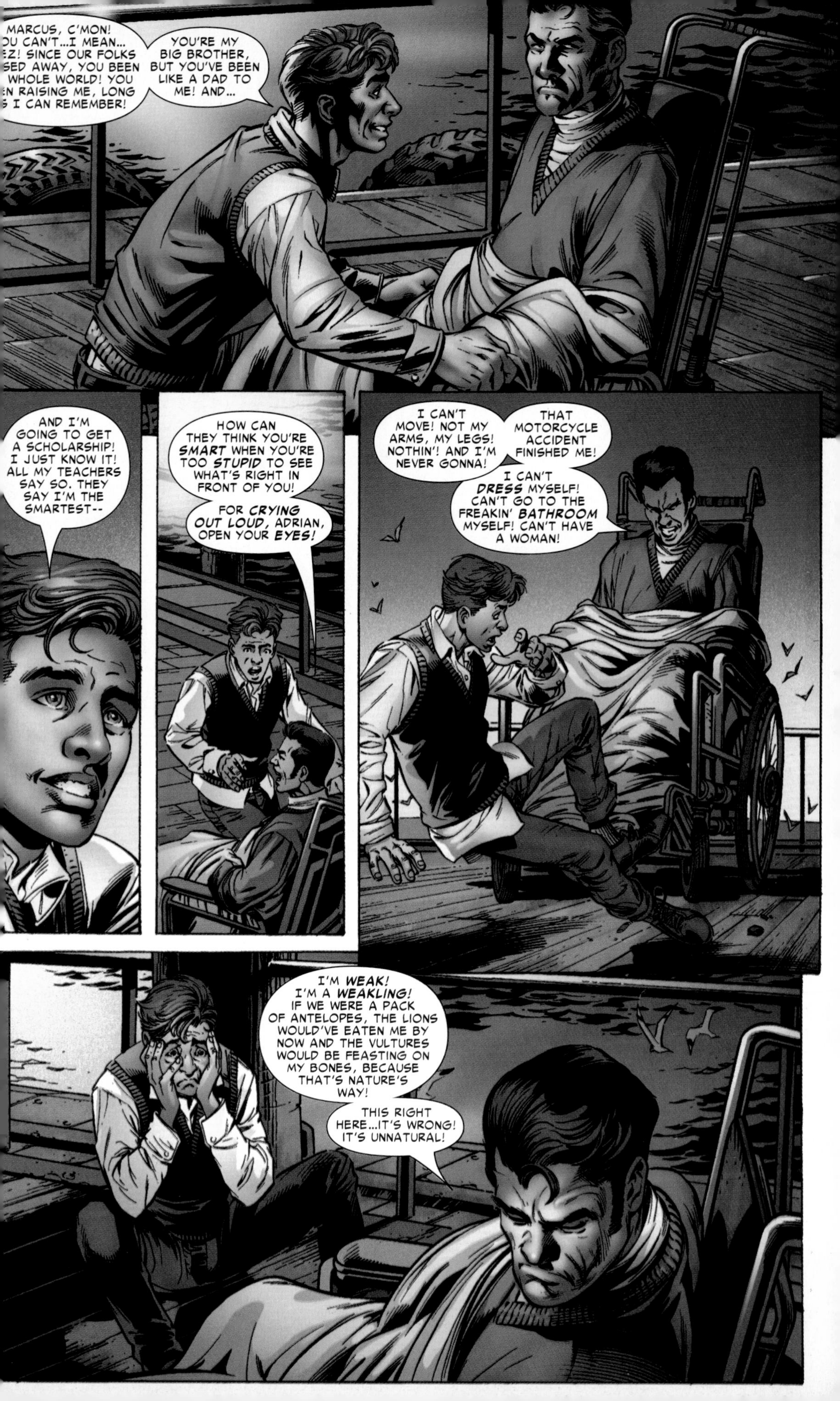

MARCUS, C'MON! OU CAN'T...I MEAN... EZ! SINCE OUR FOLKS SED AWAY, YOU BEEN WHOLE WORLD! YOU N RAISING ME, LONG S I CAN REMEMBER!
YOU'RE MY BIG BROTHER, BUT YOU'VE BEEN LIKE A DAD TO ME! AND...
AND I'M GOING TO GET A SCHOLARSHIP! I JUST KNOW IT! ALL MY TEACHERS SAY SO. THEY SAY I'M THE SMARTEST--
HOW CAN THEY THINK YOU'RE SMART WHEN YOU'RE TOO STUPID TO SEE WHAT'S RIGHT IN FRONT OF YOU!
FOR CRYING OUT LOUD, ADRIAN, OPEN YOUR EYES!
I CAN'T MOVE! NOT MY ARMS, MY LEGS! NOTHIN'! AND I'M NEVER GONNA!
THAT MOTORCYCLE ACCIDENT FINISHED ME!
I CAN'T DRESS MYSELF! CAN'T GO TO THE FREAKIN' BATHROOM MYSELF! CAN'T HAVE A WOMAN!
I'M WEAK! I'M A WEAKLING! IF WE WERE A PACK OF ANTELOPES, THE LIONS WOULD'VE EATEN ME BY NOW AND THE VULTURES WOULD BE FEASTING ON MY BONES, BECAUSE THAT'S NATURE'S WAY!
THIS RIGHT HERE...IT'S WRONG! IT'S UNNATURAL!

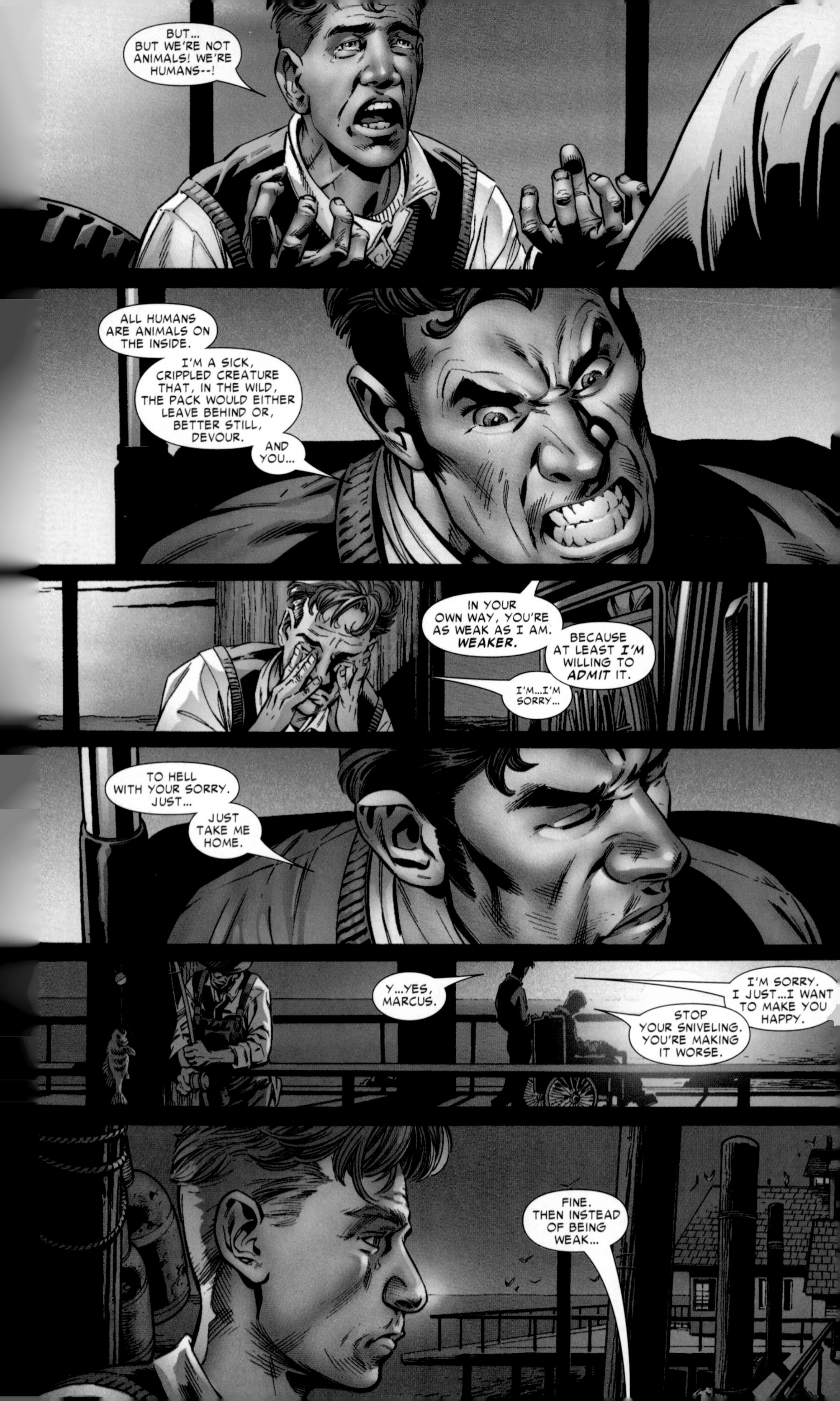

BUT... BUT WE'RE NOT ANIMALS! WE'RE HUMANS--!
ALL HUMANS ARE ANIMALS ON THE INSIDE.
I'M A SICK, CRIPPLED CREATURE THAT, IN THE WILD, THE PACK WOULD EITHER LEAVE BEHIND OR, BETTER STILL, DEVOUR.
AND YOU...
IN YOUR OWN WAY, YOU'RE AS WEAK AS I AM. WEAKER.
BECAUSE AT LEAST I'M WILLING TO ADMIT IT.
I'M...I'M SORRY...
TO HELL WITH YOUR SORRY. JUST...
JUST TAKE ME HOME.
Y...YES, MARCUS.
I'M SORRY. I JUST...I WANT TO MAKE YOU HAPPY.
STOP YOUR SNIVELING. YOU'RE MAKING IT WORSE.
FINE. THEN INSTEAD OF BEING WEAK...

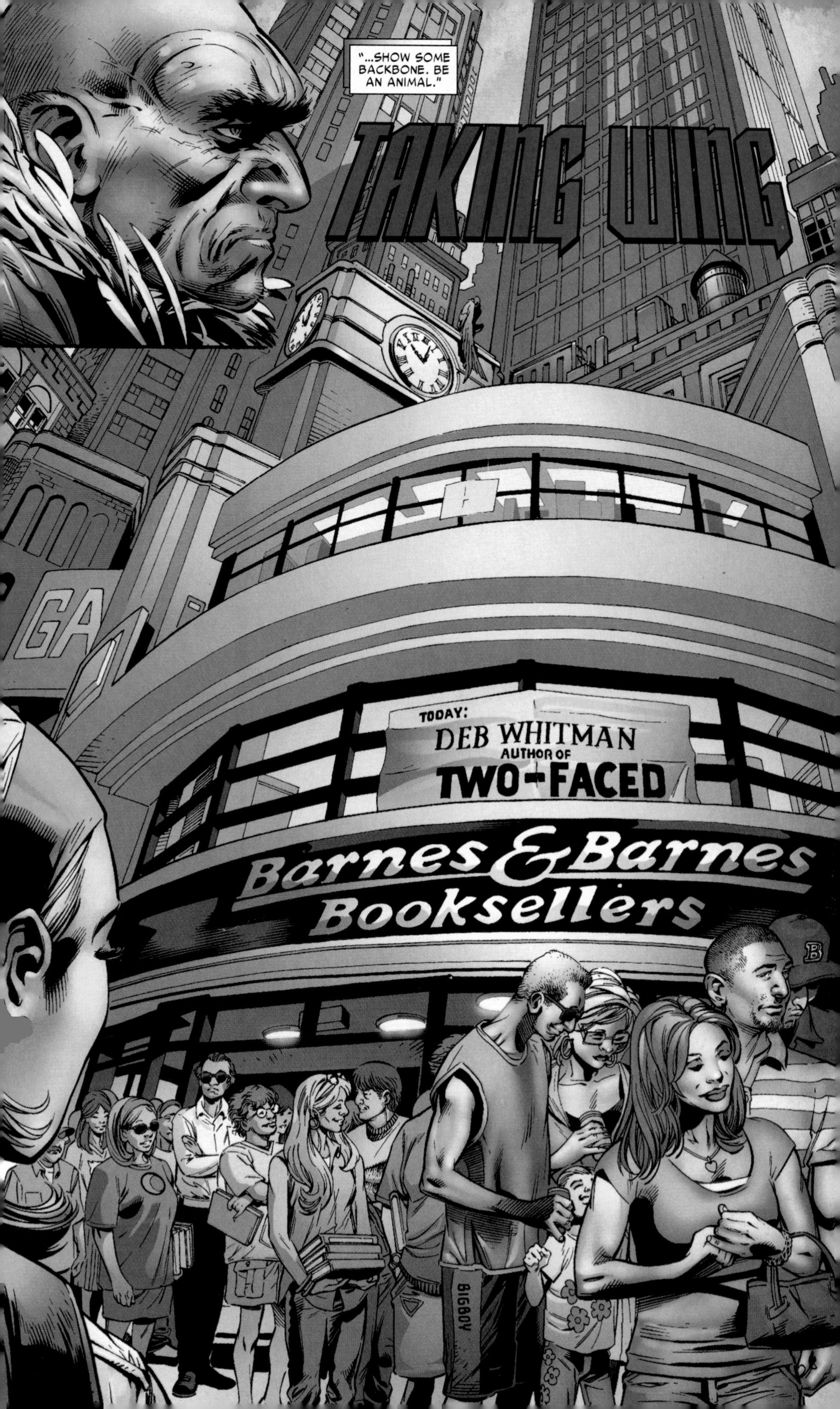

"...SHOW SOME BACKBONE. BE AN ANIMAL."
TAKING WING
TODAY:
DEB WHITMAN
AUTHOR OF
TWO-FACED
Barnes & Barnes
Booksellers
BIGBOY

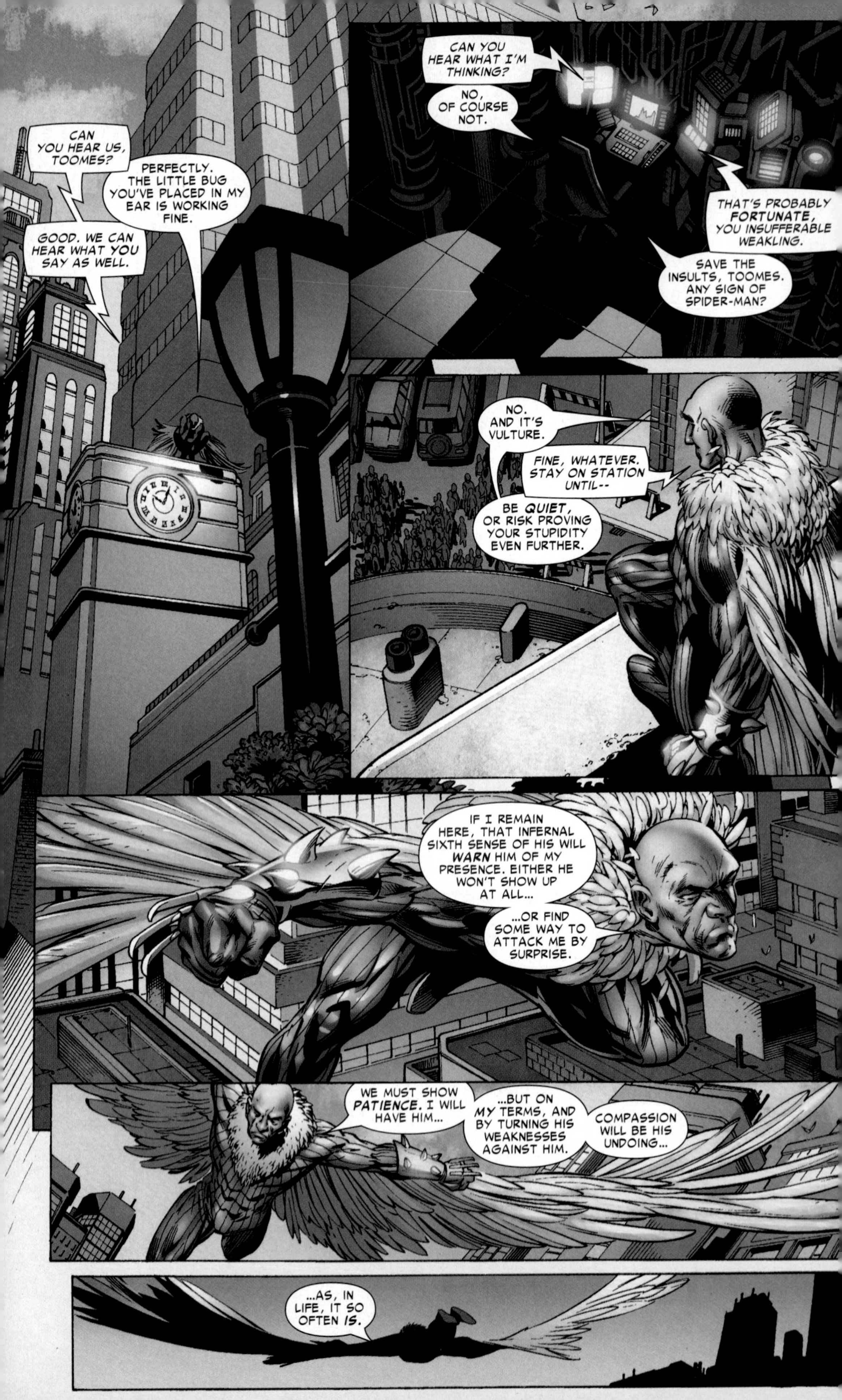
CAN YOU HEAR US, TOOMES?
PERFECTLY. THE LITTLE BUG YOU'VE PLACED IN MY EAR IS WORKING FINE.
GOOD. WE CAN HEAR WHAT YOU SAY AS WELL.
CAN YOU HEAR WHAT I'M THINKING?
NO, OF COURSE NOT.
THAT'S PROBABLY FORTUNATE, YOU INSUFFERABLE WEAKLING.
SAVE THE INSULTS, TOOMES. ANY SIGN OF SPIDER-MAN?
NO. AND IT'S VULTURE.
FINE, WHATEVER. STAY ON STATION UNTIL--
BE QUIET, OR RISK PROVING YOUR STUPIDITY EVEN FURTHER.
IF I REMAIN HERE, THAT INFERNAL SIXTH SENSE OF HIS WILL WARN HIM OF MY PRESENCE. EITHER HE WON'T SHOW UP AT ALL...
...OR FIND SOME WAY TO ATTACK ME BY SURPRISE.
WE MUST SHOW PATIENCE. I WILL HAVE HIM...
...BUT ON MY TERMS, AND BY TURNING HIS WEAKNESSES AGAINST HIM.
COMPASSION WILL BE HIS UNDOING...
...AS, IN LIFE, IT SO OFTEN IS.

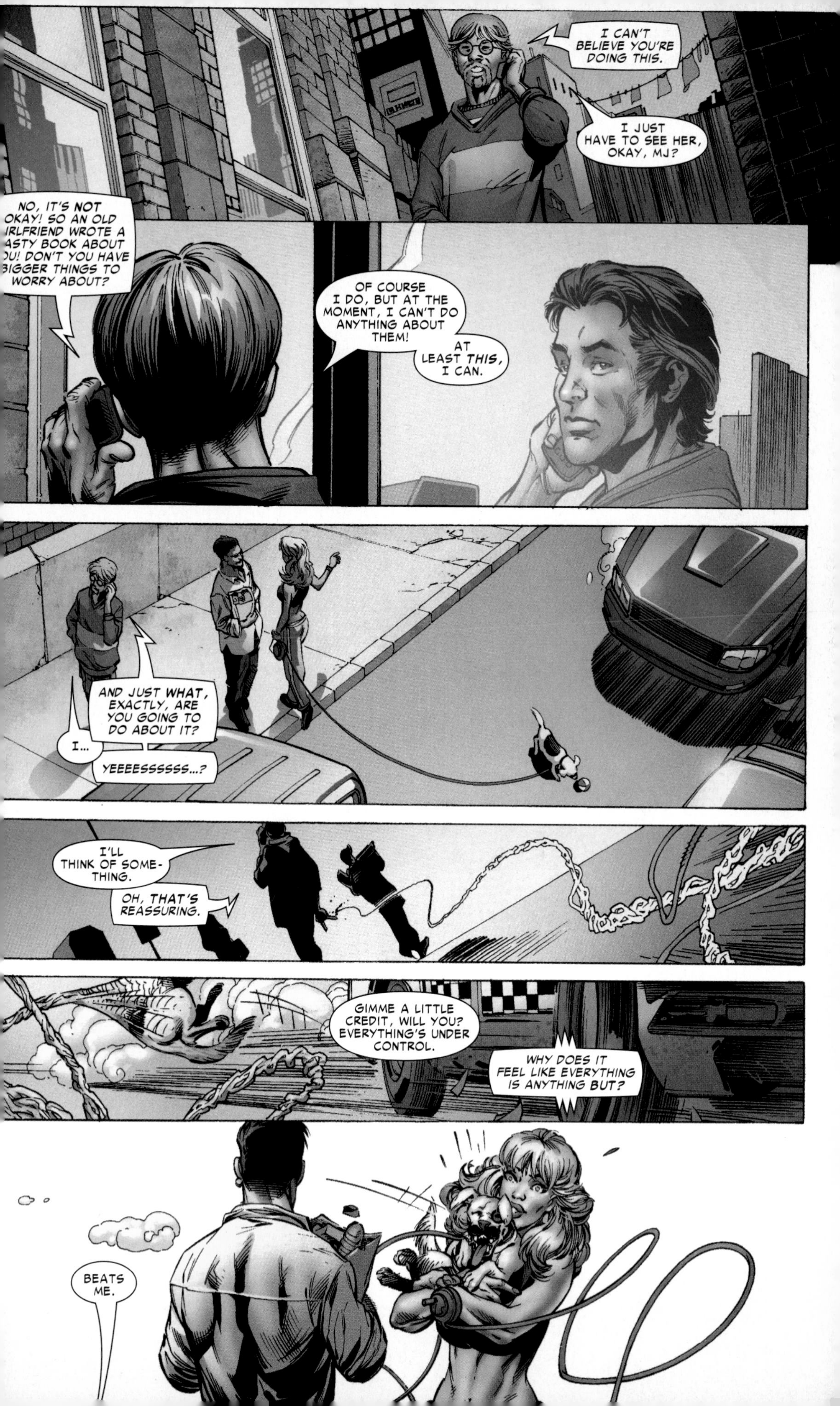

I CAN'T BELIEVE YOU'RE DOING THIS.
I JUST HAVE TO SEE HER, OKAY, MJ?
NO, IT'S NOT OKAY! SO AN OLD IRLFRIEND WROTE A ASTY BOOK ABOUT OU! DON'T YOU HAVE BIGGER THINGS TO WORRY ABOUT?
OF COURSE I DO, BUT AT THE MOMENT, I CAN'T DO ANYTHING ABOUT THEM!
AT LEAST THIS, I CAN.
AND JUST WHAT, EXACTLY, ARE YOU GOING TO DO ABOUT IT?
I...
YEEEEESSSSSS...?
I'LL THINK OF SOME-THING.
OH, THAT'S REASSURING.
GIMME A LITTLE CREDIT, WILL YOU? EVERYTHING'S UNDER CONTROL.
WHY DOES IT FEEL LIKE EVERYTHING IS ANYTHING BUT?
BEATS ME.

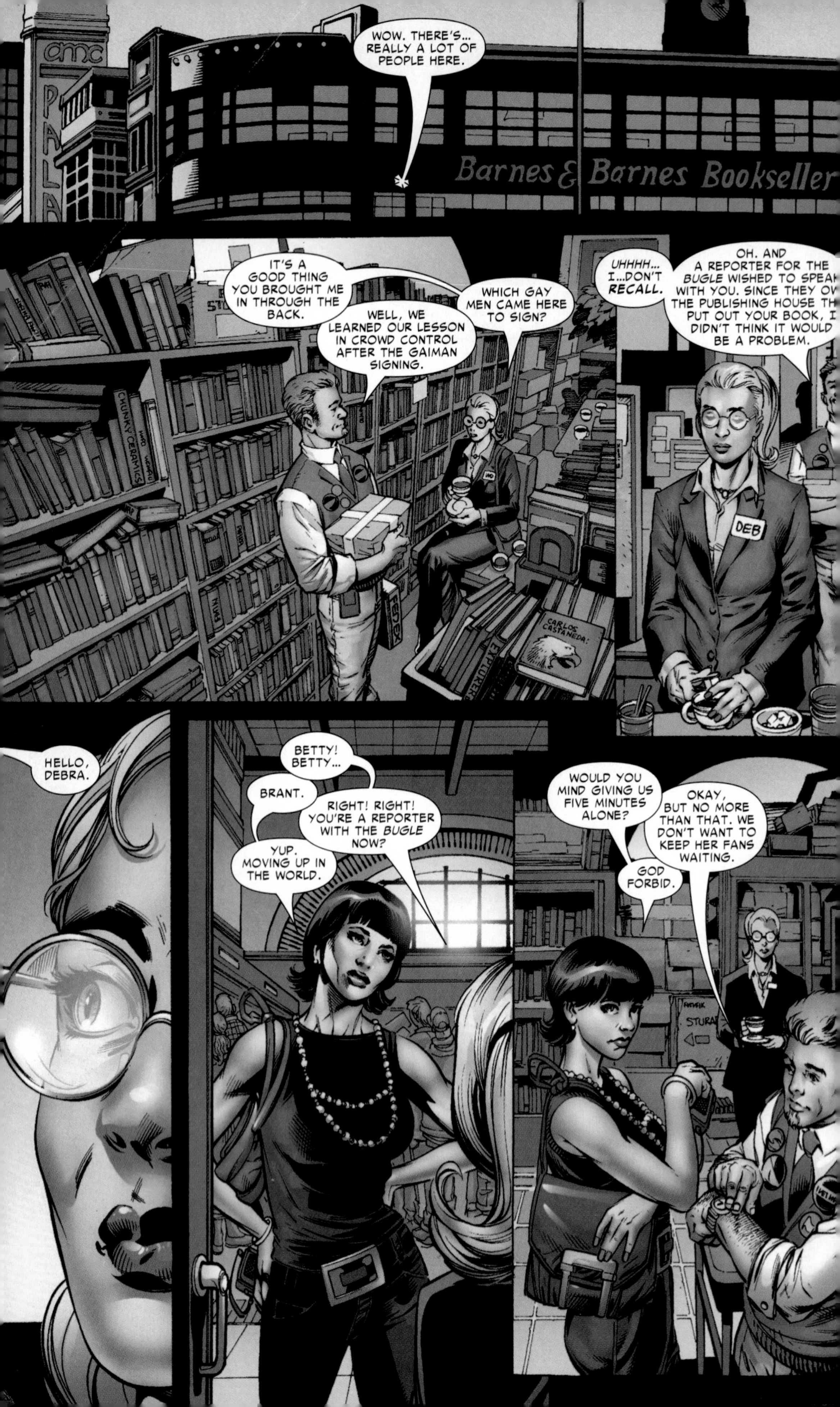
amc
PALA
WOW. THERE'S... REALLY A LOT OF PEOPLE HERE.
Barnes & Barnes Bookseller
IT'S A GOOD THING YOU BROUGHT ME IN THROUGH THE BACK.
WELL, WE LEARNED OUR LESSON IN CROWD CONTROL AFTER THE GAIMAN SIGNING.
WHICH GAY MEN CAME HERE TO SIGN?
CHUNKY CERAMICS
CARLOS CASTANEDA:
EXPLORER
UHHHH... I...DON'T RECALL.
OH. AND A REPORTER FOR THE BUGLE WISHED TO SPEAK WITH YOU. SINCE THEY OW THE PUBLISHING HOUSE TH PUT OUT YOUR BOOK, I DIDN'T THINK IT WOULD BE A PROBLEM.
DEB
HELLO, DEBRA.
BETTY! BETTY...
BRANT.
RIGHT! RIGHT! YOU'RE A REPORTER WITH THE BUGLE NOW?
YUP. MOVING UP IN THE WORLD.
WOULD YOU MIND GIVING US FIVE MINUTES ALONE?
OKAY, BUT NO MORE THAN THAT. WE DON'T WANT TO KEEP HER FANS WAITING.
GOD FORBID.

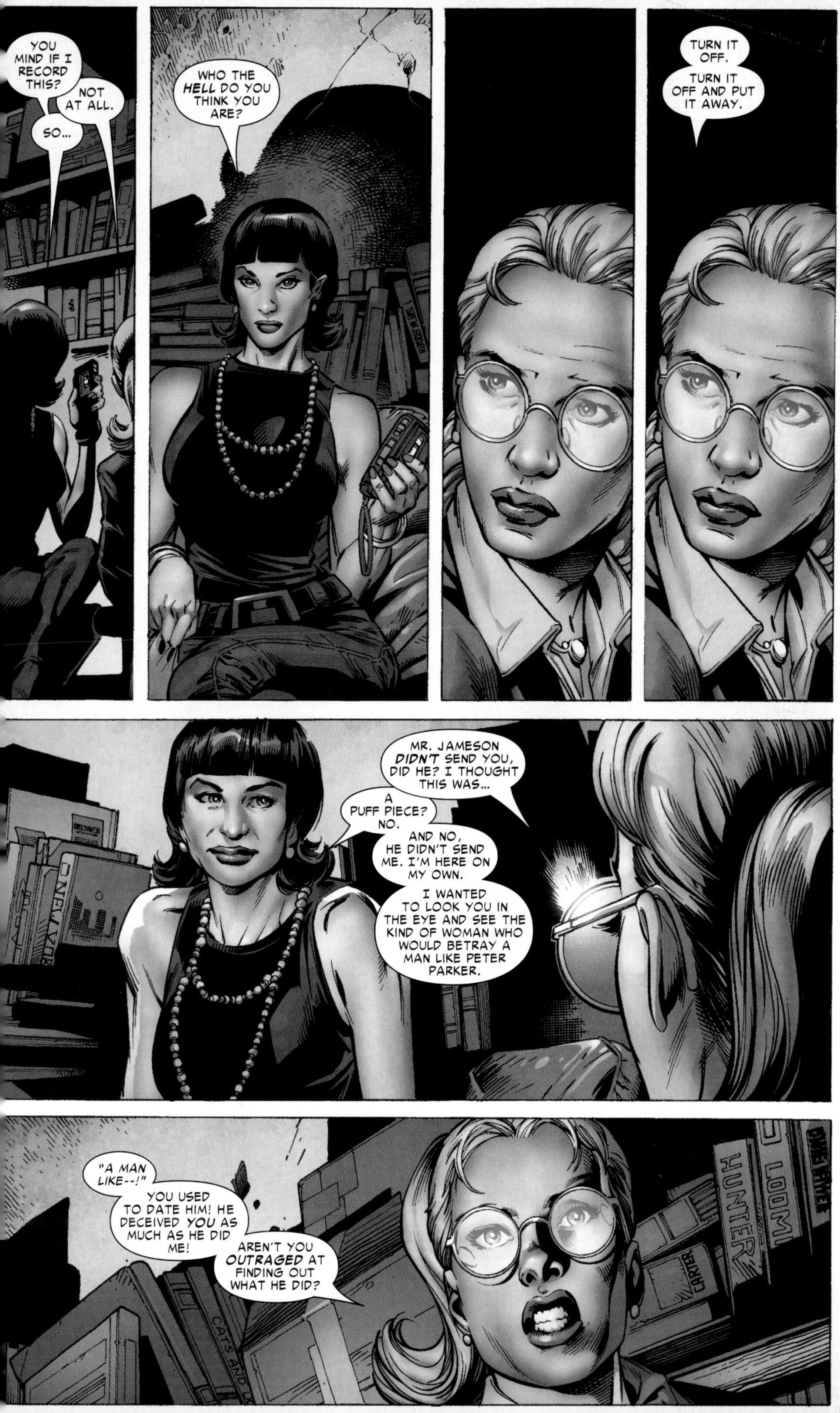

YOU MIND IF I RECORD THIS?
NOT AT ALL.
SO...
WHO THE HELL DO YOU THINK YOU ARE?
TURN IT OFF.
TURN IT OFF AND PUT IT AWAY.
MR. JAMESON DIDN'T SEND YOU, DID HE? I THOUGHT THIS WAS...
A PUFF PIECE? NO.
AND NO, HE DIDN'T SEND ME. I'M HERE ON MY OWN.
I WANTED TO LOOK YOU IN THE EYE AND SEE THE KIND OF WOMAN WHO WOULD BETRAY A MAN LIKE PETER PARKER.
"A MAN LIKE--!"
YOU USED TO DATE HIM! HE DECEIVED YOU AS MUCH AS HE DID ME!
AREN'T YOU OUTRAGED AT FINDING OUT WHAT HE DID?
HUNTER
LOOM
CARTER

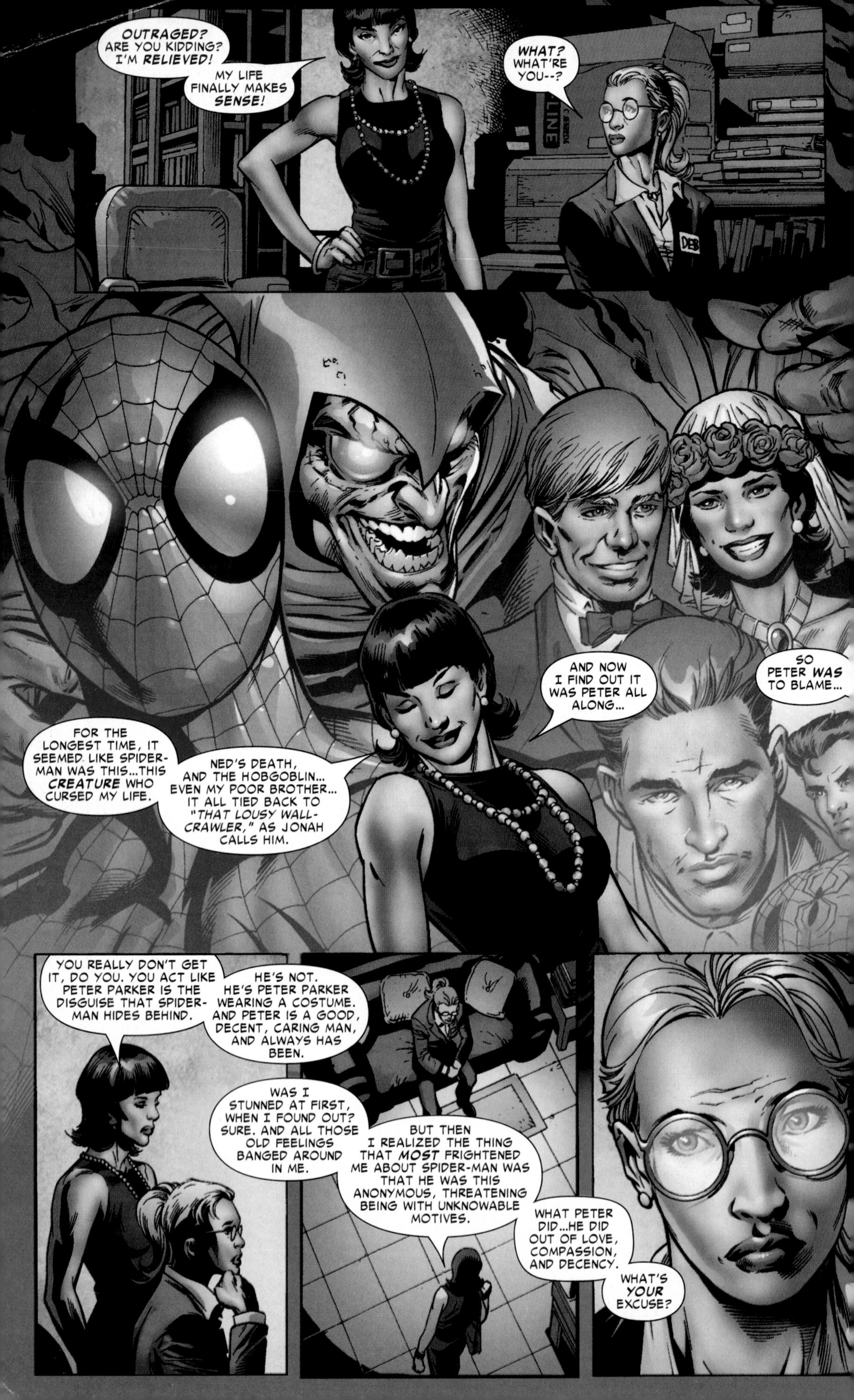
OUTRAGED? ARE YOU KIDDING? I'M RELIEVED!
MY LIFE FINALLY MAKES SENSE!
WHAT? WHAT'RE YOU--?
DEB
FOR THE LONGEST TIME, IT SEEMED LIKE SPIDER-MAN WAS THIS...THIS CREATURE WHO CURSED MY LIFE.
NED'S DEATH, AND THE HOBGOBLIN... EVEN MY POOR BROTHER... IT ALL TIED BACK TO "THAT LOUSY WALL-CRAWLER," AS JONAH CALLS HIM.
AND NOW I FIND OUT IT WAS PETER ALL ALONG...
SO PETER WAS TO BLAME...
YOU REALLY DON'T GET IT, DO YOU. YOU ACT LIKE PETER PARKER IS THE DISGUISE THAT SPIDER-MAN HIDES BEHIND.
HE'S NOT. HE'S PETER PARKER WEARING A COSTUME. AND PETER IS A GOOD, DECENT, CARING MAN, AND ALWAYS HAS BEEN.
WAS I STUNNED AT FIRST, WHEN I FOUND OUT? SURE. AND ALL THOSE OLD FEELINGS BANGED AROUND IN ME.
BUT THEN I REALIZED THE THING THAT MOST FRIGHTENED ME ABOUT SPIDER-MAN WAS THAT HE WAS THIS ANONYMOUS, THREATENING BEING WITH UNKNOWABLE MOTIVES.
WHAT PETER DID...HE DID OUT OF LOVE, COMPASSION, AND DECENCY.
WHAT'S YOUR EXCUSE?

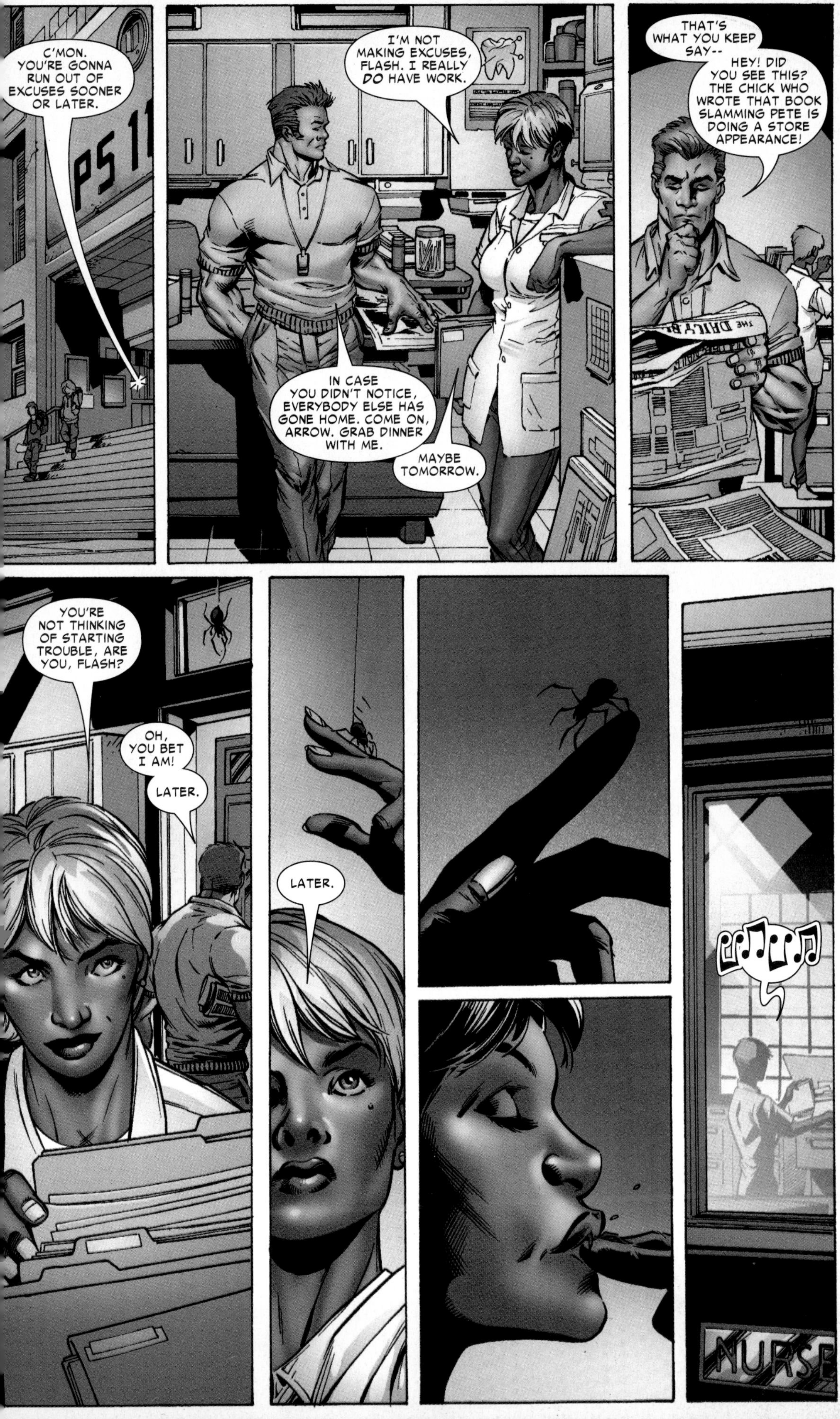
C'MON. YOU'RE GONNA RUN OUT OF EXCUSES SOONER OR LATER.
PS 11
I'M NOT MAKING EXCUSES, FLASH. I REALLY DO HAVE WORK.
IN CASE YOU DIDN'T NOTICE, EVERYBODY ELSE HAS GONE HOME. COME ON, ARROW. GRAB DINNER WITH ME.
MAYBE TOMORROW.
THAT'S WHAT YOU KEEP SAY--
HEY! DID YOU SEE THIS? THE CHICK WHO WROTE THAT BOOK SLAMMING PETE IS DOING A STORE APPEARANCE!
YOU'RE NOT THINKING OF STARTING TROUBLE, ARE YOU, FLASH?
OH, YOU BET I AM!
LATER.
LATER.
NURSE

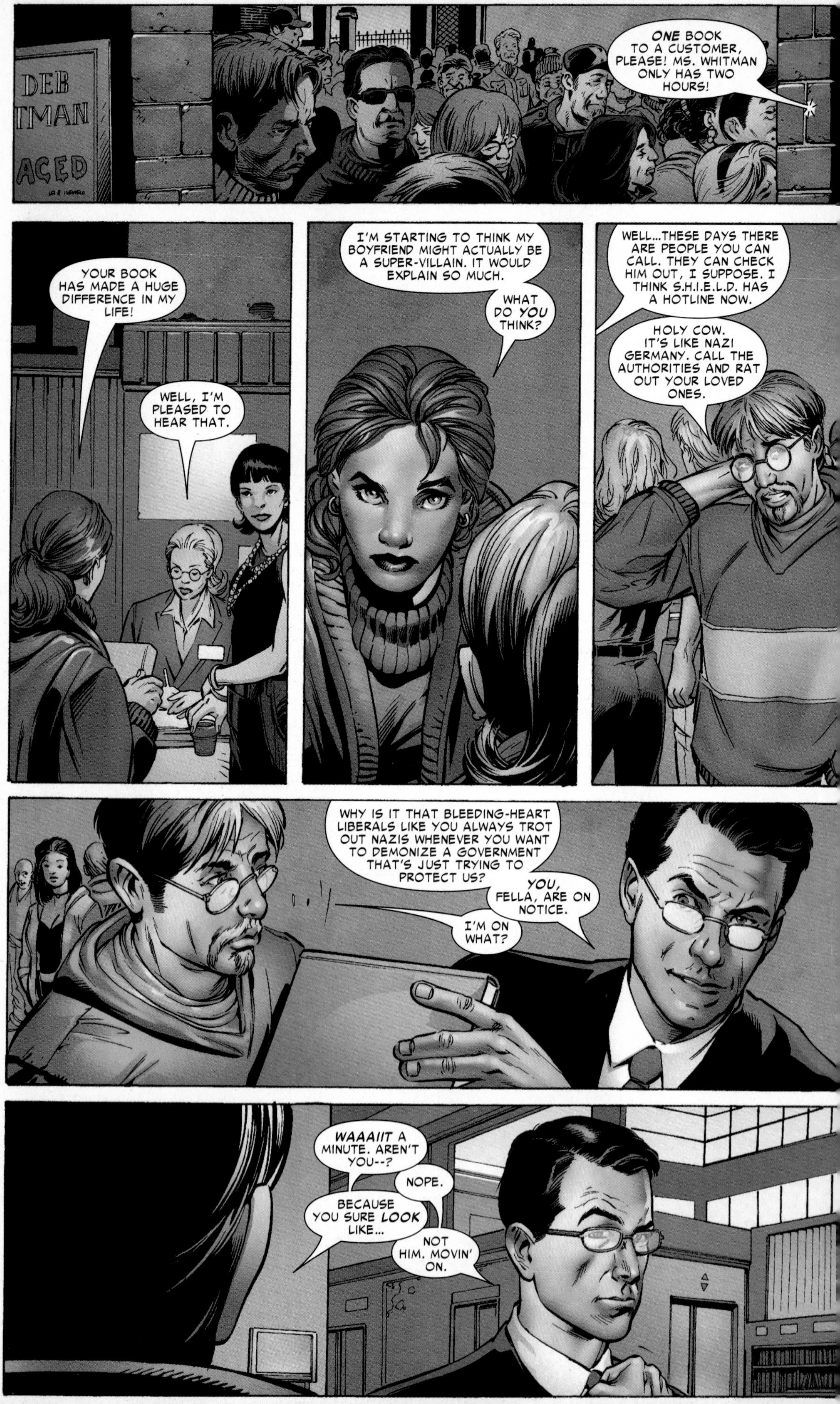
DEB
TMAN
ACED
ONE BOOK TO A CUSTOMER, PLEASE! MS. WHITMAN ONLY HAS TWO HOURS!
YOUR BOOK HAS MADE A HUGE DIFFERENCE IN MY LIFE!
WELL, I'M PLEASED TO HEAR THAT.
I'M STARTING TO THINK MY BOYFRIEND MIGHT ACTUALLY BE A SUPER-VILLAIN. IT WOULD EXPLAIN SO MUCH.
WHAT DO YOU THINK?
WELL...THESE DAYS THERE ARE PEOPLE YOU CAN CALL. THEY CAN CHECK HIM OUT, I SUPPOSE. I THINK S.H.I.E.L.D. HAS A HOTLINE NOW.
HOLY COW. IT'S LIKE NAZI GERMANY. CALL THE AUTHORITIES AND RAT OUT YOUR LOVED ONES.
WHY IS IT THAT BLEEDING-HEART LIBERALS LIKE YOU ALWAYS TROT OUT NAZIS WHENEVER YOU WANT TO DEMONIZE A GOVERNMENT THAT'S JUST TRYING TO PROTECT US?
YOU, FELLA, ARE ON NOTICE.
I'M ON WHAT?
WAAAIIT A MINUTE. AREN'T YOU--?
NOPE.
BECAUSE YOU SURE LOOK LIKE...
NOT HIM. MOVIN' ON.

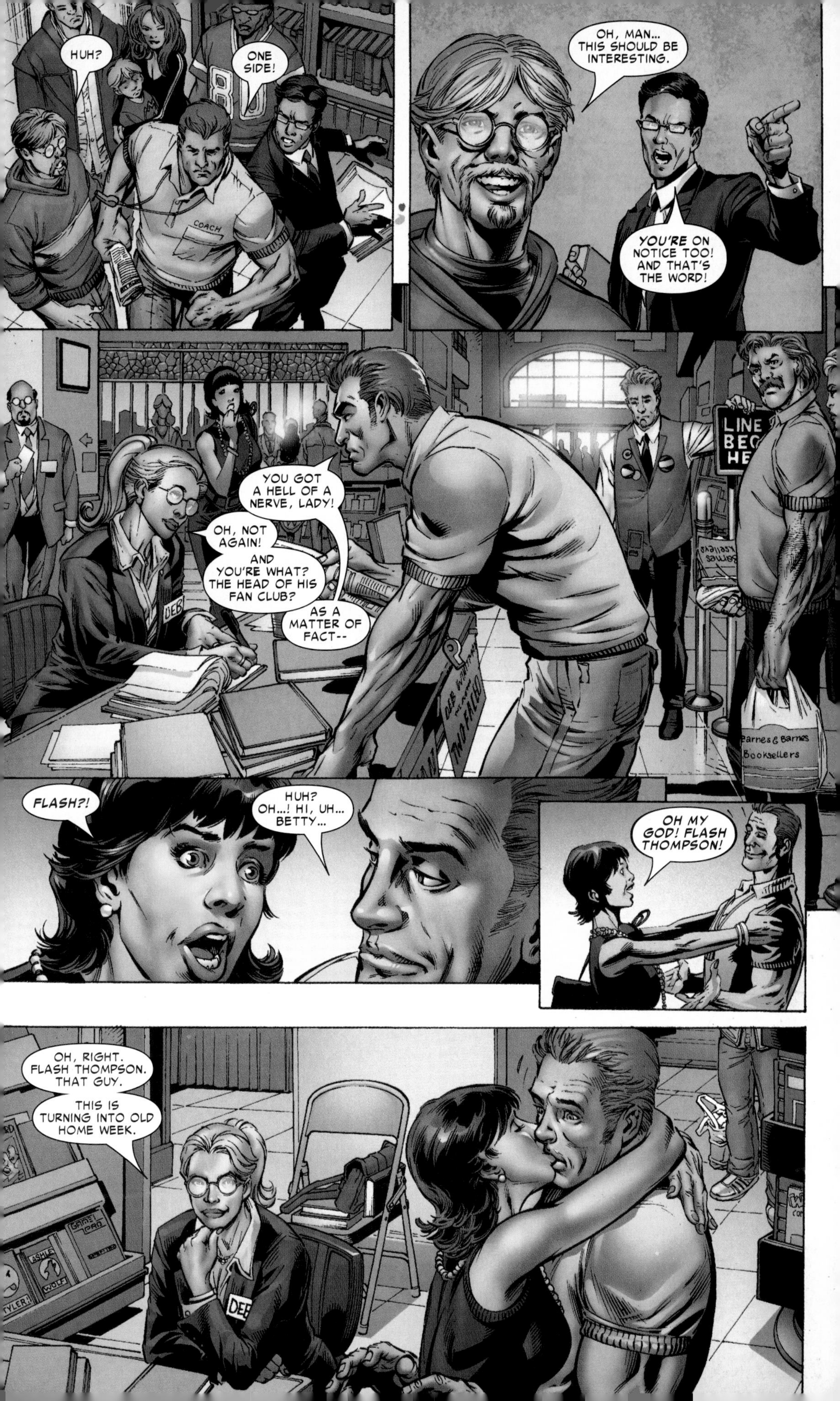
HUH?
ONE SIDE!
OH, MAN... THIS SHOULD BE INTERESTING.
YOU'RE ON NOTICE TOO! AND THAT'S THE WORD!
COACH
YOU GOT A HELL OF A NERVE, LADY!
OH, NOT AGAIN!
AND YOU'RE WHAT? THE HEAD OF HIS FAN CLUB?
AS A MATTER OF FACT--
DEB
LINE BEG HE
Barnes & Barnes Booksellers
FLASH?!
HUH? OH...! HI, UH... BETTY...
OH MY GOD! FLASH THOMPSON!
OH, RIGHT. FLASH THOMPSON. THAT GUY.
THIS IS TURNING INTO OLD HOME WEEK.
DEB

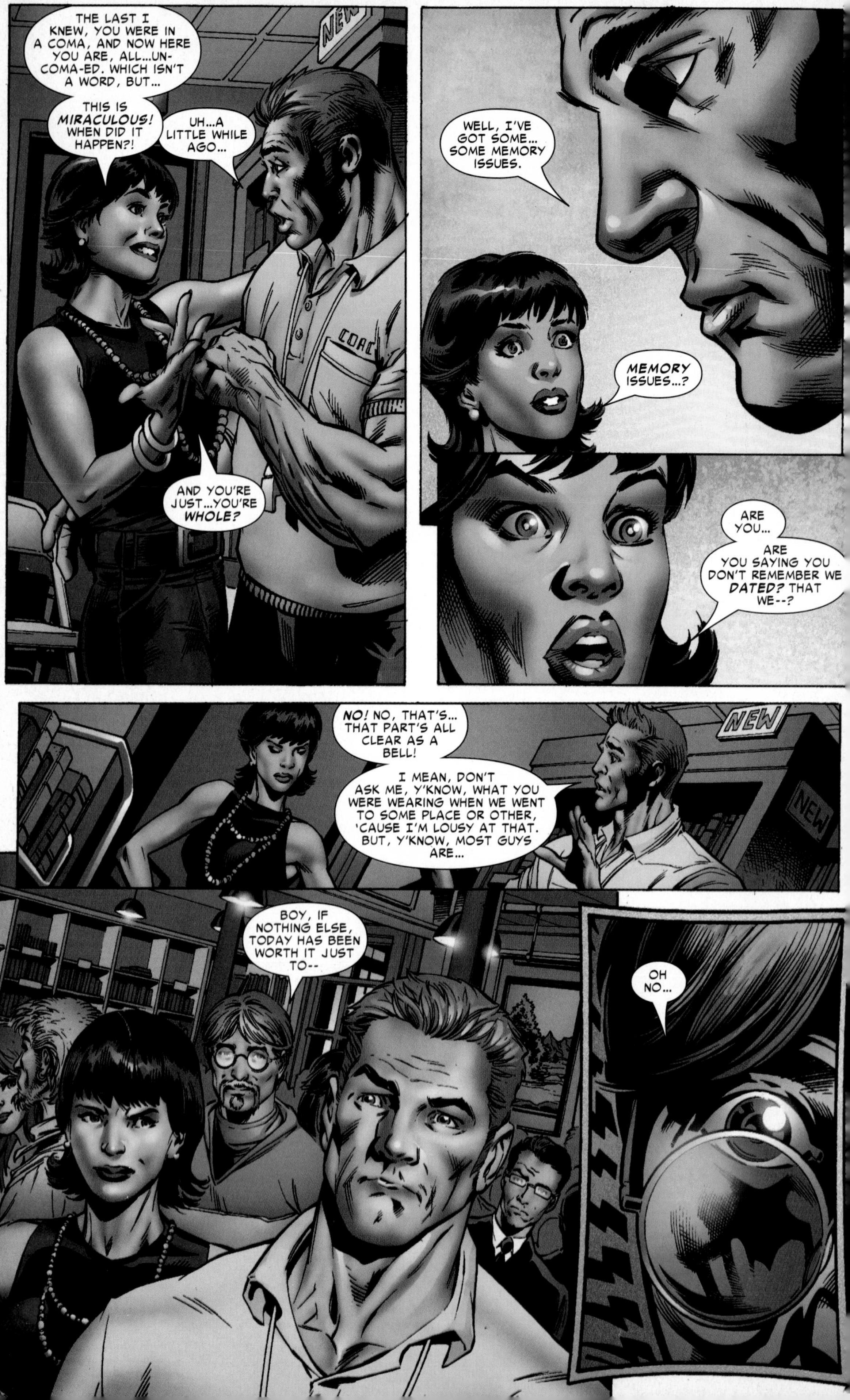
THE LAST I KNEW, YOU WERE IN A COMA, AND NOW HERE YOU ARE, ALL...UN-COMA-ED. WHICH ISN'T A WORD, BUT...
THIS IS MIRACULOUS! WHEN DID IT HAPPEN?!
UH...A LITTLE WHILE AGO...
AND YOU'RE JUST...YOU'RE WHOLE?
WELL, I'VE GOT SOME... SOME MEMORY ISSUES.
MEMORY ISSUES...?
ARE YOU...
ARE YOU SAYING YOU DON'T REMEMBER WE DATED? THAT WE--?
NO! NO, THAT'S... THAT PART'S ALL CLEAR AS A BELL!
I MEAN, DON'T ASK ME, Y'KNOW, WHAT YOU WERE WEARING WHEN WE WENT TO SOME PLACE OR OTHER, 'CAUSE I'M LOUSY AT THAT. BUT, Y'KNOW, MOST GUYS ARE...
BOY, IF NOTHING ELSE, TODAY HAS BEEN WORTH IT JUST TO--
OH NO...

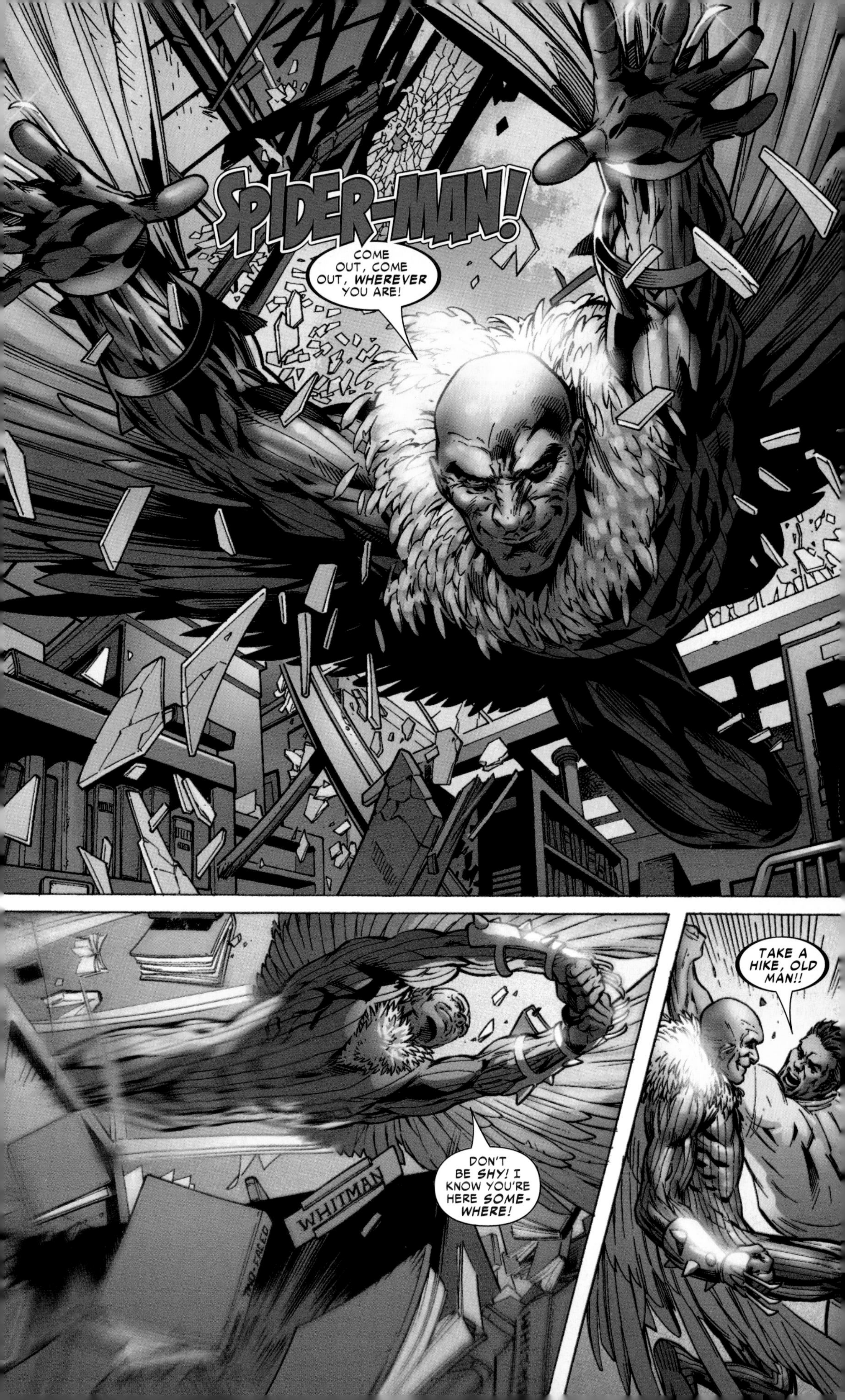
SPIDER-MAN!
COME OUT, COME OUT, WHEREVER YOU ARE!
WHITMAN
DON'T BE SHY! I KNOW YOU'RE HERE SOME-WHERE!
TAKE A HIKE, OLD MAN!!

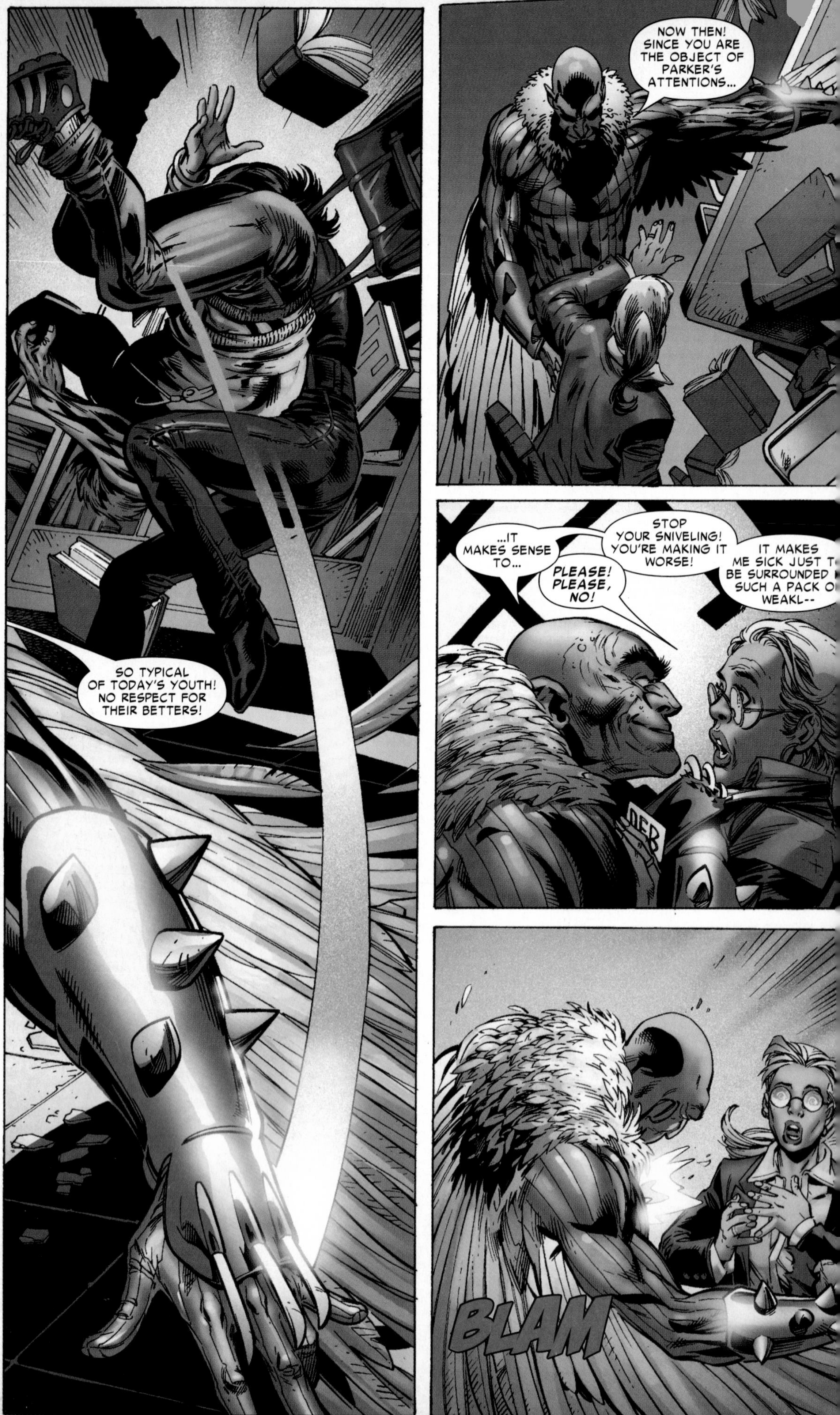

SO TYPICAL OF TODAY'S YOUTH! NO RESPECT FOR THEIR BETTERS!
NOW THEN! SINCE YOU ARE THE OBJECT OF PARKER'S ATTENTIONS...
...IT MAKES SENSE TO...
PLEASE! PLEASE, NO!
STOP YOUR SNIVELING! YOU'RE MAKING IT WORSE!
IT MAKES ME SICK JUST T BE SURROUNDED SUCH A PACK O WEAKL--
BLAM

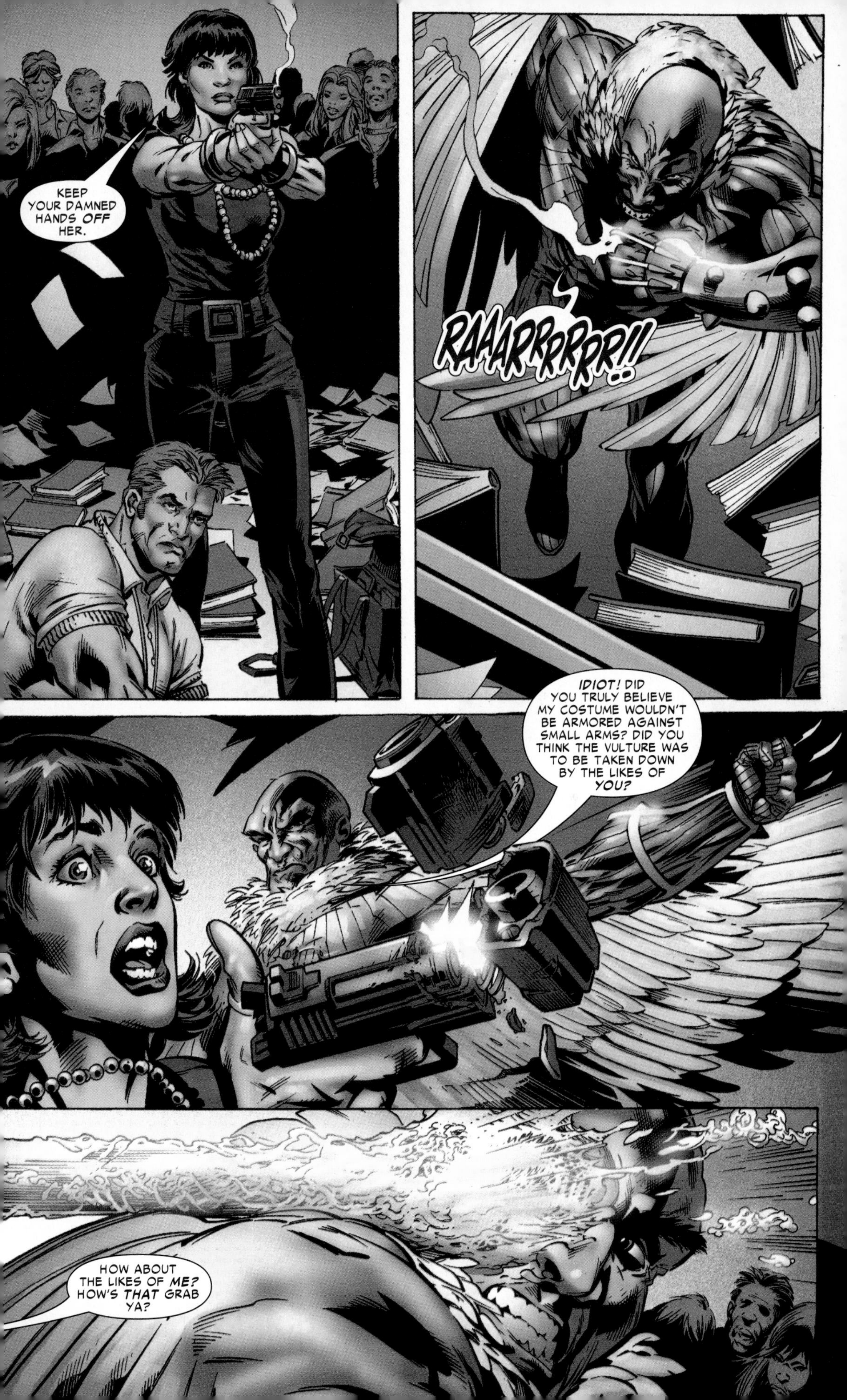
KEEP YOUR DAMNED HANDS OFF HER.
RAAARRRRRR!!
IDIOT! DID YOU TRULY BELIEVE MY COSTUME WOULDN'T BE ARMORED AGAINST SMALL ARMS? DID YOU THINK THE VULTURE WAS TO BE TAKEN DOWN BY THE LIKES OF YOU?
HOW ABOUT THE LIKES OF ME? HOW'S THAT GRAB YA?

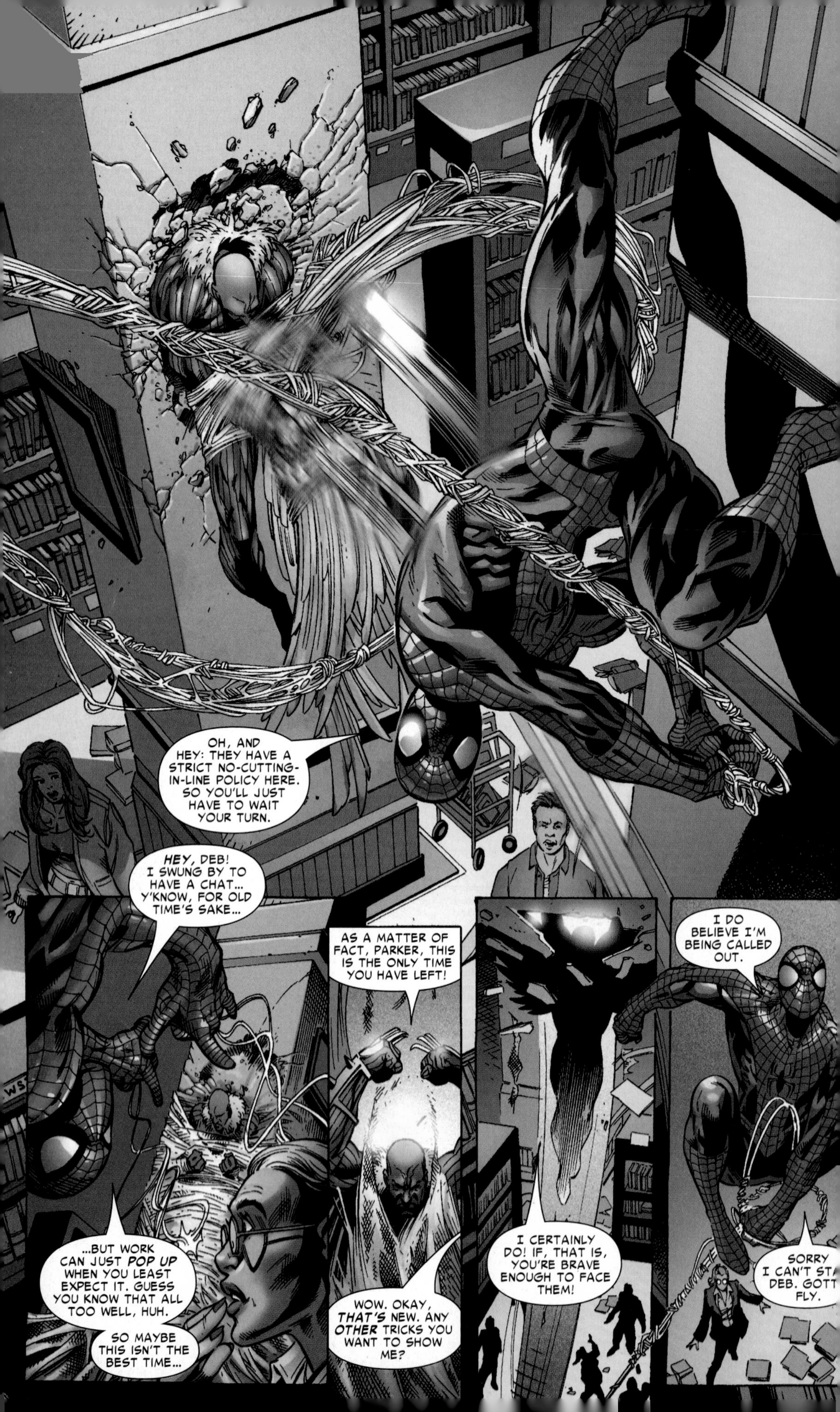
OH, AND HEY: THEY HAVE A STRICT NO-CUTTING-IN-LINE POLICY HERE. SO YOU'LL JUST HAVE TO WAIT YOUR TURN.
HEY, DEB! I SWUNG BY TO HAVE A CHAT... Y'KNOW, FOR OLD TIME'S SAKE...
...BUT WORK CAN JUST POP UP WHEN YOU LEAST EXPECT IT. GUESS YOU KNOW THAT ALL TOO WELL, HUH.
SO MAYBE THIS ISN'T THE BEST TIME...
AS A MATTER OF FACT, PARKER, THIS IS THE ONLY TIME YOU HAVE LEFT!
WOW. OKAY, THAT'S NEW. ANY OTHER TRICKS YOU WANT TO SHOW ME?
I CERTAINLY DO! IF, THAT IS, YOU'RE BRAVE ENOUGH TO FACE THEM!
I DO BELIEVE I'M BEING CALLED OUT.
SORRY I CAN'T ST DEB. GOTT FLY.

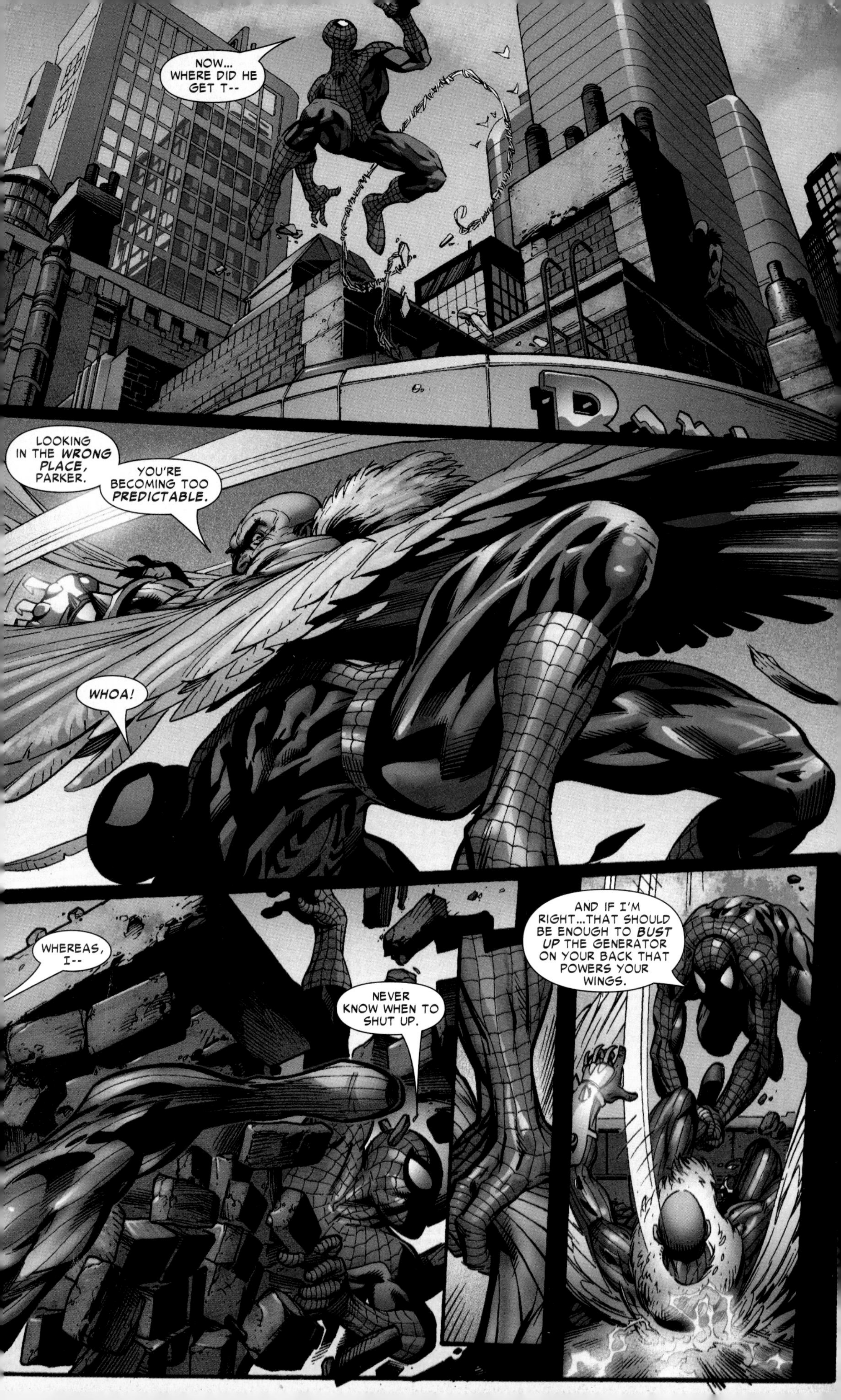
NOW... WHERE DID HE GET T--
LOOKING IN THE *WRONG PLACE*, PARKER.
YOU'RE BECOMING TOO *PREDICTABLE*.
WHOA!
WHEREAS, I--
NEVER KNOW WHEN TO SHUT UP.
AND IF I'M RIGHT...THAT SHOULD BE ENOUGH TO *BUST UP* THE GENERATOR ON YOUR BACK THAT POWERS YOUR WINGS.

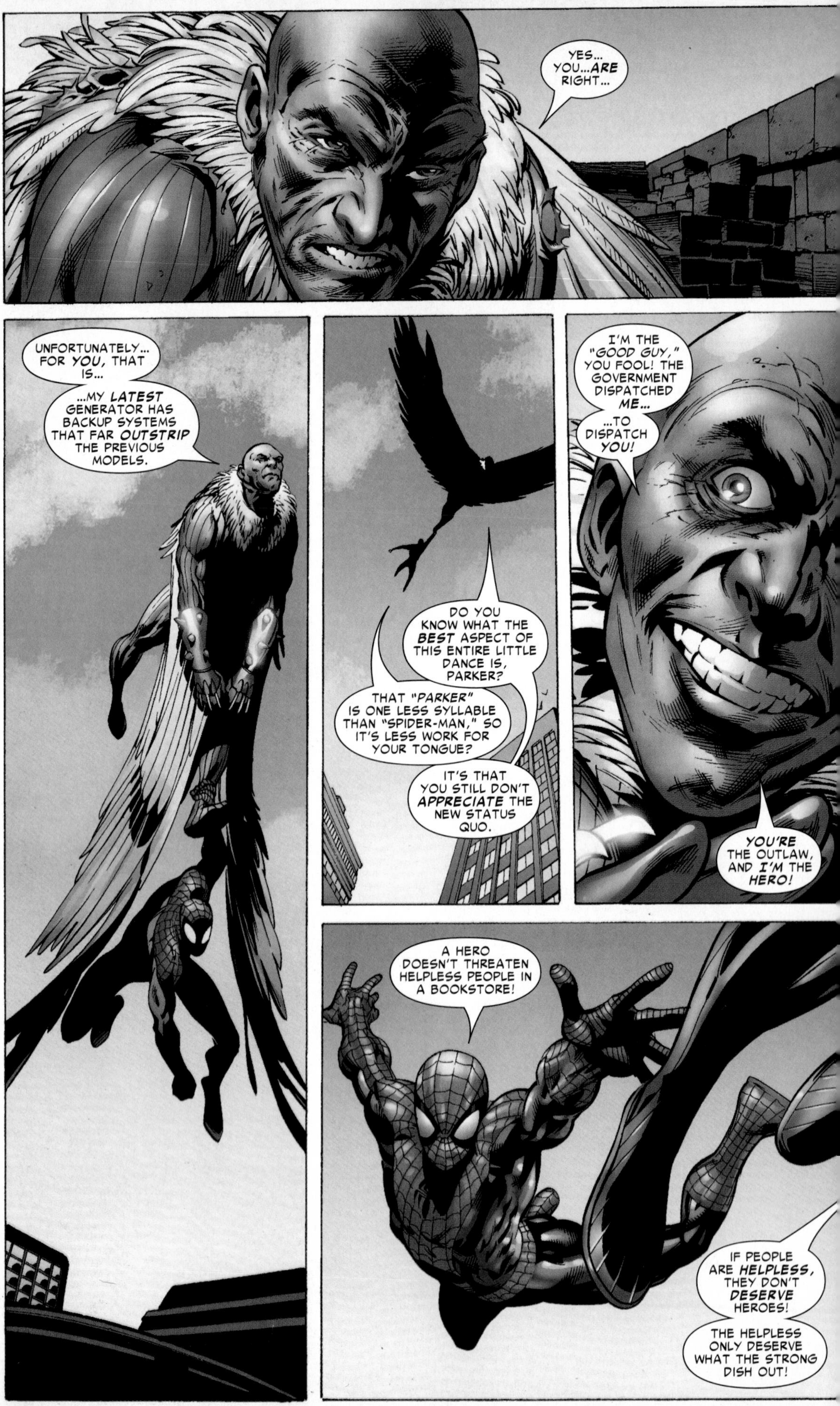
YES... YOU...ARE RIGHT...
UNFORTUNATELY... FOR YOU, THAT IS...
...MY LATEST GENERATOR HAS BACKUP SYSTEMS THAT FAR OUTSTRIP THE PREVIOUS MODELS.
DO YOU KNOW WHAT THE BEST ASPECT OF THIS ENTIRE LITTLE DANCE IS, PARKER?
THAT "PARKER" IS ONE LESS SYLLABLE THAN "SPIDER-MAN," SO IT'S LESS WORK FOR YOUR TONGUE?
IT'S THAT YOU STILL DON'T APPRECIATE THE NEW STATUS QUO.
I'M THE "GOOD GUY," YOU FOOL! THE GOVERNMENT DISPATCHED ME...
...TO DISPATCH YOU!
YOU'RE THE OUTLAW, AND I'M THE HERO!
A HERO DOESN'T THREATEN HELPLESS PEOPLE IN A BOOKSTORE!
IF PEOPLE ARE HELPLESS, THEY DON'T DESERVE HEROES!
THE HELPLESS ONLY DESERVE WHAT THE STRONG DISH OUT!

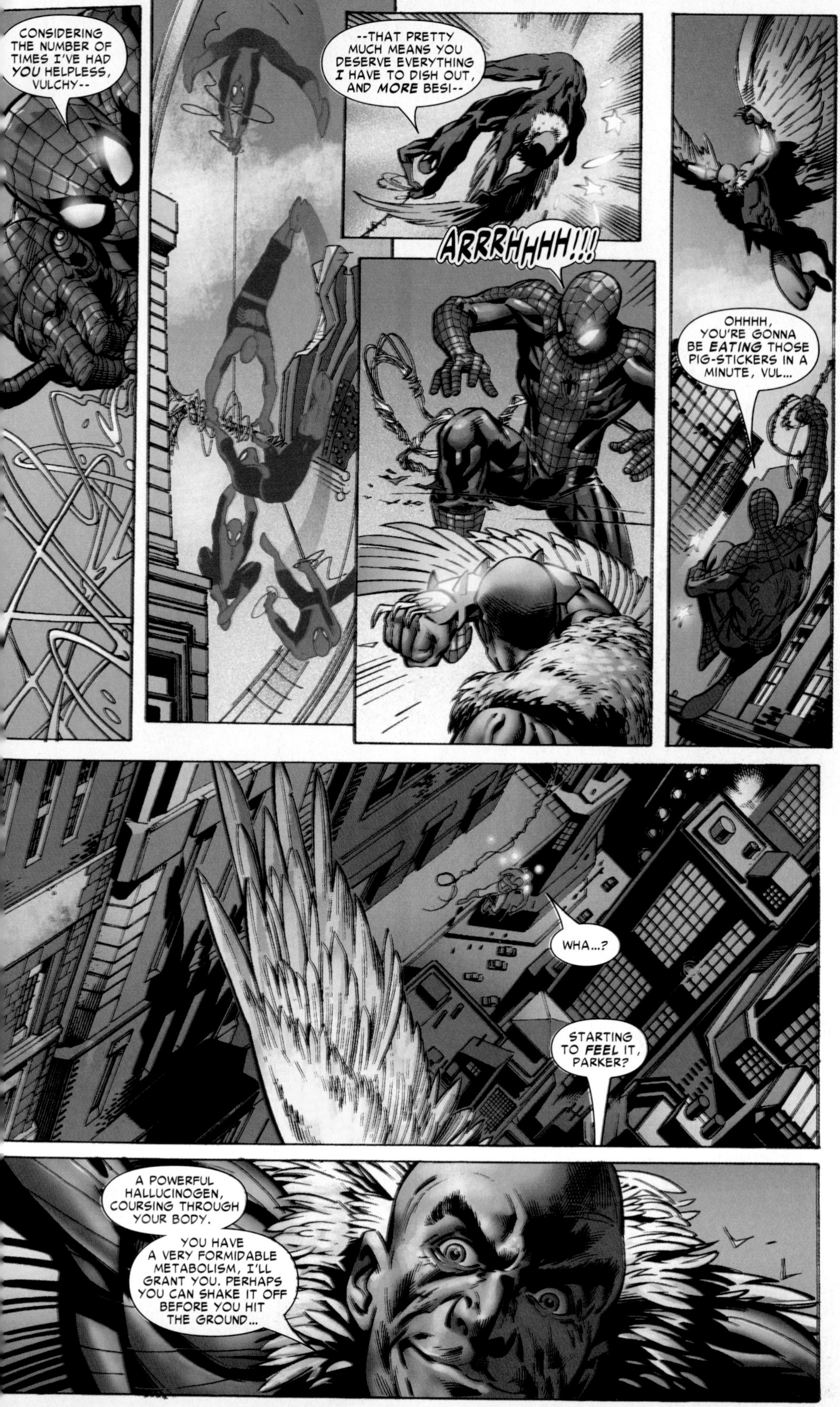

CONSIDERING THE NUMBER OF TIMES I'VE HAD YOU HELPLESS, VULCHY--
--THAT PRETTY MUCH MEANS YOU DESERVE EVERYTHING I HAVE TO DISH OUT, AND MORE BESI--
ARRRHHHH!!!
OHHHH, YOU'RE GONNA BE EATING THOSE PIG-STICKERS IN A MINUTE, VUL...
WHA...?
STARTING TO FEEL IT, PARKER?
A POWERFUL HALLUCINOGEN, COURSING THROUGH YOUR BODY.
YOU HAVE A VERY FORMIDABLE METABOLISM, I'LL GRANT YOU. PERHAPS YOU CAN SHAKE IT OFF BEFORE YOU HIT THE GROUND...

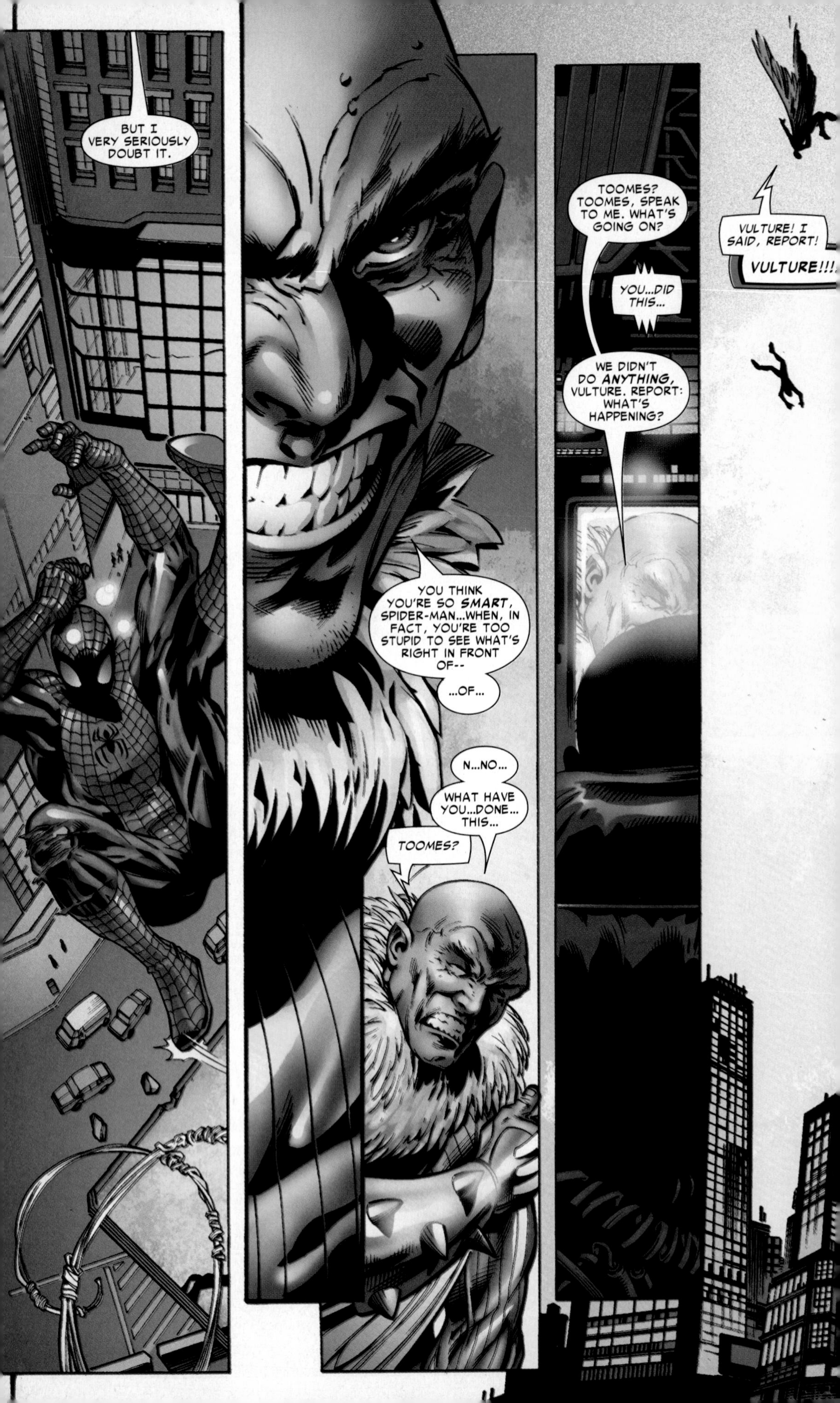
BUT I VERY SERIOUSLY DOUBT IT.
YOU THINK YOU'RE SO SMART, SPIDER-MAN...WHEN, IN FACT, YOU'RE TOO STUPID TO SEE WHAT'S RIGHT IN FRONT OF--
...OF...
N...NO...
WHAT HAVE YOU...DONE... THIS...
TOOMES?
TOOMES? TOOMES, SPEAK TO ME. WHAT'S GOING ON?
YOU...DID THIS...
WE DIDN'T DO ANYTHING, VULTURE. REPORT: WHAT'S HAPPENING?
VULTURE! I SAID, REPORT!
VULTURE!!!

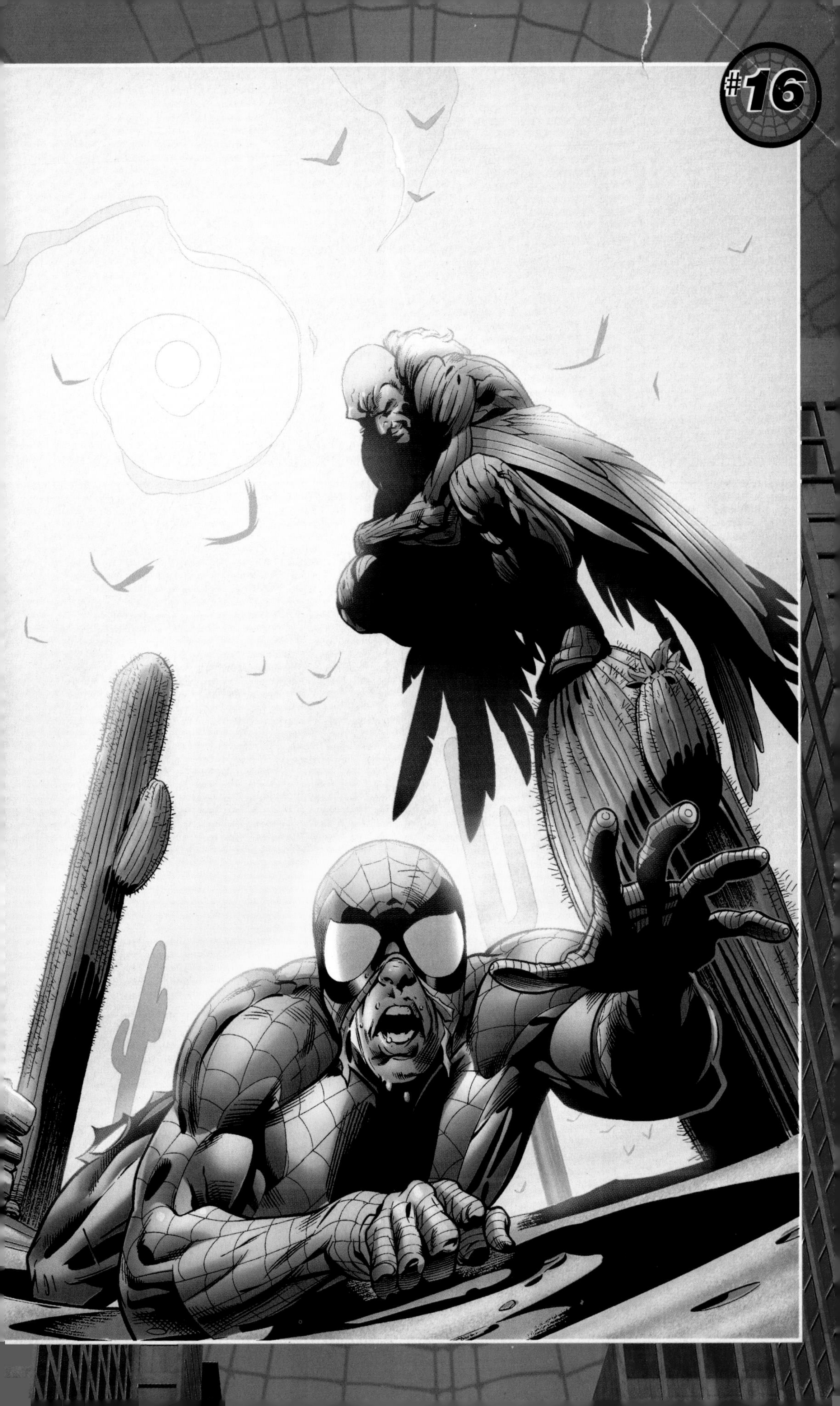
#16

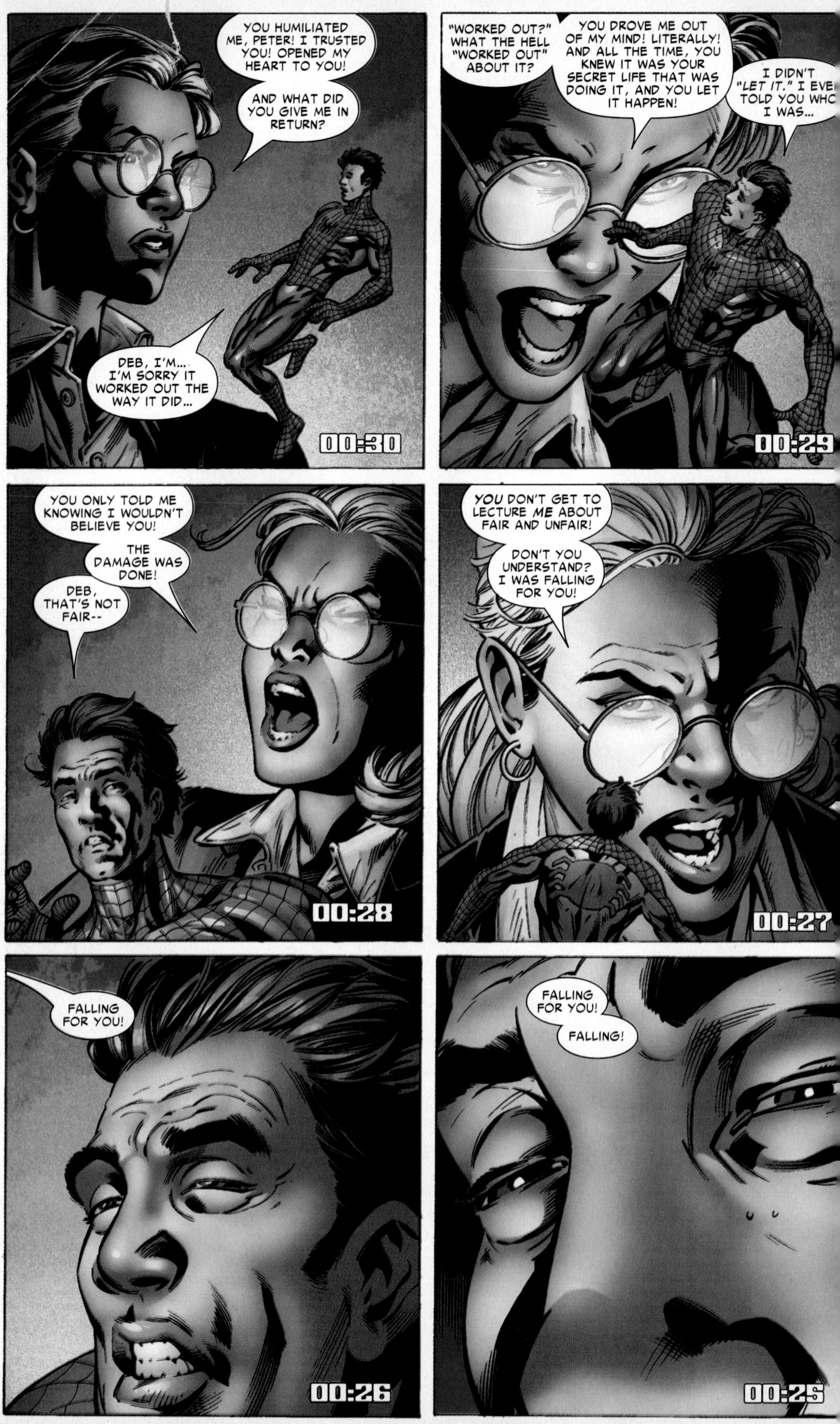
YOU HUMILIATED ME, PETER! I TRUSTED YOU! OPENED MY HEART TO YOU!
AND WHAT DID YOU GIVE ME IN RETURN?
DEB, I'M... I'M SORRY IT WORKED OUT THE WAY IT DID...
00:30
"WORKED OUT?" WHAT THE HELL "WORKED OUT" ABOUT IT?
YOU DROVE ME OUT OF MY MIND! LITERALLY! AND ALL THE TIME, YOU KNEW IT WAS YOUR SECRET LIFE THAT WAS DOING IT, AND YOU LET IT HAPPEN!
I DIDN'T "LET IT." I EVE TOLD YOU WHO I WAS...
00:29
YOU ONLY TOLD ME KNOWING I WOULDN'T BELIEVE YOU!
THE DAMAGE WAS DONE!
DEB, THAT'S NOT FAIR--
00:28
YOU DON'T GET TO LECTURE ME ABOUT FAIR AND UNFAIR!
DON'T YOU UNDERSTAND? I WAS FALLING FOR YOU!
00:27
FALLING FOR YOU!
00:26
FALLING FOR YOU!
FALLING!
00:25

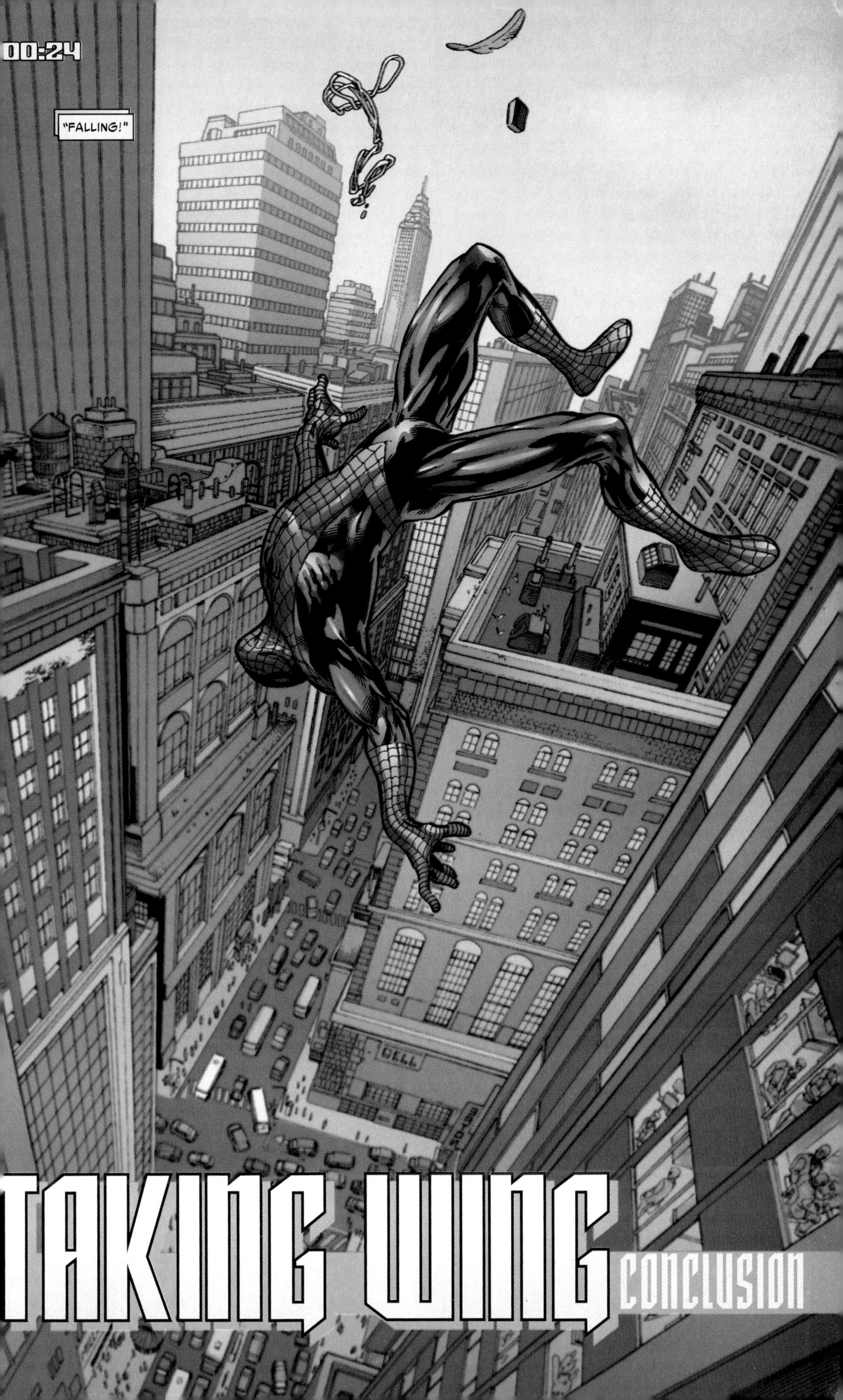
00:24
"FALLING!"
DELL
TAKING WING
CONCLUSION

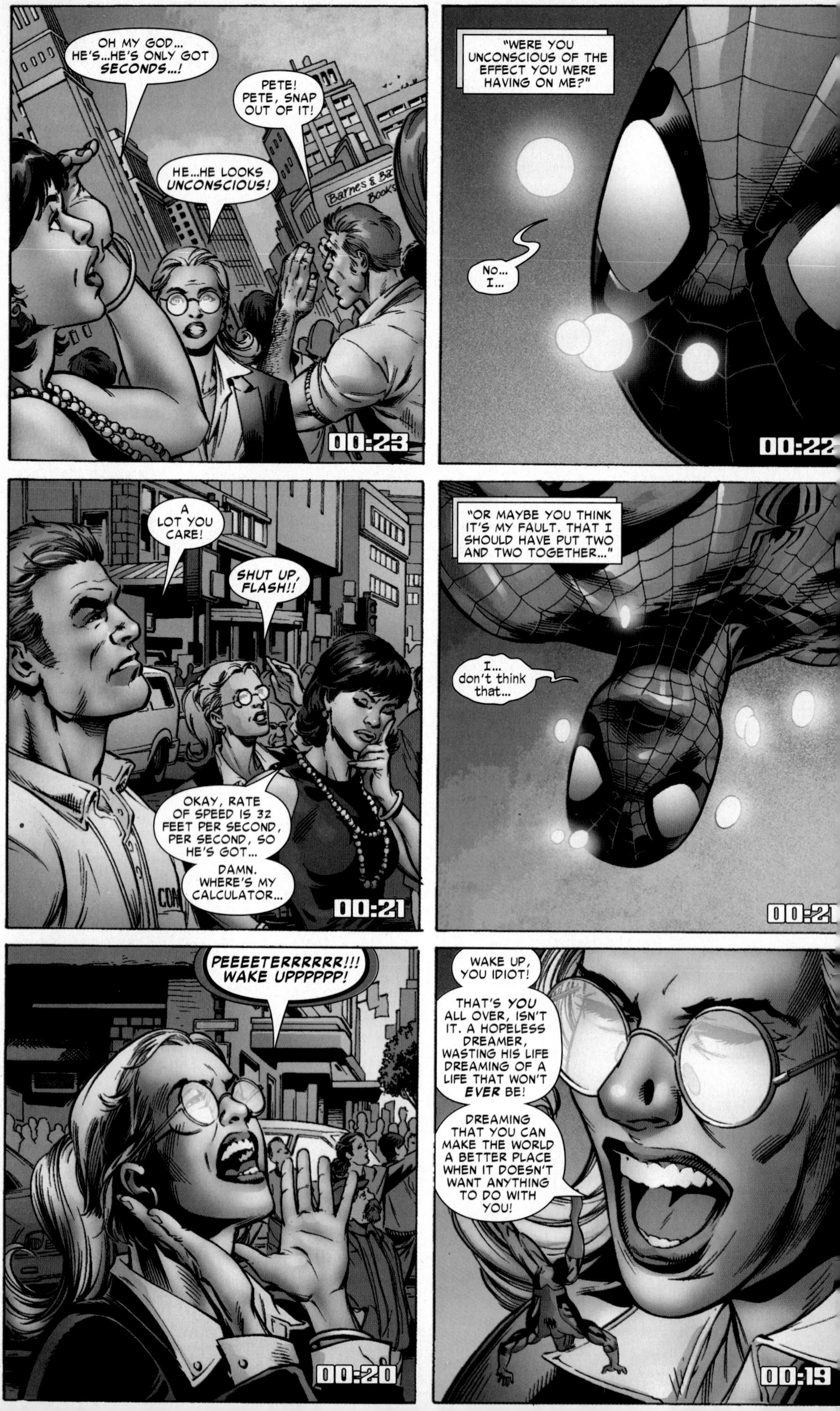

OH MY GOD... HE'S...HE'S ONLY GOT SECONDS...!
PETE! PETE, SNAP OUT OF IT!
HE...HE LOOKS UNCONSCIOUS!
Barnes & Ba... Books
00:23
"WERE YOU UNCONSCIOUS OF THE EFFECT YOU WERE HAVING ON ME?"
No... I...
00:22
A LOT YOU CARE!
SHUT UP, FLASH!!
OKAY, RATE OF SPEED IS 32 FEET PER SECOND, PER SECOND, SO HE'S GOT...
DAMN. WHERE'S MY CALCULATOR...
00:21
"OR MAYBE YOU THINK IT'S MY FAULT. THAT I SHOULD HAVE PUT TWO AND TWO TOGETHER..."
I... don't think that...
00:21
PEEEETERRRRRR!!! WAKE UPPPPPP!
00:20
WAKE UP, YOU IDIOT!
THAT'S YOU ALL OVER, ISN'T IT. A HOPELESS DREAMER, WASTING HIS LIFE DREAMING OF A LIFE THAT WON'T EVER BE!
DREAMING THAT YOU CAN MAKE THE WORLD A BETTER PLACE WHEN IT DOESN'T WANT ANYTHING TO DO WITH YOU!
00:19

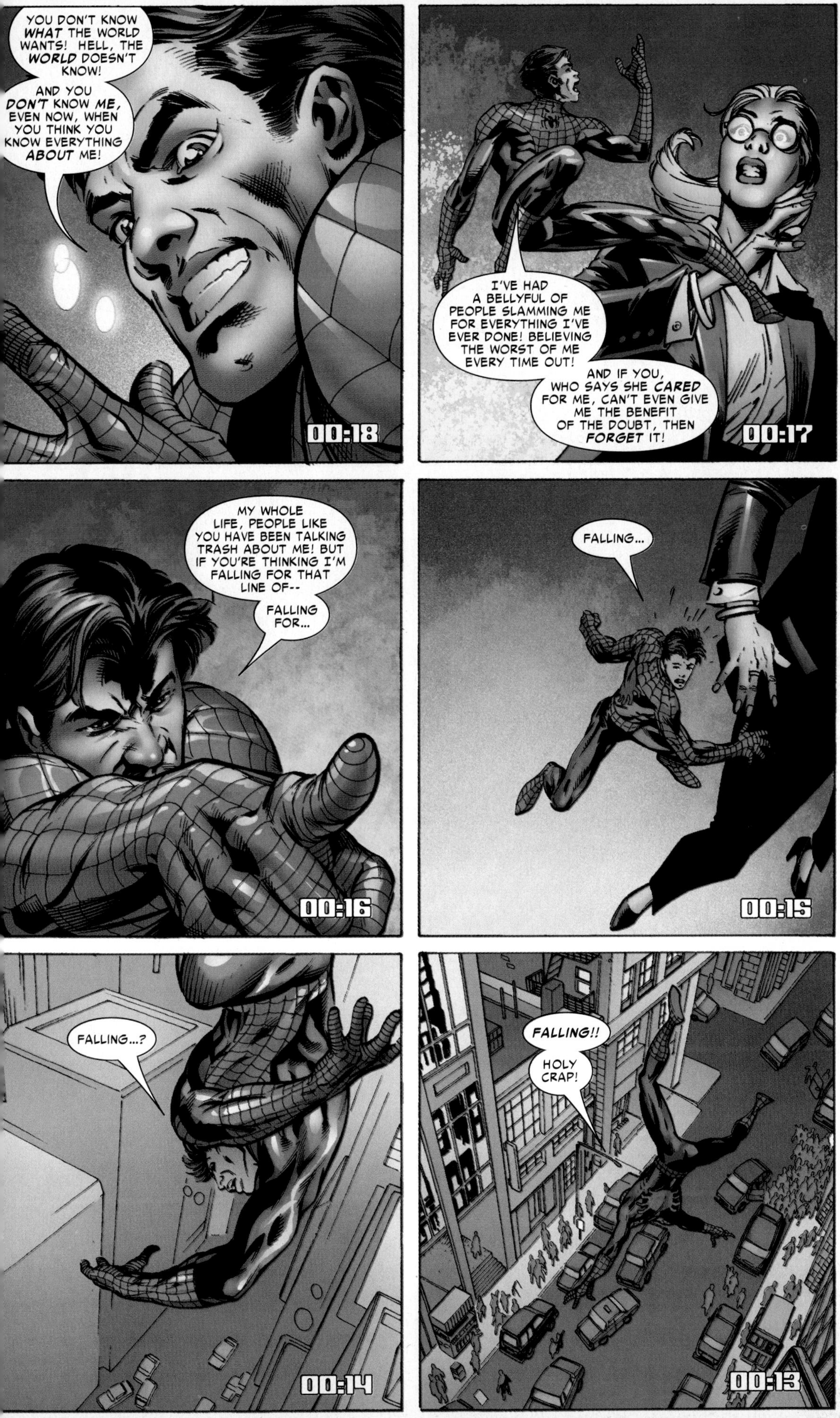
YOU DON'T KNOW *WHAT* THE WORLD WANTS! HELL, THE *WORLD* DOESN'T KNOW!
AND YOU *DON'T* KNOW *ME,* EVEN NOW, WHEN YOU THINK YOU KNOW EVERYTHING *ABOUT* ME!
00:18
I'VE HAD A BELLYFUL OF PEOPLE SLAMMING ME FOR EVERYTHING I'VE EVER DONE! BELIEVING THE WORST OF ME EVERY TIME OUT!
AND IF YOU, WHO SAYS SHE *CARED* FOR ME, CAN'T EVEN GIVE ME THE BENEFIT OF THE DOUBT, THEN *FORGET* IT!
00:17
MY WHOLE LIFE, PEOPLE LIKE YOU HAVE BEEN TALKING TRASH ABOUT ME! BUT IF YOU'RE THINKING I'M FALLING FOR THAT LINE OF--
FALLING FOR...
00:16
FALLING...
00:15
FALLING...?
00:14
FALLING!!
HOLY CRAP!
00:13

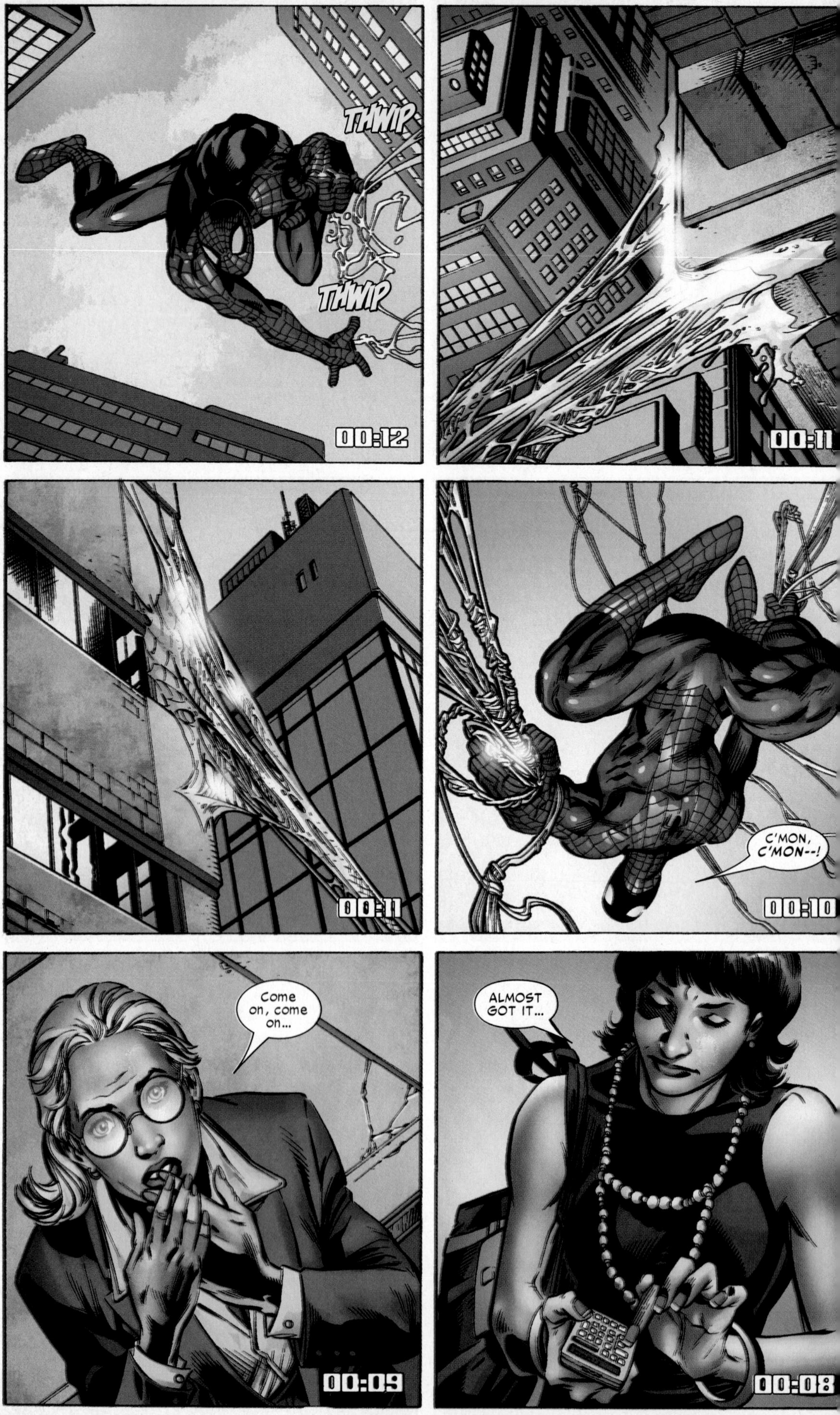
THWIP
THWIP
00:12
00:11
00:11
C'MON, C'MON--!
00:10
Come on, come on...
00:09
ALMOST GOT IT...
00:08

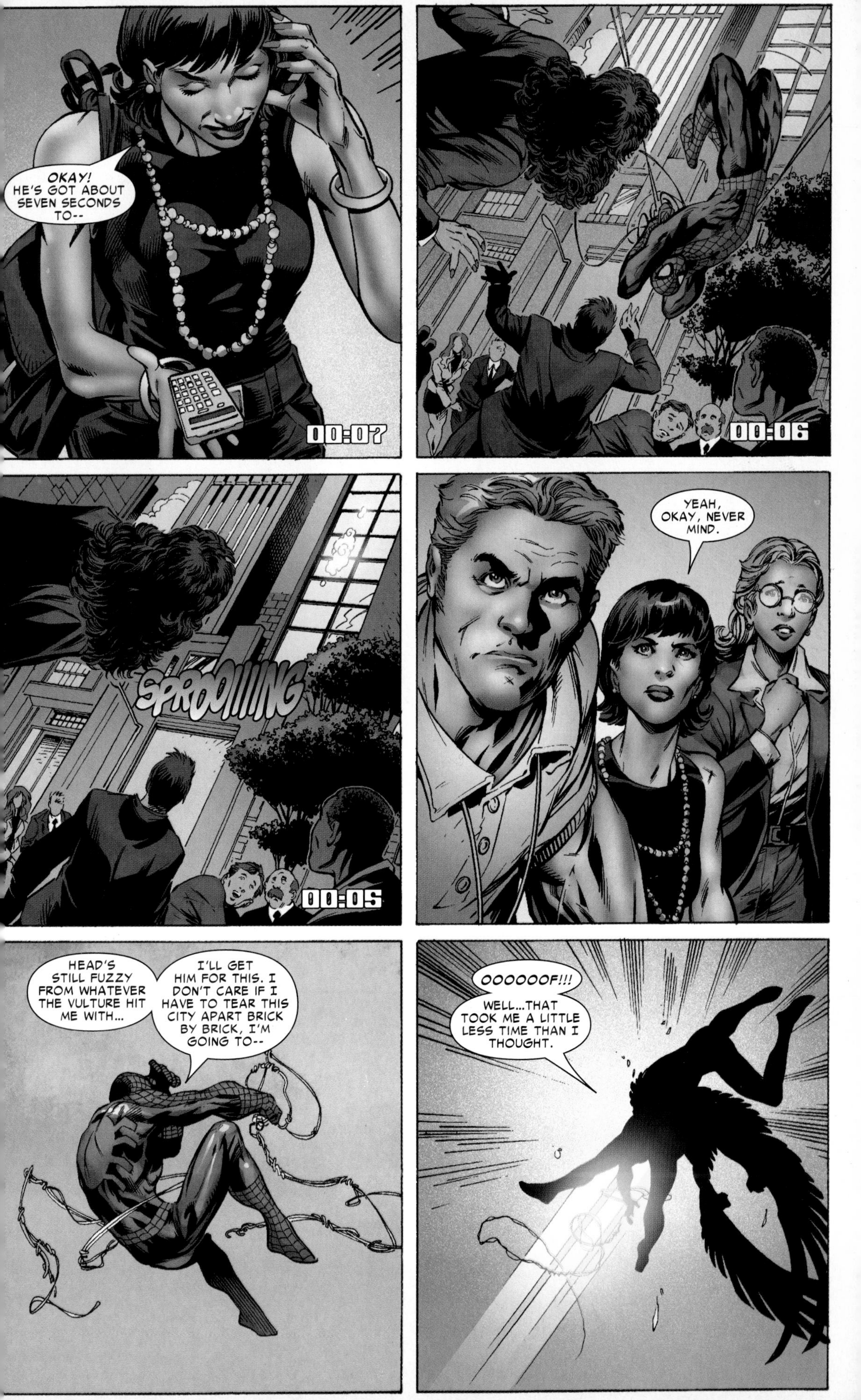
OKAY!
HE'S GOT ABOUT SEVEN SECONDS TO--
00:07
00:06
SPROOIIIING
00:05
YEAH, OKAY, NEVER MIND.
HEAD'S STILL FUZZY FROM WHATEVER THE VULTURE HIT ME WITH...
I'LL GET HIM FOR THIS. I DON'T CARE IF I HAVE TO TEAR THIS CITY APART BRICK BY BRICK, I'M GOING TO--
OOOOOOF!!!
WELL...THAT TOOK ME A LITTLE LESS TIME THAN I THOUGHT.

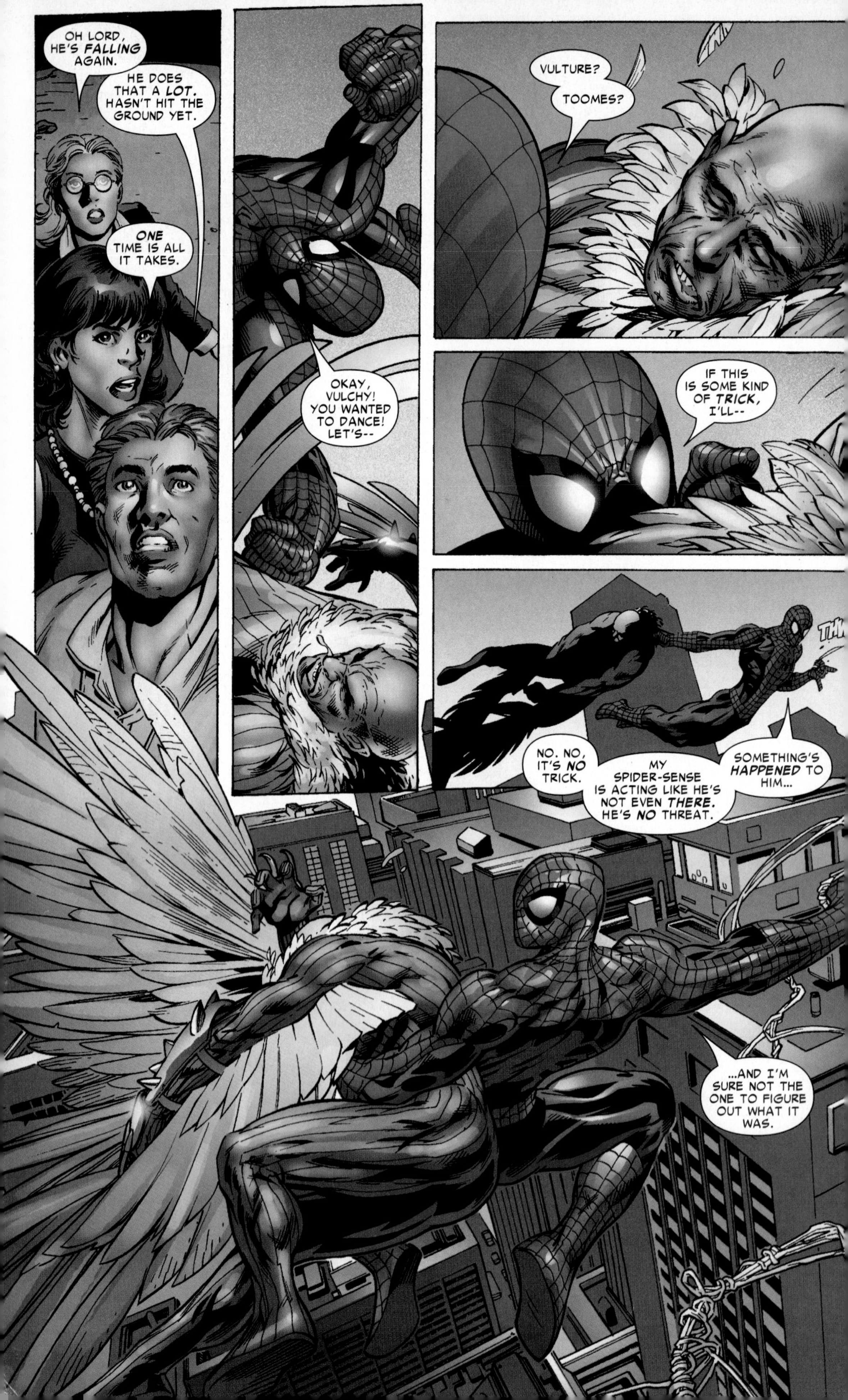
OH LORD, HE'S FALLING AGAIN.
HE DOES THAT A LOT. HASN'T HIT THE GROUND YET.
ONE TIME IS ALL IT TAKES.
OKAY, VULCHY! YOU WANTED TO DANCE! LET'S--
VULTURE?
TOOMES?
IF THIS IS SOME KIND OF TRICK, I'LL--
NO. NO, IT'S NO TRICK.
MY SPIDER-SENSE IS ACTING LIKE HE'S NOT EVEN THERE. HE'S NO THREAT.
SOMETHING'S HAPPENED TO HIM...
...AND I'M SURE NOT THE ONE TO FIGURE OUT WHAT IT WAS.

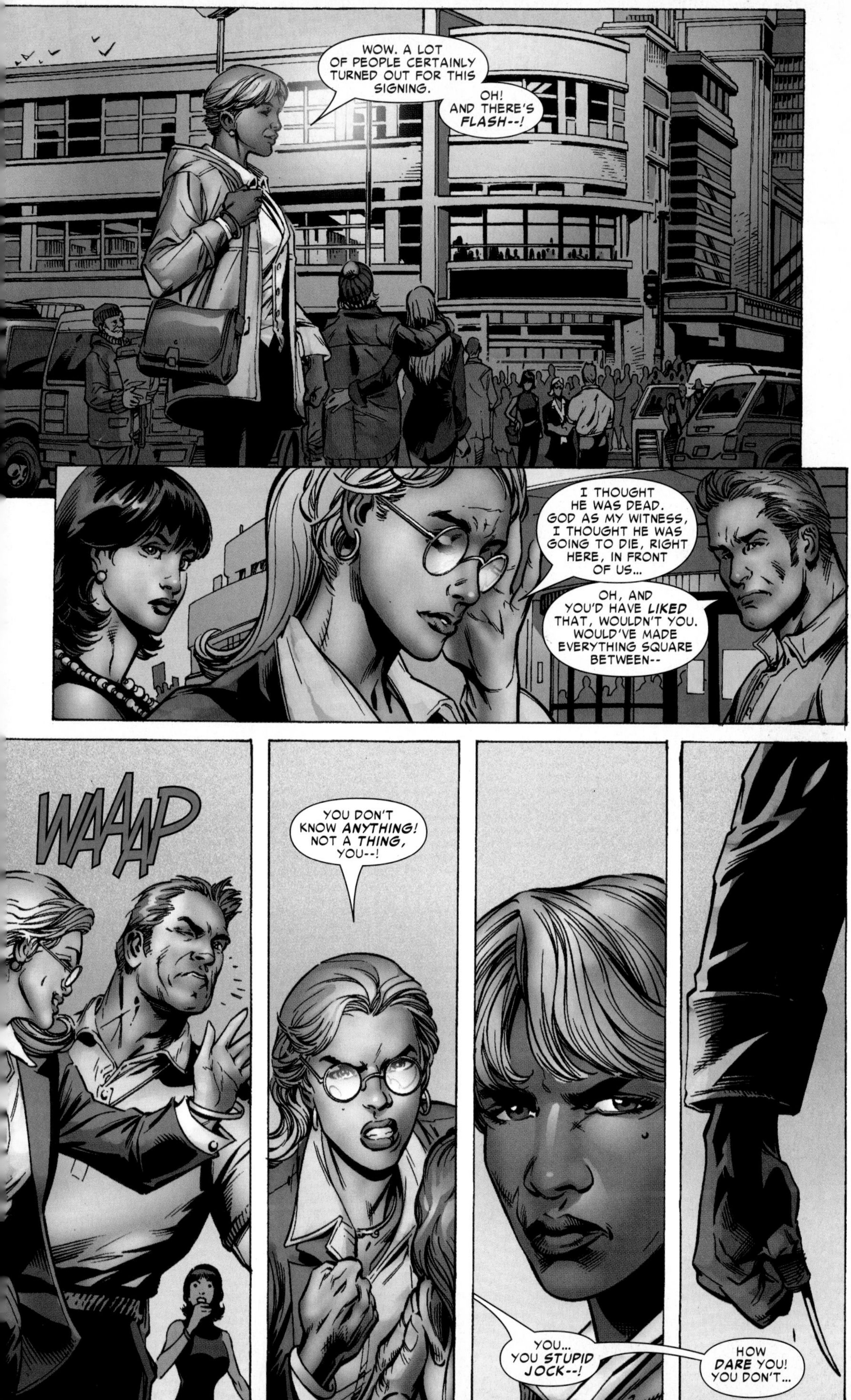
WOW. A LOT OF PEOPLE CERTAINLY TURNED OUT FOR THIS SIGNING.
OH! AND THERE'S *FLASH*--!
I THOUGHT HE WAS DEAD. GOD AS MY WITNESS, I THOUGHT HE WAS GOING TO DIE, RIGHT HERE, IN FRONT OF US...
OH, AND YOU'D HAVE *LIKED* THAT, WOULDN'T YOU. WOULD'VE MADE EVERYTHING SQUARE BETWEEN--
WAAAP
YOU DON'T KNOW *ANYTHING*! NOT A *THING*, YOU--!
YOU... YOU *STUPID JOCK*--!
HOW *DARE* YOU! YOU DON'T...

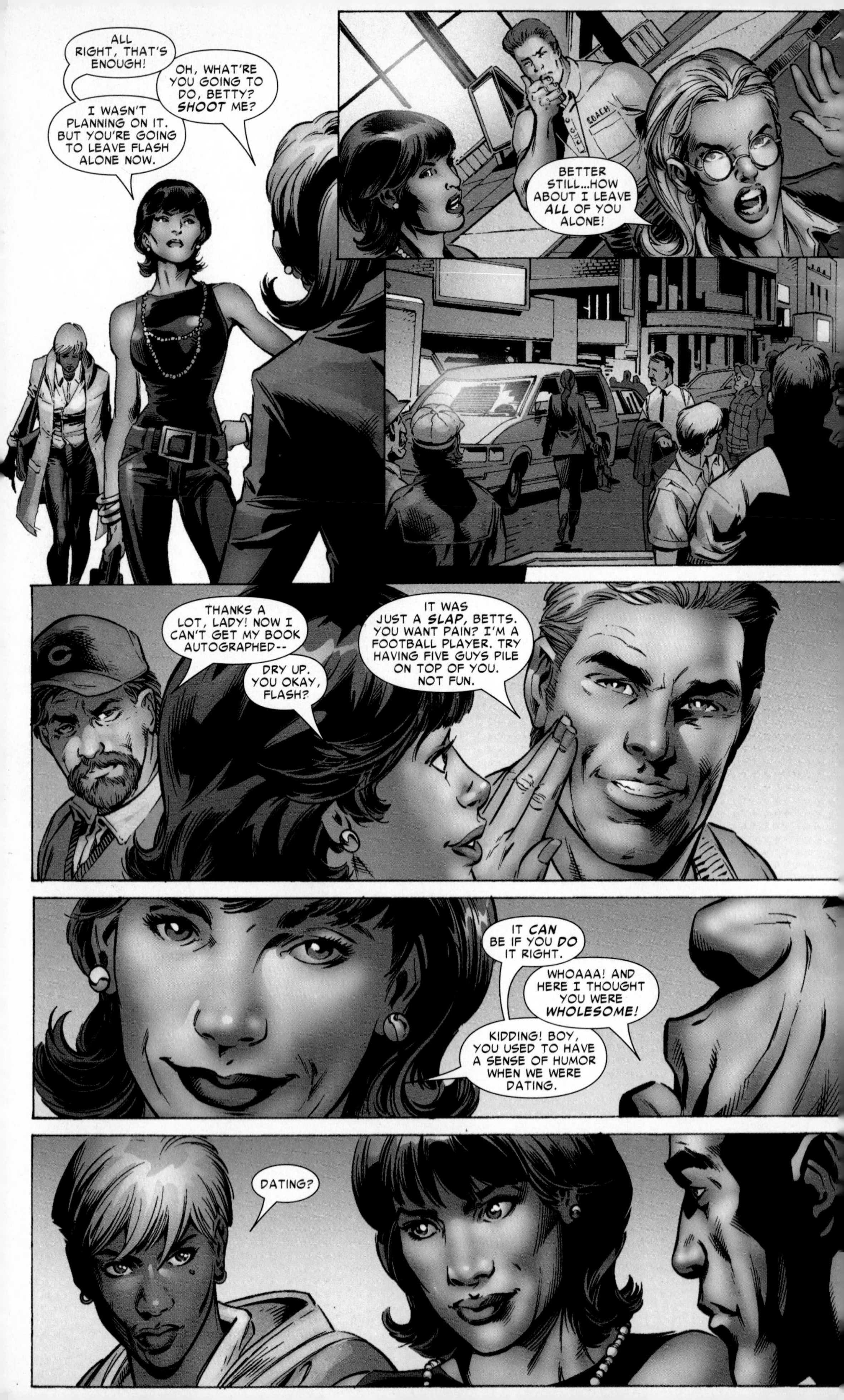

ALL RIGHT, THAT'S ENOUGH!
OH, WHAT'RE YOU GOING TO DO, BETTY? SHOOT ME?
I WASN'T PLANNING ON IT. BUT YOU'RE GOING TO LEAVE FLASH ALONE NOW.
COACH
BETTER STILL...HOW ABOUT I LEAVE ALL OF YOU ALONE!
THANKS A LOT, LADY! NOW I CAN'T GET MY BOOK AUTOGRAPHED--
DRY UP. YOU OKAY, FLASH?
IT WAS JUST A SLAP, BETTS. YOU WANT PAIN? I'M A FOOTBALL PLAYER. TRY HAVING FIVE GUYS PILE ON TOP OF YOU. NOT FUN.
IT CAN BE IF YOU DO IT RIGHT.
WHOAAA! AND HERE I THOUGHT YOU WERE WHOLESOME!
KIDDING! BOY, YOU USED TO HAVE A SENSE OF HUMOR WHEN WE WERE DATING.
DATING?

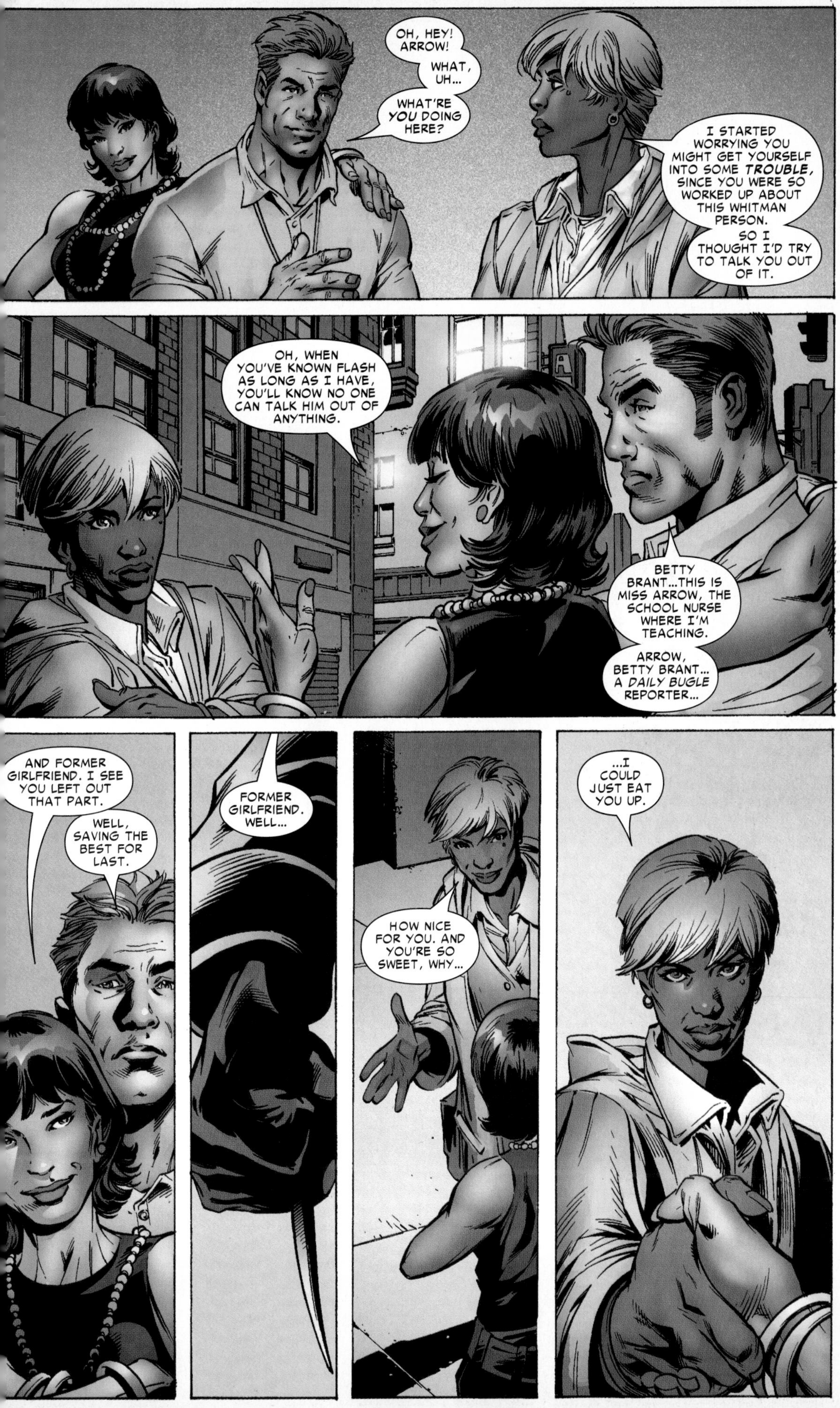
OH, HEY! ARROW!
WHAT, UH...
WHAT'RE *YOU* DOING HERE?
I STARTED WORRYING YOU MIGHT GET YOURSELF INTO SOME *TROUBLE,* SINCE YOU WERE SO WORKED UP ABOUT THIS WHITMAN PERSON.
SO I THOUGHT I'D TRY TO TALK YOU OUT OF IT.
OH, WHEN YOU'VE KNOWN FLASH AS LONG AS I HAVE, YOU'LL KNOW NO ONE CAN TALK HIM OUT OF ANYTHING.
BETTY BRANT...THIS IS MISS ARROW, THE SCHOOL NURSE WHERE I'M TEACHING.
ARROW, BETTY BRANT... A *DAILY BUGLE* REPORTER...
AND FORMER GIRLFRIEND. I SEE YOU LEFT OUT THAT PART.
WELL, SAVING THE BEST FOR LAST.
FORMER GIRLFRIEND. WELL...
HOW NICE FOR YOU. AND YOU'RE SO SWEET, WHY...
...I COULD JUST EAT YOU UP.

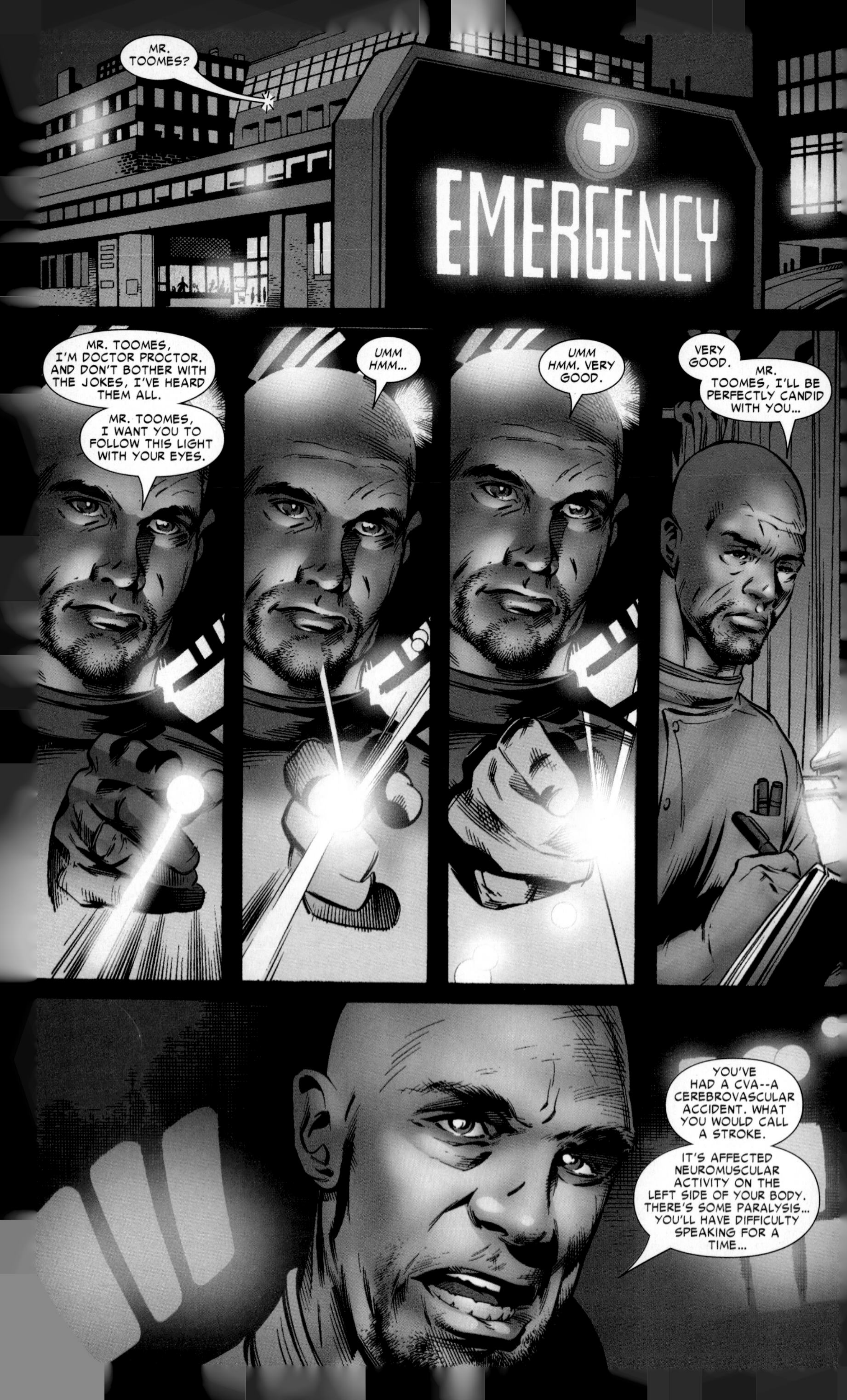
MR. TOOMES?
EMERGENCY
MR. TOOMES, I'M DOCTOR PROCTOR. AND DON'T BOTHER WITH THE JOKES, I'VE HEARD THEM ALL.
MR. TOOMES, I WANT YOU TO FOLLOW THIS LIGHT WITH YOUR EYES.
UMM HMM...
UMM HMM. VERY GOOD.
VERY GOOD.
MR. TOOMES, I'LL BE PERFECTLY CANDID WITH YOU...
YOU'VE HAD A CVA--A CEREBROVASCULAR ACCIDENT. WHAT YOU WOULD CALL A STROKE.
IT'S AFFECTED NEUROMUSCULAR ACTIVITY ON THE LEFT SIDE OF YOUR BODY. THERE'S SOME PARALYSIS... YOU'LL HAVE DIFFICULTY SPEAKING FOR A TIME...

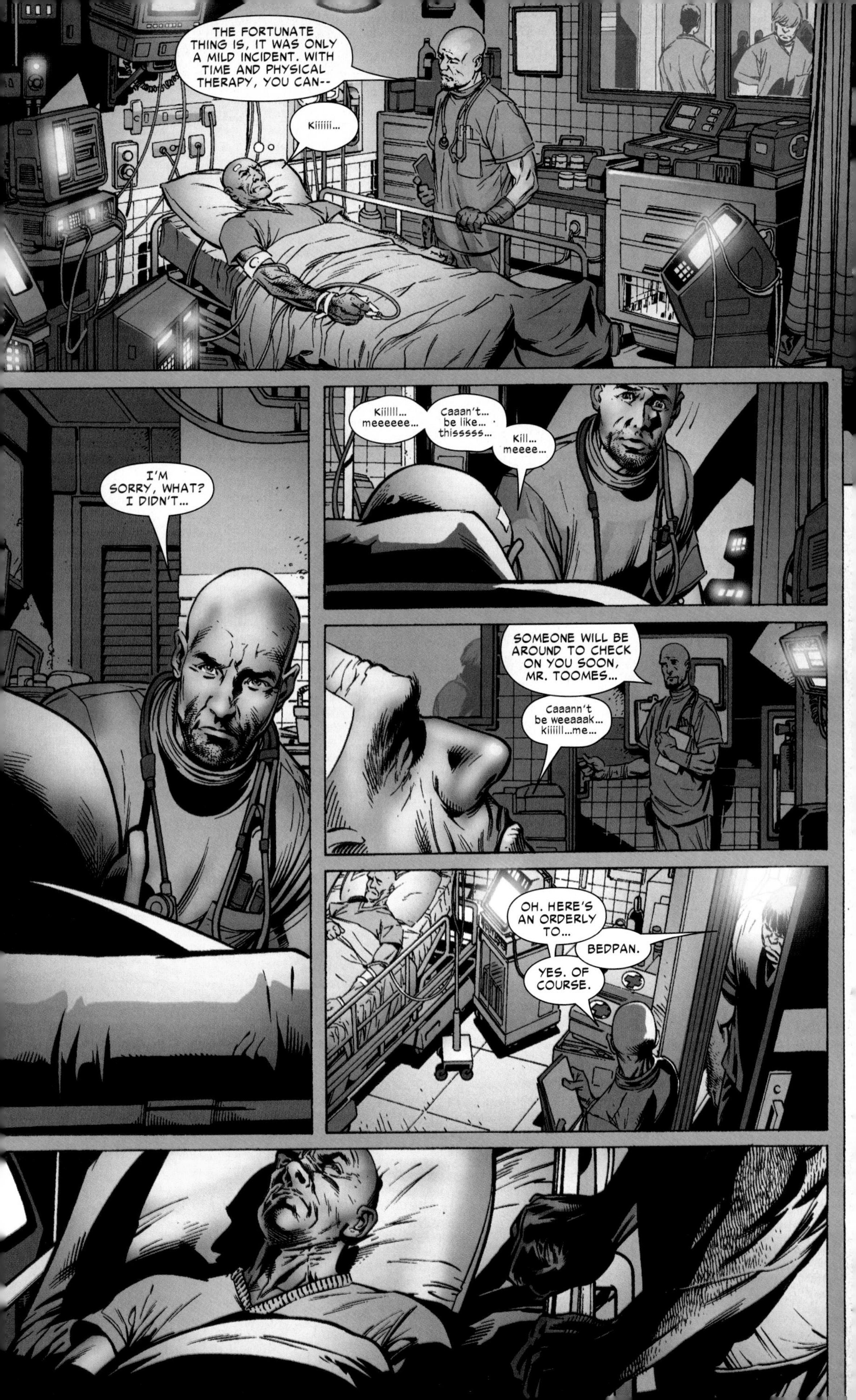
THE FORTUNATE THING IS, IT WAS ONLY A MILD INCIDENT. WITH TIME AND PHYSICAL THERAPY, YOU CAN--
Kiiiiii...
I'M SORRY, WHAT? I DIDN'T...
Kiillll... meeeeee...
Caaan't... be like... thisssss...
Kill... meeee...
SOMEONE WILL BE AROUND TO CHECK ON YOU SOON, MR. TOOMES...
Caaann't be weeaaak... kiiiill...me...
OH. HERE'S AN ORDERLY TO...
BEDPAN.
YES. OF COURSE.

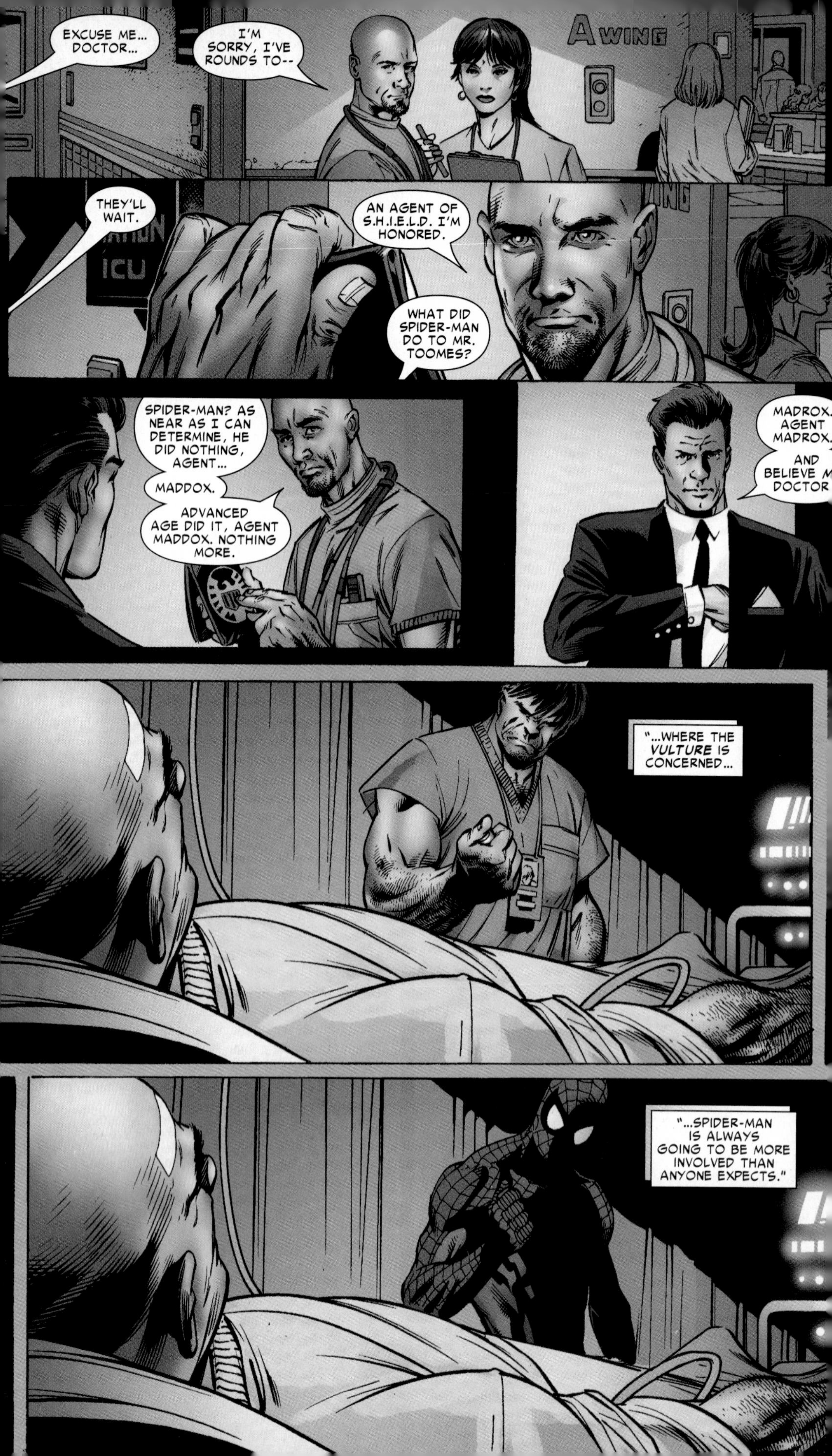
EXCUSE ME... DOCTOR...
I'M SORRY, I'VE ROUNDS TO--
A WING
THEY'LL WAIT.
ICU
AN AGENT OF S.H.I.E.L.D. I'M HONORED.
WHAT DID SPIDER-MAN DO TO MR. TOOMES?
SPIDER-MAN? AS NEAR AS I CAN DETERMINE, HE DID NOTHING, AGENT...
MADDOX.
ADVANCED AGE DID IT, AGENT MADDOX. NOTHING MORE.
MADROX. AGENT MADROX.
AND BELIEVE M DOCTOR
"...WHERE THE VULTURE IS CONCERNED...
"...SPIDER-MAN IS ALWAYS GOING TO BE MORE INVOLVED THAN ANYONE EXPECTS."

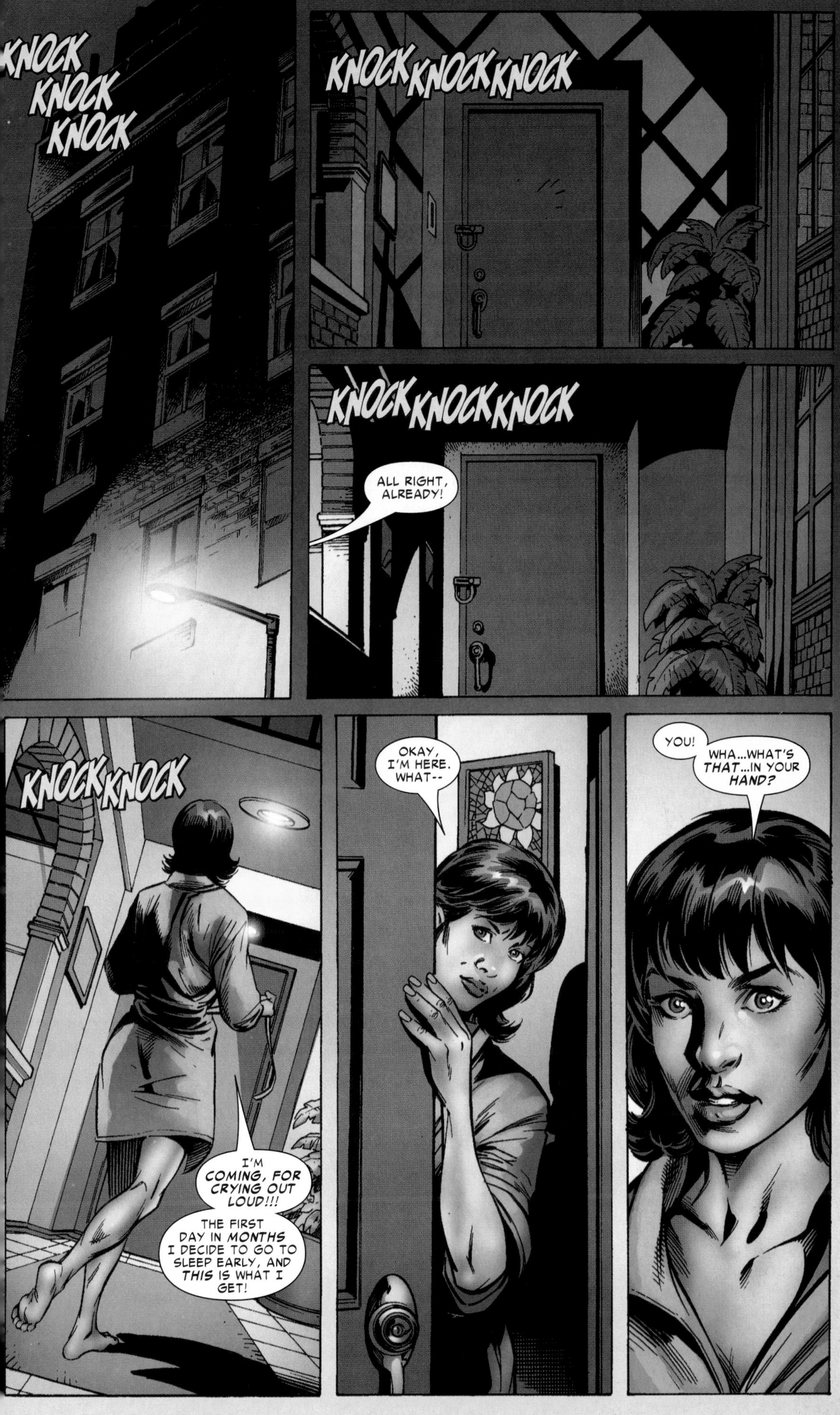
KNOCK KNOCK KNOCK
KNOCK KNOCK KNOCK
KNOCK KNOCK KNOCK
ALL RIGHT, ALREADY!
KNOCK KNOCK
I'M COMING, FOR CRYING OUT LOUD!!!
THE FIRST DAY IN MONTHS I DECIDE TO GO TO SLEEP EARLY, AND THIS IS WHAT I GET!
OKAY, I'M HERE. WHAT--
YOU!
WHA...WHAT'S THAT...IN YOUR HAND?

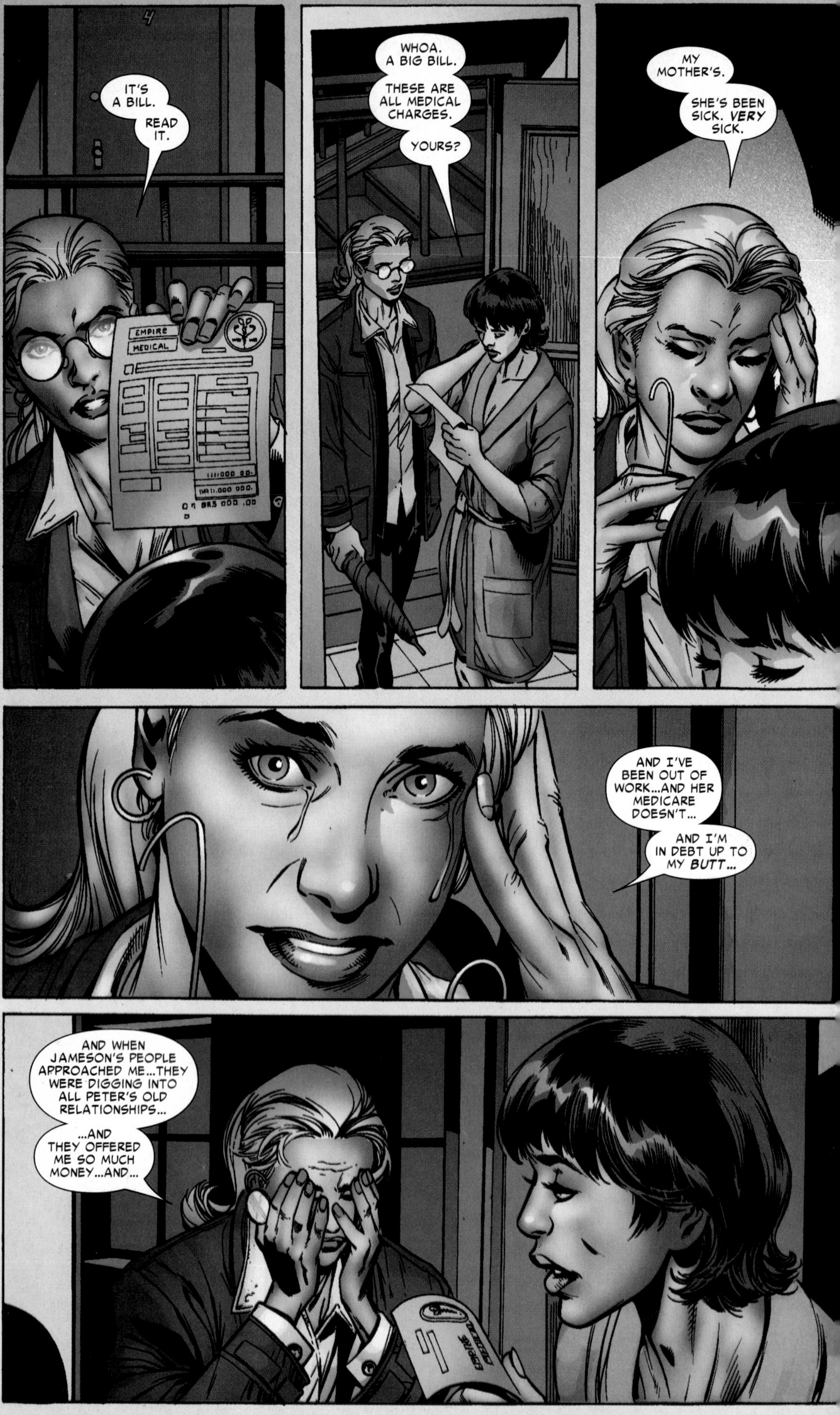
IT'S A BILL.
READ IT.
EMPIRE MEDICAL
WHOA. A BIG BILL.
THESE ARE ALL MEDICAL CHARGES.
YOURS?
MY MOTHER'S.
SHE'S BEEN SICK. VERY SICK.
AND I'VE BEEN OUT OF WORK...AND HER MEDICARE DOESN'T...
AND I'M IN DEBT UP TO MY BUTT...
AND WHEN JAMESON'S PEOPLE APPROACHED ME...THEY WERE DIGGING INTO ALL PETER'S OLD RELATIONSHIPS...
...AND THEY OFFERED ME SO MUCH MONEY...AND...

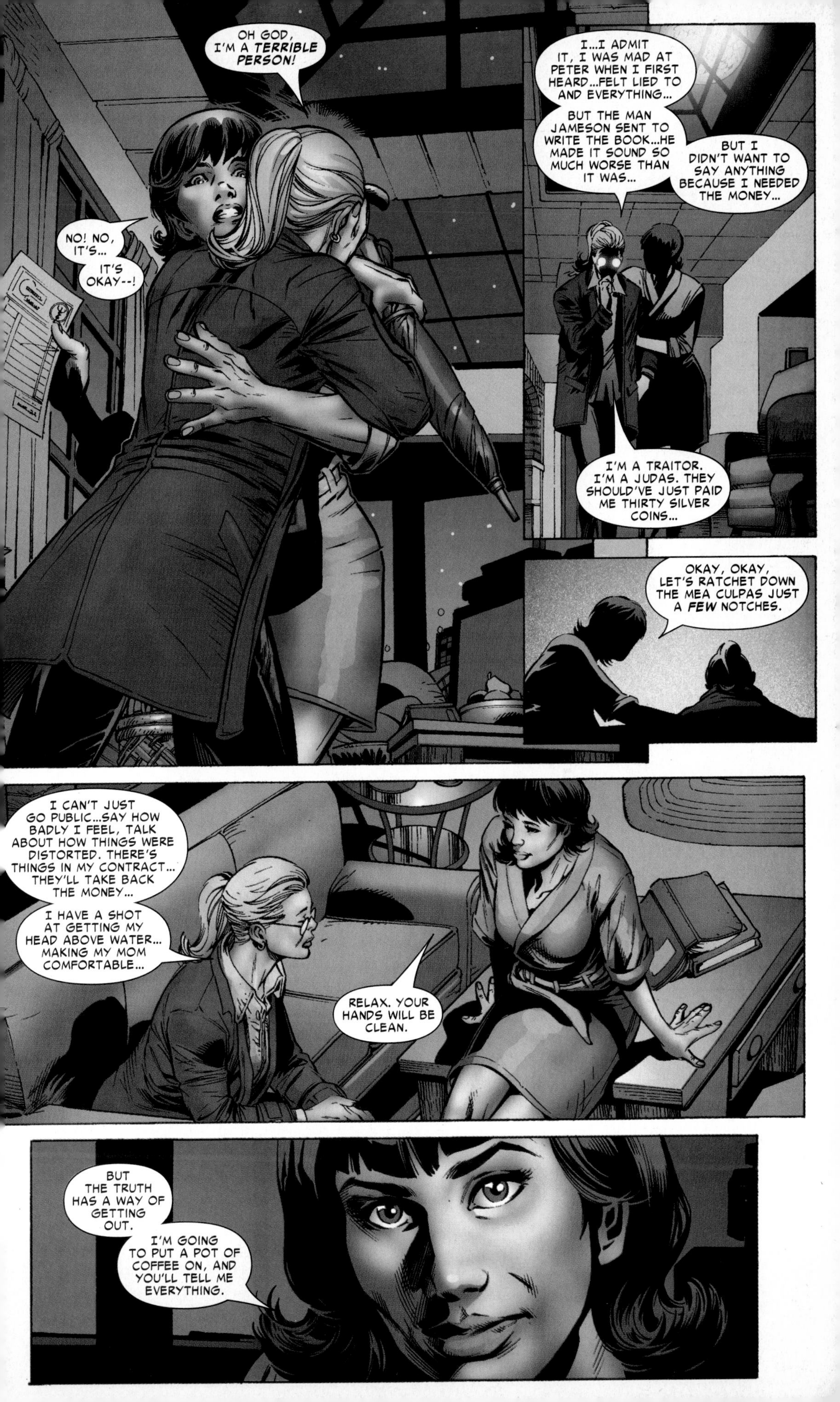

OH GOD, I'M A *TERRIBLE PERSON!*
NO! NO, IT'S...
IT'S OKAY--!
I...I ADMIT IT, I WAS MAD AT PETER WHEN I FIRST HEARD...FELT LIED TO AND EVERYTHING...
BUT THE MAN JAMESON SENT TO WRITE THE BOOK...HE MADE IT SOUND SO MUCH WORSE THAN IT WAS...
BUT I DIDN'T WANT TO SAY ANYTHING BECAUSE I NEEDED THE MONEY...
I'M A TRAITOR. I'M A JUDAS. THEY SHOULD'VE JUST PAID ME THIRTY SILVER COINS...
OKAY, OKAY, LET'S RATCHET DOWN THE MEA CULPAS JUST A *FEW* NOTCHES.
I CAN'T JUST GO PUBLIC...SAY HOW BADLY I FEEL, TALK ABOUT HOW THINGS WERE DISTORTED. THERE'S THINGS IN MY CONTRACT... THEY'LL TAKE BACK THE MONEY...
I HAVE A SHOT AT GETTING MY HEAD ABOVE WATER... MAKING MY MOM COMFORTABLE...
RELAX. YOUR HANDS WILL BE CLEAN.
BUT THE TRUTH HAS A WAY OF GETTING OUT.
I'M GOING TO PUT A POT OF COFFEE ON, AND YOU'LL TELL ME EVERYTHING.

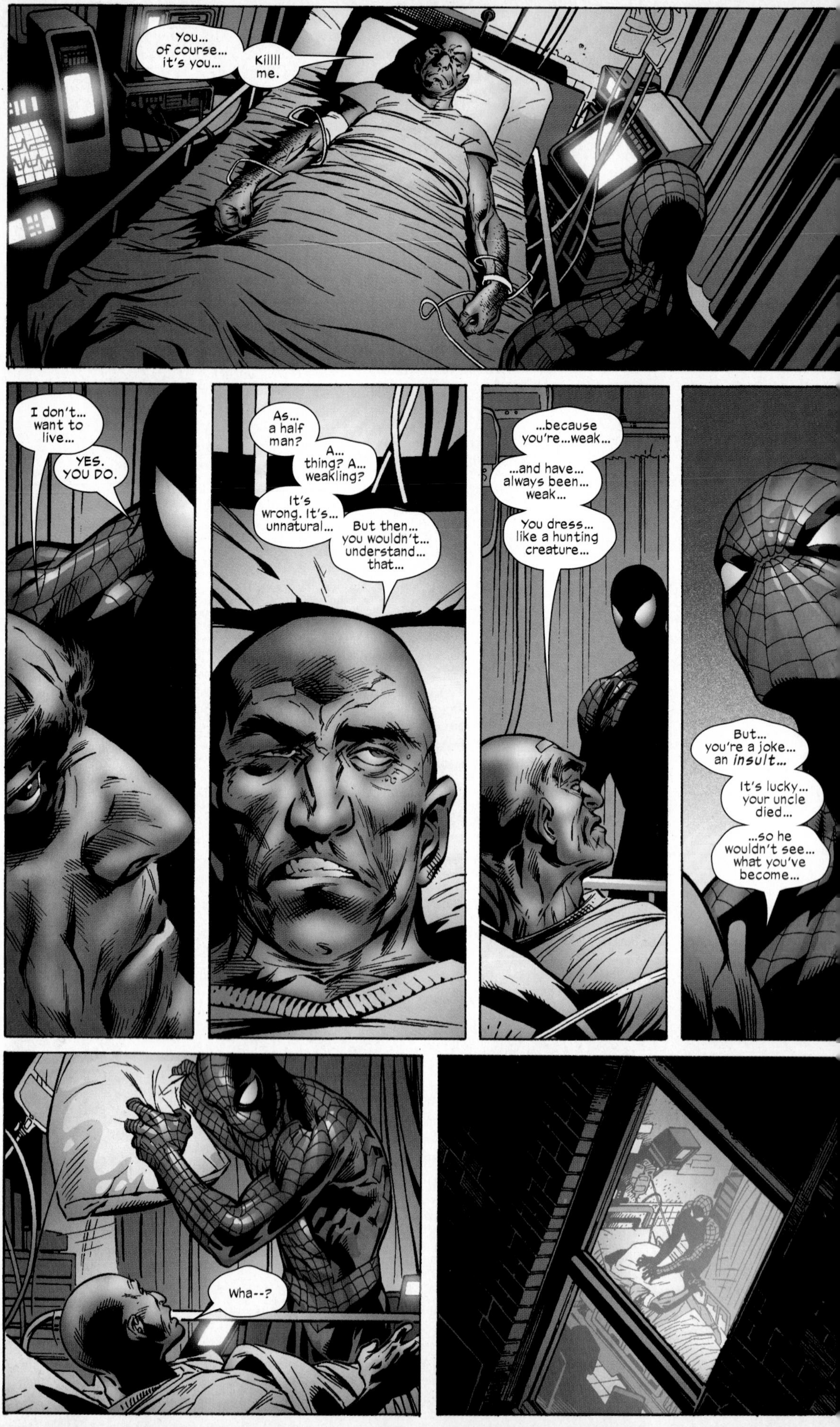

You... of course... it's you...
Killll me.
I don't... want to live...
YES. YOU DO.
As... a half man?
A... thing? A... weakling?
It's wrong. It's... unnatural...
But then... you wouldn't... understand... that...
...because you're...weak...
...and have... always been... weak...
You dress... like a hunting creature...
But... you're a joke... an *insult*...
It's lucky... your uncle died...
...so he wouldn't see... what you've become...
Wha--?

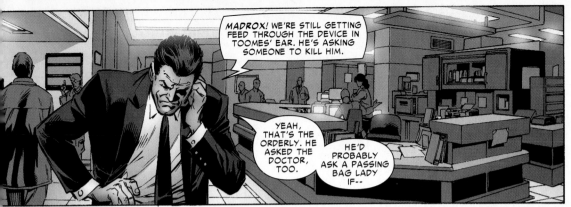

MADROX! WE'RE STILL GETTING FEED THROUGH THE DEVICE IN TOOMES' EAR. HE'S ASKING SOMEONE TO KILL HIM.

YEAH, THAT'S THE ORDERLY. HE ASKED THE DOCTOR, TOO.

HE'D PROBABLY ASK A PASSING BAG LADY IF--

BUT HE'S TALKING ABOUT SOMEONE BEING LUCKY HIS "UNCLE DIED."

UNCLE?

WE'RE GETTING ELEVATED READINGS IN ROOM 504! HEART RATE JUMPING!

504? THAT'S--

SON OF A--!

EVERYBODY STAY BACK!!

THAT'S AN ORDER!

504

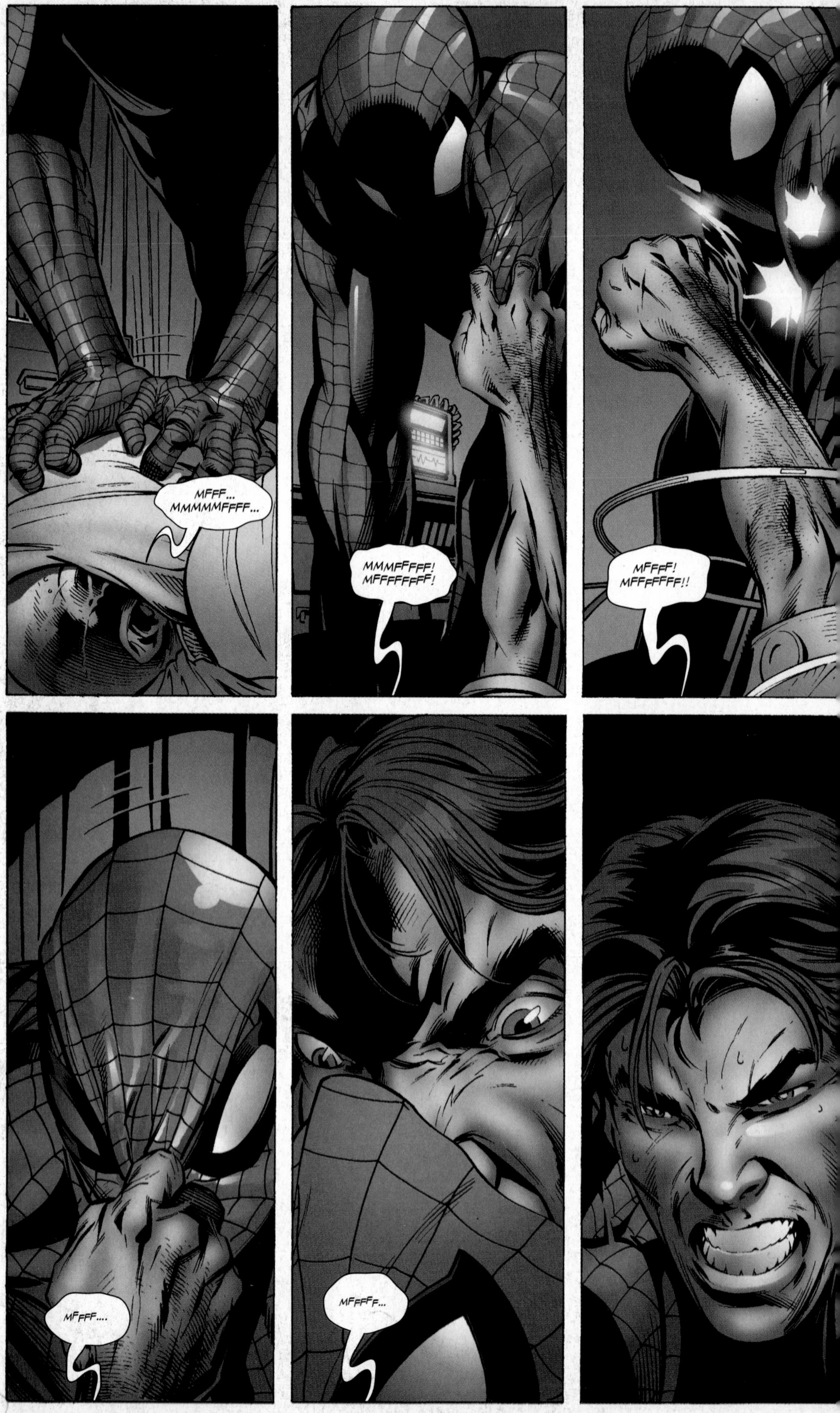
MFFF...
MMMMMFFFF...
MMMFFFFF!
MFFFFFFFF!
MFFFF!
MFFFFFFF!!
MFFFF....
MFFFFF...

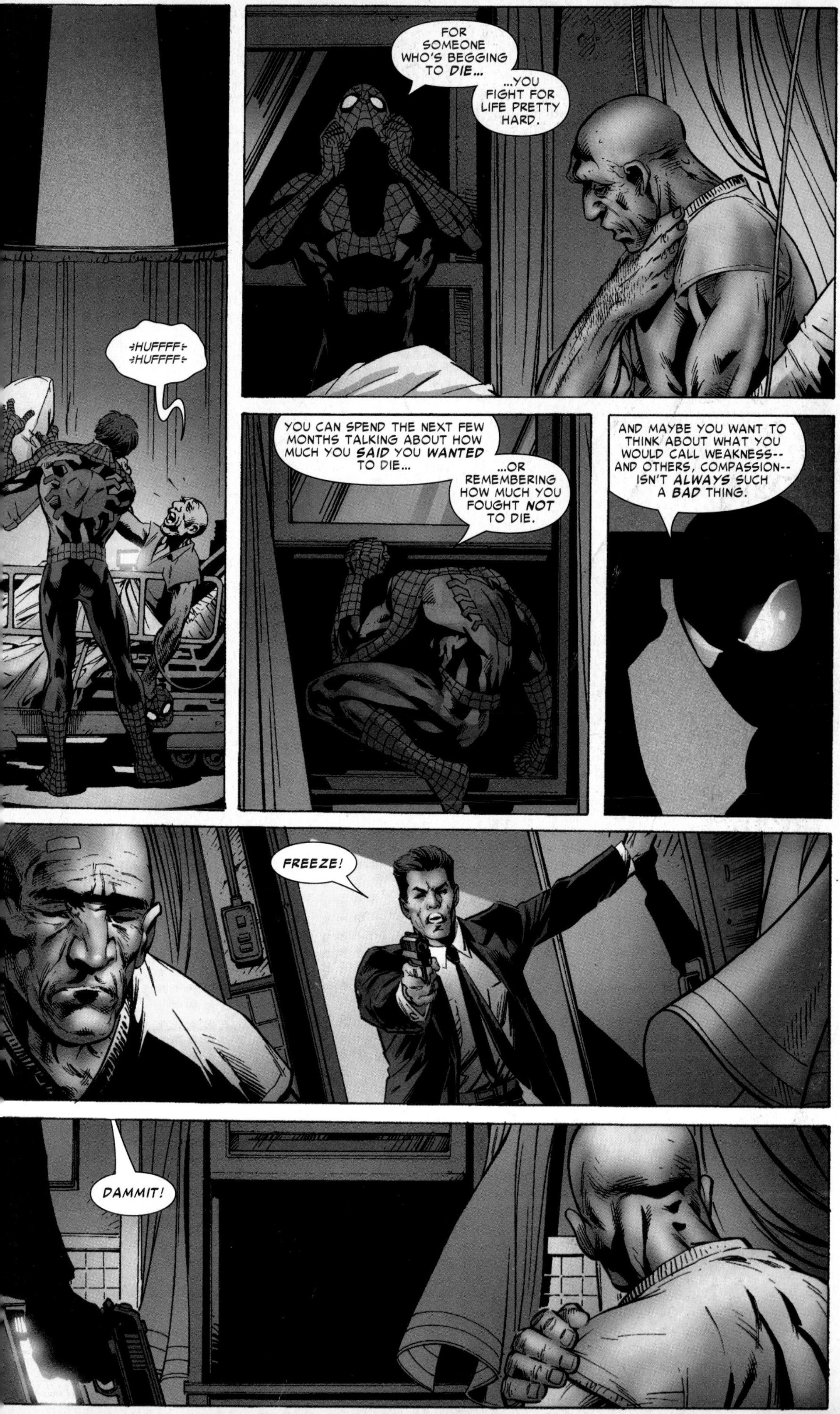

≠HUFFFF≠
≠HUFFFF≠
FOR SOMEONE WHO'S BEGGING TO DIE...
...YOU FIGHT FOR LIFE PRETTY HARD.
YOU CAN SPEND THE NEXT FEW MONTHS TALKING ABOUT HOW MUCH YOU SAID YOU WANTED TO DIE...
...OR REMEMBERING HOW MUCH YOU FOUGHT NOT TO DIE.
AND MAYBE YOU WANT TO THINK ABOUT WHAT YOU WOULD CALL WEAKNESS-- AND OTHERS, COMPASSION-- ISN'T ALWAYS SUCH A BAD THING.
FREEZE!
DAMMIT!

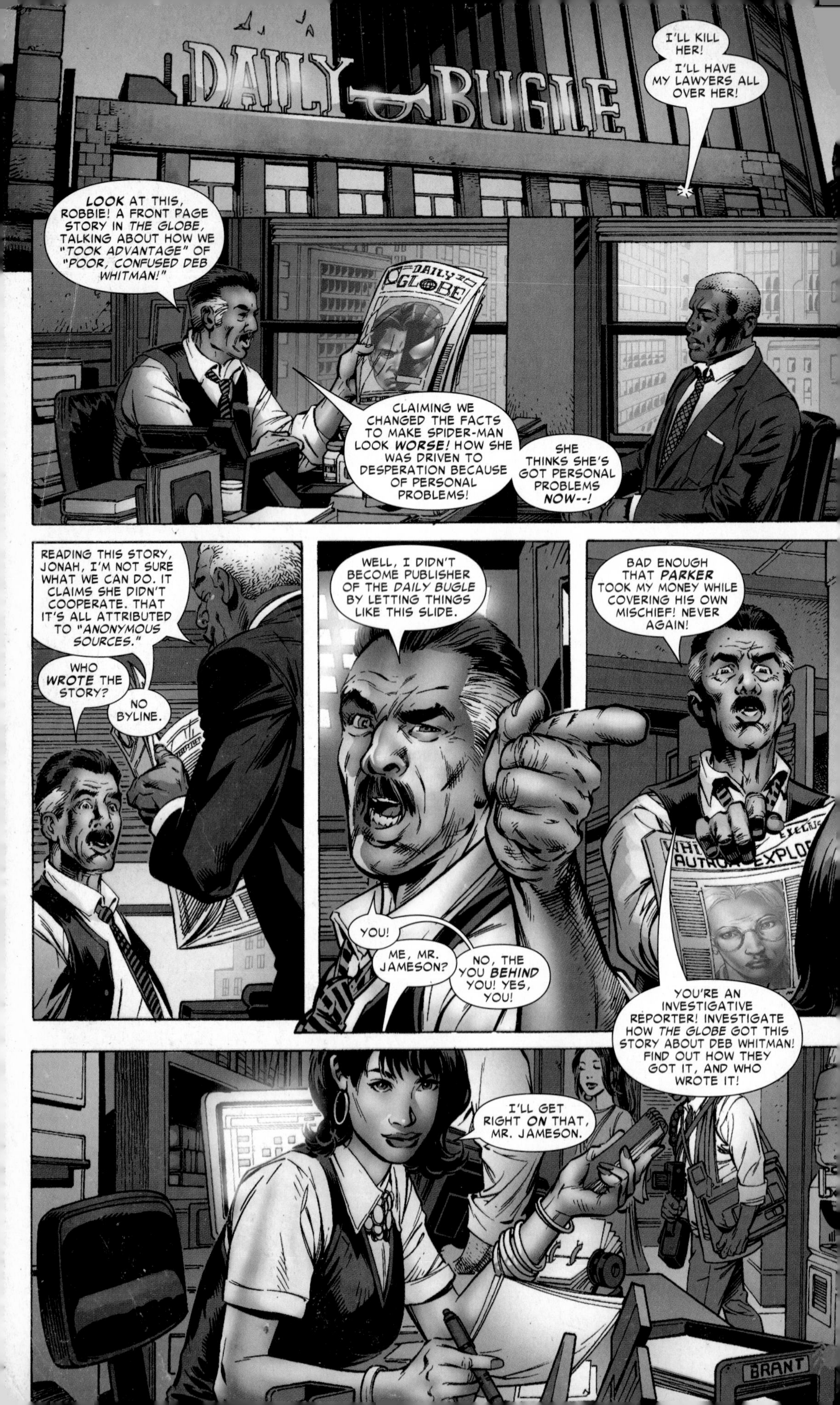
DAILY BUGLE
I'LL KILL HER! I'LL HAVE MY LAWYERS ALL OVER HER!
LOOK AT THIS, ROBBIE! A FRONT PAGE STORY IN *THE GLOBE*, TALKING ABOUT HOW WE "*TOOK ADVANTAGE*" OF "*POOR, CONFUSED DEB WHITMAN!*"
DAILY GLOBE
CLAIMING WE CHANGED THE FACTS TO MAKE SPIDER-MAN LOOK *WORSE!* HOW SHE WAS DRIVEN TO DESPERATION BECAUSE OF PERSONAL PROBLEMS!
SHE THINKS SHE'S GOT PERSONAL PROBLEMS *NOW--!*
READING THIS STORY, JONAH, I'M NOT SURE WHAT WE CAN DO. IT CLAIMS SHE DIDN'T COOPERATE. THAT IT'S ALL ATTRIBUTED TO "*ANONYMOUS SOURCES.*"
WHO *WROTE* THE STORY?
NO BYLINE.
WELL, I DIDN'T BECOME PUBLISHER OF THE *DAILY BUGLE* BY LETTING THINGS LIKE THIS SLIDE.
BAD ENOUGH THAT *PARKER* TOOK MY MONEY WHILE COVERING HIS OWN MISCHIEF! NEVER AGAIN!
YOU!
ME, MR. JAMESON?
NO, THE YOU *BEHIND* YOU! YES, YOU!
YOU'RE AN INVESTIGATIVE REPORTER! INVESTIGATE HOW *THE GLOBE* GOT THIS STORY ABOUT DEB WHITMAN! FIND OUT HOW THEY GOT IT, AND WHO WROTE IT!
I'LL GET RIGHT *ON* THAT, MR. JAMESON.
BRANT